STO

ACPL ITEM

DISCA ☑ SO-AUH-634

338.95 In81 1995

The Internationalist
business guide to Pacific
Rim & South East Asia

South East Asia

Volume 2

Business Guides to the World™

The Internationalist Publishing Company
96 Walter Street, Suite 200
Boston, MA 02131

Allen County Public Library
900 Webster Street
PO Box 2270
Fort Wayne, IN 46801-2270

The Internationalist Business Guide to Pacific Rim & South East Asia
Volume 2 of 6 volume Business Guides to the World™

Edited by Patrick W. Nee

The Internationalist Publishing Company
96 Walter Street, Suite 200
Boston, MA 02131
(617) 570-0810

Copyright © 1995 by PWN

The Internationalist is a Registered Trademark ®

All rights reserved

ISBN 0-9633905-2-X

A B C D E F G H I J

The Internationalist

Table of Contents

Introduction

The *Internationalist*® *Business Guides* for executives and investors contain the essential, core information about countries around the world. They include information about the economics of a country, its infrastructure, people, government and geography. The data has been compiled from the most authoritative government sources.

The Guides have been designed for ease of use by the busy executive or investor. The Guides are divided into six economic/geographic regions. Information is simply and precisely presented. The compact size permits use when traveling on international business. Important telephone numbers are included.

Fast moving political or economic events may affect certain elements of a country's situation, however, the basic underlying facts about a country remain constant. Those basic facts are what are covered by the guides.

COUNTRIES

AUSTRALIA

Economy

Overview: Australia has a prosperous Western-style capitalist economy, with a per capita GDP comparable to levels in industrialized West European countries. Rich in natural resources, Australia is a major exporter of agricultural products, minerals, metals, and fossil fuels. Primary products account for more than 60% of the value of total exports, so that, as in 1983-84, a downturn in world commodity prices can have a big impact on the economy. The government is pushing for increased exports of manufactured goods, but competition in international markets continues to be severe. Australia has suffered from the low growth and high unemployment characterizing the OECD countries in the early 1990s. In 1992-93 the economy recovered slowly from the prolonged recession of 1990-91, a major restraining factor being weak world demand for Australia's exports.

Unemployment has hovered around 10% and probably will remain at that level in 1994 as productivity gains rather than more jobs account for growth.

National product: GDP—purchasing power equivalent—$339.7 billion (1993)
National product real growth rate: 4% (1993)
National product per capita: $19,100 (1993)
Inflation rate (consumer prices): 1.1% (1993)
Unemployment rate: 10% (December 1993)
Budget:
revenues: $71.9 billion
expenditures: $83.1 billion, including capital expenditures of $NA (FY93)
Exports: $44.1 billion (1992)
commodities: coal, gold, meat, wool, alumina, wheat, machinery and transport equipment
partners: Japan 25%, US 11%, South Korea 6%, NZ 5.7%, UK, Taiwan, Singapore, Hong Kong (1992)
Imports: $43.6 billion (1992)
commodities: machinery and transport equipment, computers and office machines, crude oil and petroleum products
partners: US 23%, Japan 18%, UK 6%, Germany 5.7%, NZ 4% (1992)
External debt: $141.1 billion (1993)
Industrial production: growth rate 1.9% (FY93); accounts for 32% of GDP
Electricity:
capacity: 40,000,000 kW
production: 150 billion kWh
consumption per capita: 8,475 kWh (1992)
Industries: mining, industrial and transportation equipment, food processing, chemicals, steel
Agriculture: accounts for 5% of GDP and over 30% of export revenues; world's largest exporter of beef and wool, second-largest for mutton, and among top wheat exporters; major crops—wheat, barley, sugarcane, fruit; livestock - cattle, sheep, poultry
Illicit drugs: Tasmania is one of the world's major suppliers of licit opiate products; government maintains strict controls over areas

of opium poppy cultivation and output of poppy straw concentrate

Economic aid:
donor: ODA and OOF commitments (1970-89), $10.4 billion

Currency: 1 Australian dollar ($A) = 100 cents

Exchange rates: Australian dollars ($A) per US$1—1.4364 (January 1994), 1.4704 (1993), 1.3600 (1992), 1.2835 (1991), 1.2799 (1990), 1.2618 (1989)

Fiscal year: 1 July—30 June

Communications

Railroads: 40,478 km total; 7,970 km 1.600-meter gauge, 16,201 km 1.435-meter standard gauge, 16,307 km 1.067-meter gauge; 183 km dual gauge; 1,130 km electrified; government owned (except for a few hundred kilometers of privately owned track) (1985)

Highways:
total: 837,872 km
paved: 243,750 km
unpaved: gravel, crushed stone, stabilized earth 228,396 km; unimproved earth 365,726 km

Inland waterways: 8,368 km; mainly by small, shallow-draft craft

Pipelines: crude oil 2,500 km; petroleum products 500 km; natural gas 5,600 km

Ports: Adelaide, Brisbane, Cairns, Darwin, Devonport, Fremantle, Geelong, Hobart, Launceston, Mackay, Melbourne, Sydney, Townsville

Merchant marine: 83 ships (1,000 GRT or over) totaling 2,517,538 GRT/3,711,549 DWT, short-sea passenger 2, cargo 8, roll-on/roll-off cargo 7, vehicle carrier 1, oil tanker 18, chemical tanker 3, liquefied gas 5, bulk 30, combination bulk 2, container 7

Airports:
total: 481
usable: 440
with permanent-surface runways: 241
with runways over 3,659 m: 1
with runways 2,440-3,659 m: 20
with runways 1,220-2,439 m: 268

Telecommunications: good international and domestic service; 8.7 million telephones; broadcast stations—258 AM, 67 FM, 134 TV; submarine cables to New Zealand, Papua New Guinea, and Indonesia; domestic satellite service; satellite stations—4 Indian Ocean INTELSAT, 6 Pacific Ocean INTELSAT earth stations

Defense Forces

Branches: Australian Army, Royal Australian Navy, Royal Australian Air Force

Manpower availability: males age 15-49 4,885,574; fit for military service 4,239,459; reach military age (17) annually 133,337 (1994 est.)

Defense expenditures: exchange rate conversion—$7.1 billion, 2.4% of GDP (FY92/93)

Geography

Location: Southwestern Oceania, between Indonesia and New Zealand

Map references: Southeast Asia, Oceania, Antarctic Region, Standard Time Zones of the World

Area:
total area: 7,686,850 sq km
land area: 7,617,930 sq km
comparative area: slightly smaller than the US
note: includes Macquarie Island

Land boundaries: 0 km

Coastline: 25,760 km

Maritime claims:
contiguous zone: 12 nm
continental shelf: 200-m depth or to depth of exploitation
exclusive fishing zone: 200 nm
territorial sea: 12 nm

International disputes: territorial claim in Antarctica (Australian Antarctic Territory)

Climate: generally arid to semiarid; temperate in south and east; tropical in north

Terrain: mostly low plateau with deserts; fertile plain in southeast

Natural resources: bauxite, coal, iron ore, copper, tin, silver, uranium, nickel, tungsten, mineral sands, lead, zinc, diamonds, natural gas, petroleum

3 1833 02644 5855

Land use:
arable land: 6%
permanent crops: 0%
meadows and pastures: 58%
forest and woodland: 14%
other: 22%
Irrigated land: 18,800 sq km (1989 est.)
Environment:
current issues: soil erosion from overgrazing, industrial development, urbanization, and poor farming practices; soil salinity rising due to the use of poor quality water; desertification; clearing for agricultural purposes threatens the natural habitat of many unique animal and plant species; the Great Barrier Reef off the northeast coast, the largest coral reef in the world, is threatened by increased shipping and its popularity as a tourist site; limited freshwater availability
natural hazards: cyclones along the coast; subject to severe droughts
international agreements: party to—Antarctic-Environmental Protocol, Antarctic Treaty, Biodiversity, Climate Change, Endangered Species, Environmental Modification, Hazardous Wastes, Marine Dumping, Marine Life Conservation, Nuclear Test Ban, Ozone Layer Protection, Ship Pollution, Tropical Timber, Wetlands, Whaling; signed, but not ratified—Law of the Sea
Note: world's smallest continent but sixth-largest country; population concentrated along the eastern and southeastern coasts; regular, tropical, invigorating, sea breeze known as "the Doctor" occurs along the west coast in the summer

---

People

Population: 18,077,419 (July 1994 est.)
Population growth rate: 1.38% (1994 est.)
Birth rate: 14.29 births/1,000 population (1994 est.)
Death rate: 7.38 deaths/1,000 population (1994 est.)
Net migration rate: 6.91 migrant(s)/1,000 population (1994 est.)
Infant mortality rate: 7.3 deaths/1.000 live

births (1994 est.)
Life expectancy at birth:
total population: 77.57 years
male: 74.45 years
female: 80.84 years (1994 est.)
Total fertility rate: 1.83 children born/woman (1994 est.)
Nationality:
noun: Australian(s)
adjective: Australian
Ethnic divisions: Caucasian 95%, Asian 4%, aboriginal and other 1%
Religions: Anglican 26.1%, Roman Catholic 26%, other Christian 24.3%
Languages: English, native languages
Literacy: age 15 and over can read and write (1980 est.)
total population: 100%
male: 100%
female: 100%
Labor force: 8.63 million (September 1991)
by occupation: finance and services 33.8%, public and community services 22.3%, wholesale and retail trade 20.1%, manufacturing and industry 16.2%, agriculture 6.1% (1987)

Government

Names:
conventional long form: Commonwealth of Australia
conventional short form: Australia
Digraph: AS
Type: federal parliamentary state
Capital: Canberra
Administrative divisions: 6 states and 2 territories*; Australian Capital Territory*, New South Wales, Northern Territory*, Queensland, South Australia, Tasmania, Victoria, Western Australia
Dependent areas: Ashmore and Cartier Islands, Christmas Island, Cocos (Keeling) Islands, Coral Sea Islands, Heard Island and McDonald Islands, Norfolk Island
Independence: 1 January 1901 (federation of UK colonies)
National holiday: Australia Day, 26 January (1788)

The Internationalist

Constitution: 9 July 1900, effective 1 January 1901
Legal system: based on English common law; accepts compulsory ICJ jurisdiction, with reservations
Suffrage: 18 years of age; universal and compulsory
Executive branch:
chief of state: Queen ELIZABETH II (since 6 February 1952), represented by Governor General William George HAYDEN (since 16 February 1989)
head of government: Prime Minister Paul John KEATING (since 20 December 1991); Deputy Prime Minister Brian HOWE (since 4 June 1991)
cabinet: Cabinet; prime minister selects his cabinet from members of the House and Senate
Legislative branch: bicameral Federal Parliament
Senate: elections last held 13 March 1993 (next to be held by NA 1996); results—percent of vote by party NA; seats—(76 total) Liberal-National 36, Labor 30, Australian Democrats 7, Greens 2, independents 1
House of Representatives: elections last held 13 March 1993 (next to be held by NA 1996); results—percent of vote by party NA; seats—(147 total) Labor 80, Liberal-National 65, independent 2
Judicial branch: High Court
Political parties and leaders:
government: Australian Labor Party, Paul John KEATING
opposition: Liberal Party, John HEWSON; National Party, Timothy FISCHER; Australian Democratic Party, Cheryl KERNOT; Green Party, leader NA
Other political or pressure groups: Australian Democratic Labor Party (anti-Communist Labor Party splinter group); Peace and Nuclear Disarmament Action (Nuclear Disarmament Party splinter group)
Member of: AfDB, AG (observer), ANZUS, APEC, AsDB, Australia Group, BIS, C, CCC, COCOM, CP, EBRD, ESCAP, FAO, GATT, G-8, IAEA, IBRD, ICAO, ICC, ICFTU, IDA, IEA, IFAD, IFC, ILO, IMF, IMO, INMARSAT, INTELSAT, INTERPOL, IOC, IOM, ISO, ITU, LORCS, MINURSO, MTCR, NAM (guest), NEA, NSG, OECD, PCA, SPARTECA, SPC, SPF, UN, UNCTAD, UNESCO, UNFICYP, UNHCR, UNIDO, UNOSOM, UNPROFOR, UNTAC, UNTSO, UPU, WFTU, WHO, WIPO, WMO, ZC
Diplomatic representation in US:
chief of mission: Ambassador Donald RUSSELL
chancery: 1601 Massachusetts Avenue NW, Washington, DC 20036
telephone: (202) 797-3000
FAX: (202) 797-3168
consulate(s) general: Chicago, Honolulu, Houston, Los Angeles, New York, Pago Pago (American Samoa), and San Francisco
US diplomatic representation:
chief of mission: Ambassador Edward PERKINS
embassy: Moonah Place, Yarralumla, Canberra, Australian Capital Territory 2600
mailing address: APO AP 96549
telephone: [61] (6) 270-5000
FAX: [61] (6) 270-5970
consulate(s) general: Melbourne, Perth, and Sydney
consulate(s): Brisbane
Flag: blue with the flag of the UK in the upper hoist-side quadrant and a large seven-pointed star in the lower hoist-side quadrant; the remaining half is a representation of the Southern Cross constellation in white with one small five-pointed star and four, larger, seven-pointed stars

---

U.S. Government Contacts:

U.S. Trade Desk: (202) 482-2471

American Consulate General - Sydney
Commercial Sections
36th Floor, T&G Tower, Hyde Park Square
Park and Elizabeth Streets
Sydney 2000, N.S.W., Australia
APO AP 96554
Tel: 61-2-261-9200
Fax: 61-2-261-8148

American Consulate General - Melbourne
Commercial Section
553 St. Kilda Road
South Melbourne, Victoria 3004, Australia

APO AP 96551
Tel: 61-3-526-5900
Fax: 61-9-510-4660

American Consulate General - Perth
Commercial Section
246 St. George's Terrace
Perth, WA 6000, Australia
Tel: 61-9-221-1177
Fax: 61-9-325-3569

American Chamber of Commerce in Australia
60 Margaret Street
Sydney, N.S.W., 2000, Australia
Tel: 61-2-221-3055

Australian Government Contacts:

Embassy of Australia Commercial Section
1601 Massachusetts Avenue, M.W.
Washington, DC 20036
Tel: (202) 797-3201

Legal Services:

Barker Gosling Legal Group
28th Floor, 135 King Street
Sydney, New South Wales 2000, Australia
Tel: 61 02 391 3333
Fax: 61 02 391 3456
Provides a comprehensive range of legal services, both domestic and international.

Freehill, Hollingdale & Page
Australia Place, 15-17 William Street
G.P.O. Box U1942
Perth, Western Australia 6000, Australia
Tel: 61 09 327 5777
Fax: 619 322 5954
Established in 1871 with offices in London and Singapore.

Middletons Moore & Bevins
14th Floor, 241 Adelaide Street, QLD
Brisbane, Queensland 4000, Autralia
Tel: 617 221 5944
Fax: 617 229 6865
International Business and Trade, Transport

and Trading, Companies and Securities, Computer and High Technology, Commercial and General Litigation.

Travel:

International Airlines to Country:
United

International Hotels in Country:
Sydney:
Park Hyatt, Tel: 612/256-1234, Fax: 612/256-1555
The Regent, Tel: 612/238-0000, Fax: 612/251-2851
Ritz-Carlton, Tel: 612/252-4600, Fax: 612/252-4286.

BANGLADESH

150 km

Boundary representation is not necessarily authoritative.

Rangpur

Mymensingh

Rajshahi

DHAKA

Khulna

Chittagong

Bay of Bengal

Economy

Overview: Bangladesh is one of the world's poorest, most densely populated, and least developed nations. Its economy is overwhelmingly agricultural, with the cultivation of rice the single most important activity in the economy. Major impediments to growth include frequent cyclones and floods, government interference with the economy, a rapidly growing labor force that cannot be absorbed by agriculture, a low level of industrialization, failure to fully exploit energy resources (natural gas), and inefficient and inadequate power supplies. Excellent rice crops and expansion of the export garment industry helped growth in FY92 and FY93. Policy reforms intended to reduce government regulation of private industry and promote public-sector efficiency have been announced but are being implemented only slowly.
National product: GDP—purchasing power equivalent—$122 billion (1993 est.)
National product real growth rate: 4.3% (FY93)
National product per capita: $1.000 (1993 est.)
Inflation rate (consumer prices): 1.4% (FY93)
Unemployment rate: NA%
Budget:
revenues: $2.5 billion
expenditures: $3.7 billion, including capital expenditures of $NA (FY92)
Exports: $2.1 billion (FY93)
commodities: garments, jute and jute goods, leather, shrimp
partners: US 33%, Western Europe 39% (Germany 8.4%, Italy 6%) (FY92 est.)
Imports: $3.5 billion (FY93)
commodities: capital goods, petroleum, food, textiles
partners: Hong Kong 7.5%, Singapore 7.4%, China 7.4%, Japan 7.1% (FY92 est.)
External debt: $13.5 billion (June 1993)
Industrial production: growth rate 6.9% (FY93 est.); accounts for 9.4% of GDP
Electricity:
capacity: 2,400,000 kW
production: 9 billion kWh
consumption per capita: 75 kWh (1992)
Industries: jute manufacturing, cotton textiles, food processing, steel, fertilizer
Agriculture: accounts for 33% of GDP, 65% of employment, and one-fifth of exports; world's largest exporter of jute; commercial products—jute, rice, wheat, tea, sugarcane, potatoes, beef, milk, poultry; shortages include wheat, vegetable oils, cotton
Illicit drugs: transit country for illegal drugs produced in neighboring countries
Economic aid:
recipient: US commitments, including Ex-Im (FY70-89), $3.4 billion; Western (non-US) countries, ODA and OOF bilateral commitments (1980-89), $11.65 million; OPEC bilateral aid (1979-89), $6.52 million; Communist countries (1970-89), $1.5 billion
Currency: 1 taka (Tk) = 100 poiska
Exchange rates: taka (Tk) per US$1— 40.064 (January 1994), 39.567 (1993), 38.951

(1992), 36.596 (1991), 34.569 (1990), 32.270 (1989)

Fiscal year: 1 July—30 June

Communications

Railroads: 2,892 km total (1986); 1,914 km 1.000-meter gauge, 978 km 1.676-meter broad gauge
Highways:
total: 7,240 km
paved: 3,840 km
unpaved: 3,400 km (1985)
Inland waterways: 5,150-8,046 km navigable waterways (includes 2,575-3,058 km main cargo routes)
Pipelines: natural gas 1,220 km
Ports: Chittagong, Chalna
Merchant marine: 41 ships (1,000 GRT or over) totaling 312,172 GRT/458,131 DWT, cargo 33, oil tanker 2, refrigerated cargo 3, bulk 3
Airports:
total: 16
usable: 12
with permanent-surface runways: 12
with runways over 3,659 m: 0
with runways 2,440-3,659 m: 4
with runways 1,220-2,439 m: 6
Telecommunications: adequate international radio communications and landline service; poor domestic telephone service; 241.250 telephones—only one telephone for each 522 persons; fair broadcast service; broadcast stations—9 AM, 6 FM, 11 TV; 2 Indian Ocean INTELSAT satellite earth stations

Defense Forces

Branches: Army, Navy, Air Force
paramilitary forces: Bangladesh Rifles, Bangladesh Ansars, Armed Police Reserve, Defense Parties, National Cadet Corps
Manpower availability: males age 15-49 31,955,948; fit for military service 18,967,602
Defense expenditures: exchange rate conversion—$355 million, 1.5% of GDP (FY92/93)

Geography

Location: Southern Asia, at the head of the Bay of Bengal, almost completely surrounded by India
Map references: Asia, Standard Time Zones of the World
Area:
total area: 144,000 sq km
land area: 133,910 sq km
comparative area: slightly smaller than Wisconsin
Land boundaries: total 4,246 km, Burma 193 km, India 4,053 km
Coastline: 580 km
Maritime claims:
contiguous zone: 18 nm
continental shelf: up to outer limits of continental margin
exclusive economic zone: 200 nm
territorial sea: 12 nm
International disputes: a portion of the boundary with India is in dispute; water-sharing problems with upstream riparian India over the Ganges
Climate: tropical; cool, dry winter (October to March); hot, humid summer (March to June); cool, rainy monsoon (June to October)
Terrain: mostly flat alluvial plain; hilly in southeast
Natural resources: natural gas, arable land, timber
Land use:
arable land: 67%
permanent crops: 2%
meadows and pastures: 4%
forest and woodland: 16%
other: 11%
Irrigated land: 27,380 sq km (1989)
Environment:
current issues: many people are landless and forced to live on and cultivate flood-prone land; limited access to potable water; water-borne diseases prevalent; water pollution especially of fishing areas results from the use of commercial pesticides; intermittent water shortages because of falling water tables in the northern and central parts of the country; soil degradation; deforestation·

severe overpopulation
natural hazards: vulnerable to droughts,
cyclones; much of the country routinely
flooded during the summer monsoon season
international agreements: party to—
Endangered Species, Environmental
Modification, Hazardous Wastes, Nuclear Test
Ban, Ozone Layer Protection; signed, but not
ratified—Biodiversity, Climate Change, Law
of the Sea

People

Population: 125,149,469 (July 1994 est.)
Population growth rate: 2.33% (1994 est.)
Birth rate: 35.02 births/1,000 population
(1994 est.)
Death rate: 11.68 deaths/1,000 population
(1994 est.)
Net migration rate: 0 migrant(s)/1,000
population (1994 est.)
Infant mortality rate: 106.9 deaths/1,000
live births (1994 est.)
Life expectancy at birth:
total population: 55.08 years
male: 55.35 years
female: 54.8 years (1994 est.)
Total fertility rate: 4.47 children
born/woman (1994 est.)
Nationality:
noun: Bangladeshi(s)
adjective: Bangladesh
Ethnic divisions: Bengali 98%, Biharis
250,000, tribals less than 1 million
Religions: Muslim 83%, Hindu 16%,
Buddhist, Christian, other
Languages: Bangla (official), English
Literacy: age 15 and over can read and write
(1990 est.)
total population: 35%
male: 47%
female: 22%
Labor force: 50.1 million
by occupation: agriculture 65%, services 21%,
industry and mining 14% (1989)
note: extensive export of labor to Saudi
Arabia, UAE, and Oman (1991)

Government

Names:
conventional long form: People's Republic of
Bangladesh
conventional short form: Bangladesh
former: East Pakistan
Digraph: BG
Type: republic
Capital: Dhaka
Administrative divisions: 64 districts
(zillagulo, singular—zilla); Bagerhat,
Bandarban, Barguna, Barisal, Bhola, Bogra,
Brahmanbaria, Chandpur, Chapai Nawabganj,
Chattagram, Chuadanga, Comilla, Cox's
Bazar, Dhaka, Dinajpur, Faridpur, Feni,
Gaibandha, Gazipur, Gopalganj, Habiganj,
Jaipurhat, Jamalpur, Jessore, Jhalakati,
Jhenaidah, Khagrachari, Khulna, Kishorganj,
Kurigram, Kushtia, Laksmipur, Lalmonirhat,
Madaripur, Magura, Manikganj, Meherpur,
Moulavibazar, Munshiganj, Mymensingh,
Naogaon, Narail, Narayanganj, Narsingdi,
Nator, Netrakona, Nilphamari, Noakhali,
Pabna, Panchagar, Parbattya Chattagram,
Patuakhali, Pirojpur, Rajbari, Rajshahi,
Rangpur, Satkhira, Shariyatpur, Sherpur,
Sirajganj, Sunamganj, Sylhet, Tangail,
Thakurgaon
Independence: 16 December 1971 (from
Pakistan)
National holiday: Independence Day, 26
March (1971)
Constitution: 4 November 1972, effective 16
December 1972, suspended following coup of
24 March 1982, restored 10 November 1986,
amended many times
Legal system: based on English common law
Suffrage: 18 years of age; universal
Executive branch:
chief of state: President Abdur Rahman
BISWAS (since 8 October 1991); election last
held 8 October 1991 (next to be held by NA
October 1996); results—Abdur Rahman
BISWAS received 52.1% of parliamentary
vote
head of government: Prime Minister Khaleda
ZIAur RAHMAN (since 20 March 1991)
cabinet: Council of Ministers; appointed by

the president
Legislative branch: unicameral
National Parliament (Jatiya Sangsad):
elections last held 27 February 1991 (next to be
held NA February 1996); results—percent of
vote by party NA; seats—(330 total, 300
elected and 30 seats reserved for women) BNP
168, AL 93, JP 35, JI 20, BCP 5, National
Awami Party (Muzaffar) 1, Workers Party 1,
JSD 1, Ganotantri Party 1, Islami Oikya Jote 1,
NDP 1, independents 3
Judicial branch: Supreme Court
Political parties and leaders: Bangladesh
Nationalist Party (BNP), Khaleda ZIAur
RAHMAN; Awami League (AL), Sheikh
Hasina WAJED; Jatiyo Party (JP), Hussain
Mohammad ERSHAD (in jail); Jamaat-E-
Islami (JI), Ali KHAN; Bangladesh
Communist Party (BCP), Saifuddin Ahmed
MANIK; National Awami Party (Muzaffar);
Workers Party, leader NA; Jatiyo Samajtantik
Dal (JSD), Serajul ALAM KHAN; Ganotantri
Party, leader NA; Islami Oikya Jote, leader
NA; National Democratic Party (NDP), leader
NA; Muslim League, Khan A. SABUR;
Democratic League, Khondakar
MUSHTAQUE Ahmed; Democratic League,
Khondakar MUSHTAQUE Ahmed; United
People's Party, Kazi ZAFAR Ahmed
Member of: AsDB, C, CCC, CP, ESCAP,
FAO, G-77, GATT, IAEA, IBRD, ICAO,
ICFTU, IDA, IDB, IFAD, IFC, ILO, IMF,
IMO, INTELSAT, INTERPOL, IOC, IOM,
ISO, ITU, LORCS, MINURSO, NAM, OIC,
SAARC, UN, UNCTAD, UNESCO, UNIDO,
UNIKOM, UNOMIG, UNOMOZ, UNOMUR,
UNOSOM, UNPROFOR, UNTAC, UPU,
WCL, WHO, WFTU, WIPO, WMO, WTO
Diplomatic representation in US:
chief of mission: Ambassador Abul AHSAN
chancery: 2201 Wisconsin Avenue NW,
Washington, DC 20007
telephone: (202) 342-8372 through 8376
consulate(s) general: New York
US diplomatic representation:
chief of mission: Ambassador David
MERRILL
embassy: Diplomatic Enclave, Madani
Avenue, Baridhara, Dhaka
mailing address: G. P. O. Box 323, Dhaka

1212
telephone: [880] (2) 884700-22
FAX: [880] (2) 883-744
Flag: green with a large red disk slightly to the
hoist side of center; green is the traditional
color of Islam

U.S. Government Contacts:

U.S. Trade Desk: (202) 482-2954

Bangladesh Government Contacts:

Mr. M. Mokammel Haque
Executive Chairman
Board of Investment of Bangladesh
Shelpa Bhaban
Motijheel C/A.
Dhaka
Tel: 8802 861140, 405121-8
Fax: 880-2-833626

Legal Services:

Dr. Kamal Hossain & Associates
Chamber Building, 2nd Floor
122-124, Motijheel C/A
Dhaka
Tel: 880-2-864966, 232946, 407086
Fax: 880-2-833075

The Law Associates
Globe Chamber, 2nd Floor
104, Motijheel C/A
Dhaka
Tel: 880-2-234098, 252694, 863927
Fax: 880-2-863927

K.S. Zamaa & Associates
Advocate Bangladesh Supreme Court
Chamber: 35 Shidheswary Circular Road
Dhaka - 1217
Tel: 880-2-834696
Fax: 880-2-889376

Consultants:

Bangladesh Consultants Ltd.
34 Dhanmondi R/A, Road 16 (New)
Dhaka - 1209
Tel: 880-2-317019, 319559, 319208

Engineering & Planning Services:

Bangladesh Engineering & Technological Services, Ltd., (Bets)
11, Motijheel C/A., Dhaka
Tel: 880-2-235984, 235328
Fax: 880-2-81300 & 833188

Engineers & Consultants Bangladesh Ltd. (ECBL)
17, Bakshibazar. Dhaka - 1211
Tel: 880-2-862735-36
Fax: 880-2-864711

Engineering & Planning Consultants Ltd.
43, Dilkusha C/A. Dhaka
Tel: 880-2-234141, 833654, 235533

BHUTAN

75 km

Economy

Overview: The economy, one of the world's least developed, is based on agriculture and forestry, which provide the main livelihood for 90% of the population and account for about 50% of GDP. Rugged mountains dominate the terrain and make the building of roads and other infrastructure difficult and expensive. The economy is closely aligned with that of India through strong trade and monetary links. The industrial sector is small and technologically backward, with most production of the cottage industry type. Most development projects, such as road construction, rely on Indian migrant labor. Bhutan's hydropower potential and its attraction for tourists are its most important natural resources; however, the government limits the number of tourists to 4,000 per year to minimize foreign influence. Much of the impetus for growth has come from large public-sector companies. Nevertheless, in recent years, Bhutan has shifted toward decentralized development planning and greater private initiative. The government privatized several large public-sector firms, is revamping its trade regime and liberalizing administerial procedures over industrial licensing. The government's industrial contribution to GDP decreased from 13% in 1988 to about 10% in 1992.

National product: GDP—purchasing power equivalent—$500 million (1993 est.)
National product real growth rate: 5% (FY93 est.)
National product per capita: $700 (1993 est.)
Inflation rate (consumer prices): 11% (October 1993)
Unemployment rate: NA%
Budget:
revenues: $100 million
expenditures: $112 million, including capital expenditures of $60 million (FY92 est.)
note: the government of India finances nearly one-quarter of Bhutan's budget expenditures
Exports: $66 million (f.o.b., FY93 est.)
commodities: cardamon, gypsum, timber, handicrafts, cement, fruit, electricity (to India), precious stones, spices
partners: India 82%, Bangladesh, Singapore
Imports: $125 million (c.i.f., FY93 est.)
commodities: fuel and lubricants, grain, machinery and parts, vehicles, fabrics
partners: India 60%, Japan, Germany, US, UK
External debt: $141 million (June 1993)
Industrial production: growth rate NA%; accounts for 8% of GDP; primarily cottage industry and home based handicrafts
Electricity:
capacity: 336,000 kW
production: 1.5422 billion kWh
consumption per capita: 2,203 kWh (25.8% is exported to India leaving 1,633 kWh per capita; 1990-91)
Industries: cement, wood products, processed fruits, alcoholic beverages, calcium carbide
Agriculture: accounts for 45% of GDP; based on subsistence farming and animal husbandry;

self-sufficient in food except for foodgrains; other production—rice, corn, root crops, citrus fruit, dairy products, eggs

Economic aid:
recipient: Western (non-US) countries, ODA and OOF bilateral commitments (1970-89), $115 million; OPEC bilateral aid (1979-89), $11 million

Currency: 1 ngultrum (Nu) = 100 chetrum; note—Indian currency is also legal tender

Exchange rates: ngultrum (Nu) per US$1—31.370 (January 1994), 30.493 (1993), 25.918 (1992), 22.742 (1991), 17.504 (1990), 16.226 (1989); note—the Bhutanese ngultrum is at par with the Indian rupee

Fiscal year: 1 July—30 June

Communications

Highways:
total: 2,165 km
paved: NA
unpaved: gravel 1,703 km
undifferentiated: 462 km

Airports:
total: 2
usable: 2
with permanent-surface runways: 1
with runways over 3,659 m: 0
with runways 2,440-3,659 m: 0
with runways 1,220-2,439 m: 2

Telecommunications: domestic telephone service is very poor with very few telephones in use; international telephone and telegraph service is by land line through India; a satellite earth station was planned (1990); broadcast stations—1 AM, 1 FM, no TV (1990)

Defense Forces

Branches: Royal Bhutan Army, Palace Guard, Militia

Manpower availability: males age 15-49 424,558; fit for military service 226,851; reach military age (18) annually 17,310 (1994 est.)

Defense expenditures: exchange rate conversion—$NA, NA% of GDP

Geography

Location: Southern Asia, in the Himalayas, between China and India

Map references: Asia, Standard Time Zones of the World

Area:
total area: 47,000 sq km
land area: 47,000 sq km
comparative area: slightly more than half the size of Indiana

Land boundaries: total 1,075 km, China 470 km, India 605 km

Coastline: 0 km (landlocked)

Maritime claims: none; landlocked

International disputes: none

Climate: varies; tropical in southern plains; cool winters and hot summers in central valleys; severe winters and cool summers in Himalayas

Terrain: mostly mountainous with some fertile valleys and savanna

Natural resources: timber, hydropower, gypsum, calcium carbide

Land use:
arable land: 2%
permanent crops: 0%
meadows and pastures: 5%
forest and woodland: 70%
other: 23%

Irrigated land: 340 sq km (1989 est.)

Environment:
current issues: soil erosion; limited access to safe drinking water
natural hazards: violent storms coming down from the Himalayas are the source of the country's name which translates as Land of the Thunder Dragon
international agreements: party to—Nuclear Test Ban; signed, but not ratified—Biodiversity, Climate Change, Law of the Sea

Note: landlocked; strategic location between China and India; controls several key Himalayan mountain passes

People

Population: 716,380 (July 1994 est.)
note: other estimates range as high as 1.7 million (July 1994 est.)

Population growth rate: 2.34% (1994 est.)
Birth rate: 39.31 births/1,000 population (1994 est.)
Death rate: 15.93 deaths/1,000 population (1994 est.)
Net migration rate: 0 migrant(s)/1,000 population (1994 est.)
Infant mortality rate: 121 deaths/1,000 live births (1994 est.)
Life expectancy at birth:
total population: 50.6 years
male: 51.15 years
female: 50.03 years (1994 est.)
Total fertility rate: 5.42 children born/woman (1994 est.)
Nationality:
noun: Bhutanese (singular and plural)
adjective: Bhutanese
Ethnic divisions: Bhote 50%, ethnic Nepalese 35%, indigenous or migrant tribes 15%
Religions: Lamaistic Buddhism 75%, Indian- and Nepalese-influenced Hinduism 25%
Languages: Dzongkha (official), Bhotes speak various Tibetan dialects; Nepalese speak various Nepalese dialects
Literacy:
total population: NA%
male: NA%
female: NA%
Labor force: NA
by occupation: agriculture 93%, services 5%, industry and commerce 2%
note: massive lack of skilled labor

Government

Names:
conventional long form: Kingdom of Bhutan
conventional short form: Bhutan
Digraph: BT
Type: monarchy; special treaty relationship with India
Capital: Thimphu
Administrative divisions: 18 districts (dzongkhag, singular and plural); Bumthang, Chhukha, Chirang, Daga, Geylegphug, Ha, Lhuntshi, Mongar, Paro, Pemagatsel, Punakha, Samchi, Samdrup Jongkhar, Shemgang, Tashigang, Thimphu, Tongsa, Wangdi Phodrang
Independence: 8 August 1949 (from India)
National holiday: National Day, 17 December (1907) (Ugyen Wangchuck became first hereditary king)
Constitution: no written constitution or bill of rights
Legal system: based on Indian law and English common law; has not accepted compulsory ICJ jurisdiction
Suffrage: each family has one vote in village-level elections
Executive branch:
Chief of State and Head of Government: King Jigme Singye WANGCHUCK (since 24 July 1972)
Royal Advisory Council (Lodoi Tsokde): nominated by the king
cabinet: Council of Ministers (Lhengye Shungtsog); appointed by the king
Legislative branch: unicameral National Assembly (Tshogdu); no national elections
Judicial branch: High Court
Political parties and leaders: no legal parties
Other political or pressure groups: Buddhist clergy; Indian merchant community; ethnic Nepalese organizations leading militant antigovernment campaign
Member of: AsDB, CP, ESCAP, FAO, G-77, IBRD, ICAO, IDA, IFAD, IMF, INTELSAT, IOC, ITU, NAM, SAARC, UN, UNCTAD, UNESCO, UNIDO, UPU, WHO
Diplomatic representation in US: no formal diplomatic relations; the Bhutanese mission to the UN in New York has consular jurisdiction in the US
consulate(s) general: New York
US diplomatic representation: no formal diplomatic relations, although informal contact is maintained between the Bhutanese and US Embassies in New Delhi (India)
Flag: divided diagonally from the lower hoist side corner; the upper triangle is orange and the lower triangle is red; centered along the dividing line is a large black and white dragon facing away from the hoist side

BRUNEI

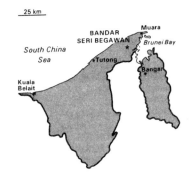

25 km

BANDAR
SERI BEGAWAN · Muara
· Brunei Bay

South China
Sea · Tutong

· Bangar

Kuala
Belait

Economy

Overview: The economy is a mixture of foreign and domestic entrepreneurship, government regulation and welfare measures, and village tradition. It is almost totally supported by exports of crude oil and natural gas, with revenues from the petroleum sector accounting for more than 50% of GDP. Per capita GDP is among the highest in the Third World, and substantial income from overseas investment supplements domestic production. The government provides for all medical services and subsidizes food and housing.
National product: GDP—exchange rate conversion—$2.5 billion (1991 est.)
National product real growth rate: 1% (1991)
National product per capita: $9,000 (1991 est.)
Inflation rate (consumer prices): 2% (1993 est.)
Unemployment rate: 3.7% (1989)
Budget:
revenues: $1.3 billion
expenditures: $1.5 billion, including capital expenditures of $255 million (1989 est.)
Exports: $2.3 billion (f.o.b., 1992 est.)
commodities: crude oil, liquefied natural gas, petroleum products
partners: Japan 53%, UK 12%, South Korea 9%, Thailand 7%, Singapore 5% (1990)

Imports: $2 billion (c.i.f., 1992 est.)
commodities: machinery and transport equipment, manufactured goods, food, chemicals
partners: Singapore 35%, UK 26%, Switzerland 9%, US 9%, Japan 5% (1990)
External debt: $0
Industrial production: growth rate 12.9% (1987); accounts for 52.4% of GDP
Electricity:
capacity: 310,000 kW
production: 890 million kWh
consumption per capita: 3,300 kWh (1990)
Industries: petroleum, petroleum refining, liquefied natural gas, construction
Agriculture: imports about 80% of its food needs; principal crops and livestock include rice, cassava, bananas, buffaloes, and pigs
Economic aid:
recipient: US commitments, including Ex-Im (FY70-87), $20.6 million; Western (non-US) countries, ODA and OOF bilateral commitments (1970-89), $153 million
Currency: 1 Bruneian dollar (B$) = 100 cents
Exchange rates: Bruneian dollars (B$) per US$1—1.6032 (January 1994), 1.6158 (1993), 1.6290 (1992), 1.7276 (1991), 1.8125 (1990), 1.9503 (1989); note—the Bruneian dollar is at par with the Singapore dollar
Fiscal year: calendar year

Communications

Railroads: 13 km 0.610-meter narrow-gauge private line
Highways:
total: 1,090 km
paved: bituminous 370 km (with another 52 km under construction)
unpaved: gravel or earth 720 km
Inland waterways: 209 km; navigable by craft drawing less than 1.2 meters
Pipelines: crude oil 135 km; petroleum products 418 km; natural gas 920 km
Ports: Kuala Belait, Muara
Merchant marine: 7 liquefied gas carrier (1,000 GRT or over) totaling 348,476 GRT/340,635 DWT
Airports:
total: 2

usable: 2
with permanent-surface runways: 1
with runway over 3,659 m: 1
with runway 2,440-3,659 m: 0
with runway 1,220-2,439 m: 1
Telecommunications: service throughout country is adequate for present needs; international service good to adjacent Malaysia; radiobroadcast coverage good; 33,000 telephones (1987); broadcast stations—4 AM/FM, 1 TV; 74,000 radio receivers (1987); satellite earth stations—1 Indian Ocean INTELSAT and 1 Pacific Ocean INTELSAT

Defense Forces

Branches: Land Force, Navy, Air Force, Royal Brunei Police
Manpower availability: males age 15-49 79,486; fit for military service 46,258; reach military age (18) annually 2,756 (1994 est.)
Defense expenditures: exchange rate conversion—$300 million, 9% of GDP (1990)

Geography

Location: Southeastern Asia, on the northern coast of Borneo almost completely surrounded by Malaysia
Map references: Asia, Oceania, Southeast Asia, Standard Time Zones of the World
Area:
total area: 5,770 sq km
land area: 5,270 sq km
comparative area: slightly larger than Delaware
Land boundaries: total 381 km, Malysia 381 km
Coastline: 161 km
Maritime claims:
exclusive fishing zone: 200 nm
territorial sea: 12 nm
International disputes: may wish to purchase the Malaysian salient that divides the country; all of the Spratly Islands are claimed by China, Taiwan, and Vietnam; parts of them are claimed by Malaysia and the Philippines; in 1984, Brunei established an exclusive fishing zone that encompasses Louisa Reef, but has not publicly claimed the island

Climate: tropical; hot, humid, rainy
Terrain: flat coastal plain rises to mountains in east; hilly lowland in west
Natural resources: petroleum, natural gas, timber
Land use:
arable land: 1%
permanent crops: 1%
meadows and pastures: 1%
forest and woodland: 79%
other: 18%
Irrigated land: 10 sq km (1989 est.)
Environment:
current issues: NA
international agreements: party to—Ozone Layer Protection, Ship Pollution; signed, but not ratified—Law of the Sea
natural hazards: typhoons, earthquakes, and severe flooding are rare
Note: close to vital sea lanes through South China Sea linking Indian and Pacific Oceans; two parts physically separated by Malaysia; almost an enclave of Malaysia

People

Population: 284,653 (July 1994 est.)
Population growth rate: 2.7% (1994 est.)
Birth rate: 26.18 births/1,000 population (1994 est.)
Death rate: 5.04 deaths/1,000 population (1994 est.)
Net migration rate: 5.81 migrant(s)/1,000 population (1994 est.)
Infant mortality rate: 25.2 deaths/1,000 live births (1994 est.)
Life expectancy at birth:
total population: 71.1 years
male: 69.46 years
female: 72.78 years (1994 est.)
Total fertility rate: 3.43 children born/woman (1994 est.)
Nationality:
noun: Bruneian(s)
adjective: Bruneian
Ethnic divisions: Malay 64%, Chinese 20%, other 16%
Religions: Muslim (official) 63%, Buddhism 14%, Christian 8%, indigenous beliefs and other 15% (1981)

Languages: Malay (official), English, Chinese
Literacy: age 15 and over can read and write (1981)
total population: 77%
male: 85%
female: 69%
Labor force: 89,000 (includes members of the Army)
by occupation: government 47.5%, production of oil, natural gas, services, and construction 41.9%, agriculture, forestry, and fishing 3.8% (1986)
note: 33% of labor force is foreign (1988)

Government

Names:
conventional long form: Negara Brunei Darussalam
conventional short form: Brunei
Digraph: BX
Type: constitutional sultanate
Capital: Bandar Seri Begawan
Administrative divisions: 4 districts (daerah-daerah, singular—daerah); Belait, Brunei and Muara, Temburong, Tutong
Independence: 1 January 1984 (from UK)
National holiday: National Day 23 February (1984)
Constitution: 29 September 1959 (some provisions suspended under a State of Emergency since December 1962, others since independence on 1 January 1984)
Legal system: based on Islamic law
Suffrage: none
Executive branch:
chief of state and head of government: Sultan and Prime Minister His Majesty Paduka Seri Baginda Sultan Haji HASSANAL Bolkiah Mu'izzaddin Waddaulah (since 5 October 1967)
cabinet: Council of Cabinet Ministers; composed chiefly of members of the royal family
Legislative branch: unicameral
Legislative Council (Majlis Masyuarat Megeri): elections last held in March 1962; in 1970 the Council was changed to an appointive body by decree of the sultan; an elected

legislative Council is being considered as part of constitution reform, but elections are unlikely for several years
Judicial branch: Supreme Court
Political parties and leaders: Brunei United National Party (inactive), Anak HASANUDDIN, chairman; Brunei National Democratic Party (the first legal political party and now banned), leader NA
Member of: APEC, ASEAN, C, ESCAP, FAO, G-77, GATT, ICAO, IDB, IMO, INTELSAT (nonsignatory user), INTERPOL, IOC, ISO (correspondent), ITU, NAM, OIC, UN, UNCTAD, UPU, UNTAC, WHO, WMO
Diplomatic representation in US:
chief of mission: Ambassador JAYA bin Abdul Latif
chancery: 2600 Virginia Avenue NW, Suite 300, Washington, DC 20037
telephone: (202) 342-0159
FAX: (202) 342-0158
US diplomatic representation:
chief of mission: Ambassador Theresa A. TULL
embassy: Third Floor, Teck Guan Plaza, Jalan Sultan, Bandar Seri Begawan
mailing address: American Embassy Box B, APO AP 96440
telephone: [673] (2) 229-670
FAX: [673] (2) 225-293
Flag: yellow with two diagonal bands of white (top, almost double width) and black starting from the upper hoist side; the national emblem in red is superimposed at the center; the emblem includes a swallow-tailed flag on top of a winged column within an upturned crescent above a scroll and flanked by two upraised hands

U.S. Government Contacts:

U.S. Trade Desk: (202) 482-3877

Brunei Government Contacts:

Ministry of Industry and Primary Resources
Bandar Seri Begawan, 1220
Brunei Darussalam
Tel: 673-2-244822
Fax: 673-2-244811

Travel:

International Hotels in Country:
Bandar Seri Begawan
Sheraton Utama, Tel: 673-2-244272, Fax: 673-2-221579
Brunei Hotel, Tel: 673-2-242372, Fax: 673-2-226196.

BURMA

Economy

Overview: Burma has a mixed economy with about 70% private activity, mainly in agriculture, light industry, and transport, and with about 30% state-controlled activity, mainly in energy, heavy industry, and foreign trade. Government policy in the last five years, 1989-93, has aimed at revitalizing the economy after four decades of tight central planning. Thus, private activity has markedly increased; foreign investment has been encouraged, so far with moderate success; and efforts continue to increase the efficiency of state enterprises. Published estimates of Burma's foreign trade are greatly understated because of the volume of black market trade. A major ongoing problem is the failure to achieve monetary and fiscal stability. Inflation has been running at 25% to 30% annually. Good weather helped boost GDP by perhaps 5% in 1993. Although Burma remains a poor Asian country, its rich resources furnish the potential for substantial long-term increases in income, exports, and living standards.

National product: GDP—purchasing power equivalent—$41 billion (1993 est.)

National product real growth rate: 5% (1993 est.)

National product per capita: $950 (1993 est.)

Inflation rate (consumer prices): 30% (1993 est.)

Unemployment rate: NA%

Budget:
revenues: $8.1 billion
expenditures: $11.6 billion, including capital expenditures of $NA (1992)

Exports: $613.4 million (FY93)
commodities: pulses and beans, teak, rice, hardwood
partners: Singapore, China, Thailand, India, Hong Kong

Imports: $1.02 billion (FY93)
commodities: machinery, transport equipment, chemicals, food products
partners: Japan, China, Thailand, Singapore, Malaysia

External debt: $4 billion (1992)

Industrial production: growth rate 4.9% (FY93 est.); accounts for 10% of GDP

Electricity:
capacity: 1,100,000 kW
production: 2.8 billion kWh
consumption per capita: 65 kWh (1992)

Industries: agricultural processing; textiles and footwear; wood and wood products; petroleum refining; mining of copper, tin, tungsten, iron; construction materials; pharmaceuticals; fertilizer

Agriculture: accounts for 40% of GDP and 66% of employment (including fish and forestry); self-sufficient in food; principal crops—paddy rice, corn, oilseed, sugarcane, pulses; world's largest stand of hardwood trees; rice and timber account for 55% of export revenues

Illicit drugs: world's largest illicit producer of opium (2,575 metric tons in 1993) and minor producer of cannabis for the international drug trade; opium production has doubled since the collapse of Rangoon's antinarcotic programs

Economic aid:
recipient: US commitments, including Ex-Im (FY70-89), $158 million; Western (non-US) countries, ODA and OOF bilateral commitments (1970-89), $3.9 billion; Communist countries (1970-89), $424 million

Currency: 1 kyat (K) = 100 pyas

Exchange rates: kyats (K) per US$1— 6.2301 (December 1993), 6.1570 (1993),

6.1045 (1992), 6.2837 (1991), 6.3386 (1990), 6.7049 (1989); unofficial—105
Fiscal year: 1 April—31 March

Communications

Railroads: 3,991 km total, all government owned; 3,878 km 1.000-meter gauge, 113 km narrow-gauge industrial lines; 362 km double track
Highways:
total: 27,000 km
paved: bituminous 3,200 km
unpaved: gravel, improved earth 17,700 km; unimproved earth 6,100 km
Inland waterways: 12,800 km; 3,200 km navigable by large commercial vessels
Pipelines: crude oil 1,343 km; natural gas 330 km
Ports: Rangoon, Moulmein, Bassein
Merchant marine: 47 ships (1,000 GRT or over) totaling 665,628 GRT/941,512 DWT, passenger-cargo 3, cargo 15, refrigerated cargo 5, vehicle carrier 2, container 2, oil tanker 2, chemical 1, combination ore/oil 1, bulk 15, combination bulk 1
Airports:
total: 83
usable: 78
with permanent-surface runways: 24
with runways over 3,659 m: 0
with runways 2,440-3,659 m: 3
with runways 1,220-2,439 m: 38
Telecommunications: meets minimum requirements for local and intercity service for business and government; international service is good; 53,000 telephones (1986); radiobroadcast coverage is limited to the most populous areas; broadcast stations—2 AM, 1 FM, 1 TV (1985); 1 Indian Ocean INTELSAT earth station

Defense Forces

Branches: Army, Navy, Air Force
Manpower availability: males age 15-49 11,199,531; females age 15-49 11,273,643; males fit for military service 5,979,710; females fit for military service 6,034,810; males reach military age (18) annually 445,933 (1994 est.); females reach military age (18) annually 430,738 (1994 est.); both sexes liable for military service
Defense expenditures: exchange rate conversion—$NA, NA% of GDP

Geography

Location: Southeastern Asia, bordering the Bay of Bengal, between Bangladesh and Thailand
Map references: Asia, Southeast Asia, Standard Time Zones of the World
Area:
total area: 678,500 sq km
land area: 657,740 sq km
comparative area: slightly smaller than Texas
Land boundaries: total 5,876 km, Bangladesh 193 km, China 2,185 km, India 1,463 km, Laos 235 km, Thailand 1,800 km
Coastline: 1,930 km
Maritime claims:
contiguous zone: 24 nm
continental shelf: 200 nm or to the edge of continental margin
exclusive economic zone: 200 nm
territorial sea: 12 nm
International disputes: none
Climate: tropical monsoon; cloudy, rainy, hot, humid summers (southwest monsoon, June to September); less cloudy, scant rainfall, mild temperatures, lower humidity during winter (northeast monsoon, December to April)
Terrain: central lowlands ringed by steep, rugged highlands
Natural resources: petroleum, timber, tin, antimony, zinc, copper, tungsten, lead, coal, some marble, limestone, precious stones, natural gas
Land use:
arable land: 15%
permanent crops: 1%
meadows and pastures: 1%
forest and woodland: 49%
other: 34%
Irrigated land: 10,180 sq km (1989)
Environment:
current issues: deforestation

natural hazards: subject to destructive earthquakes and cyclones; flooding and landslides common during rainy season (June to September)
international agreements: party to—Nuclear Test Ban, Ozone Layer Protection, Ship Pollution, Tropical Timber; signed, but not ratified—Biodiversity, Climate Change, Law of the Sea
Note: strategic location near major Indian Ocean shipping lanes

People

Population: 44,277,014 (July 1994 est.)
Population growth rate: 1.86% (1994 est.)
Birth rate: 28.45 births/1,000 population (1994 est.)
Death rate: 9.84 deaths/1,000 population (1994 est.)
Net migration rate: 0 migrant(s)/1,000 population (1994 est.)
Infant mortality rate: 63.7 deaths/1,000 live births (1994 est.)
Life expectancy at birth:
total population: 59.98 years
male: 57.94 years
female: 62.15 years (1994 est.)
Total fertility rate: 3.64 children born/woman (1994 est.)
Nationality:
noun: Burmese (singular and plural)
adjective: Burmese
Ethnic divisions: Burman 68%, Shan 9%, Karen 7%, Rakhine 4%, Chinese 3%, Mon 2%, Indian 2%, other 5%
Religions: Buddhist 89%, Christian 4% (Baptist 3%, Roman Catholic 1%), Muslim 4%, animist beliefs 1%, other 2%
Languages: Burmese; minority ethnic groups have their own languages
Literacy: age 15 and over can read and write (1990 est.)
total population: 81%
male: 89%
female: 72%
Labor force: 16.007 million (1992)
by occupation: agriculture 65.2%, industry 14.3%, trade 10.1%, government 6.3%, other 4.1% (FY89 est.)

Government

Names:
conventional long form: Union of Burma
conventional short form: Burma
local long form: Pyidaungzu Myanma Naingngandaw (translated by the US Government as Union of Myanma and by the Burmese as Union of Myanmar)
local short form: Myanma Naingngandaw
former: Socialist Republic of the Union of Burma
Digraph: BM
Type: military regime
Capital: Rangoon (sometimes translated as Yangon)
Administrative divisions: 7 divisions* (yin-mya, singular—yin) and 7 states (pyine-mya, singular—pyine); Chin State, Irrawaddy*, Kachin State, Karan State, Kayah State, Magwe*, Mandalay*, Mon State, Pegu*, Rakhine State, Rangoon*, Sagaing*, Shan State, Tenasserim*
Independence: 4 January 1948 (from UK)
National holiday: Independence Day, 4 January (1948)
Constitution: 3 January 1974 (suspended since 18 September 1988); National Convention started on 9 January 1993 to draft chapter headings for a new constitution
Legal system: has not accepted compulsory ICJ jurisdiction
Suffrage: 18 years of age; universal
Executive branch:
chief of state and head of government: Chairman of the State Law and Order Restoration Council Gen. THAN SHWE (since 23 April 1992)
State Law and Order Restoration Council: military junta which assumed power 18 September 1988
Legislative branch:
People's Assembly (Pyithu Hluttaw): last held 27 May 1990, but Assembly never convened; results—NLD 80%; seats—(485 total) NLD 396, the regime-favored NUP 10, other 79; was dissolved after the coup of 18 September 1988
Judicial branch: none; Council of People's Justices was abolished after the coup of 18 September 1988

Political parties and leaders: Union Solidarity and Development Association (USDA), leader NA; National Unity Party (NUP; proregime), THA KYAW; National League for Democracy (NLD), U AUNG SHWE

Other political or pressure groups: National Coalition Government of the Union of Burma (NCGUB), headed by the elected prime minister SEIN WIN (consists of individuals legitimately elected to Parliament but not recognized by the military regime; the group fled to a border area and joined with insurgents in December 1990 to form a parallel government; Kachin Independence Army (KIA); United Wa State Army (UWSA); Karen National Union (KNU); several Shan factions, including the Mong Tai Army (MTA); All Burma Student Democratic Front (ABSDF)

Member of: AsDB, CCC, CP, ESCAP, FAO, G-77, GATT, IAEA, IBRD, ICAO, IDA, IFAD, IFC, ILO, IMF, IMO, INTELSAT (nonsignatory user), INTERPOL, IOC, ITU, LORCS, NAM, UN, UNCTAD, UNESCO, UNIDO, UPU, WHO, WMO

Diplomatic representation in US:
chief of mission: Ambassador U THAUNG
chancery: 2300 S Street NW, Washington, DC 20008
telephone: (202) 332-9044 or 9045
consulate(s) general: New York

US diplomatic representation:
chief of mission: (vacant); Deputy Chief of Mission, Charge d'Affaires Franklin P. HUDDLE, Jr.
embassy: 581 Merchant Street, Rangoon
mailing address: American Embassy, Box B, APO AP 96546
telephone: [95] (1) 82055, 82181
FAX: [95] (1) 80409

Flag: red with a blue rectangle in the upper hoist-side corner bearing, all in white, 14 five-pointed stars encircling a cogwheel containing a stalk of rice; the 14 stars represent the 14 administrative divisions

---

U.S. Government Contacts:

U.S. Trade Desk: (202) 482-3877

CAMBODIA

125 km

Bătdâmbâng · Siĕmréab · Stœ̆ng Trêng · Tonle Sap · Krâchéh · **PHNOM PENH** ★ · Kâmpóng Saôm · Gulf of Thailand

Boundary representation is not necessarily authoritative.

Economy

Overview: The Cambodian economy—virtually destroyed by decades of war—is slowly recovering. Government leaders are moving toward restoring fiscal and monetary discipline and have established good working relations with international financial institutions. Despite such positive developments, the reconstruction effort faces many tough challenges. Rural Cambodia, where 90% of almost ten million Khmer live, remains mired in poverty. The almost total lack of basic infrastructure in the countryside will hinder development and will contribute to a growing imbalance in growth between urban and rural areas over the near term. Moreover, the new government's lack of experience in administering economic and technical assistance programs, and rampant corruption among officials, will slow the growth of critical public sector investment. Inflation for 1993 as a whole was 60%, less than a quarter of the 1992 rate, and was declining during the year. The government hoped the rate would fall to 10% in early 1994.

National product: GDP—purchasing power equivalent—$6 billion (1993 est.)

National product real growth rate: 7.5% (1993 est.)

National product per capita: $600 (1993 est.)

Inflation rate (consumer prices): 60% (1993 est.)

Unemployment rate: NA%

Budget:
revenues: $350 million
expenditures: $350 million, including capital expenditures of $133 million (1994 est.)

Exports: $70 million (f.o.b., 1992 est.)
commodities: natural rubber, rice, pepper, raw timber
partners: Thailand, Japan, India, Singapore, Malaysia, China, Vietnam

Imports: $360 million (c.i.f., 1992 est.)
commodities: international food aid; fuels, consumer goods, machinery
partners: Japan, India, Singapore, Malaysia, Thailand, China, Vietnam

External debt: total outstanding bilateral official debt to OECD members $248 million (yearend 1991), plus 840 million ruble debt to former CEMA countries

Industrial production: growth rate 15.6%; accounts for 10% of GDP

Electricity:
capacity: 35,000 kW
production: 70 million kWh
consumption per capita: 9 kWh (1990)

Industries: rice milling, fishing, wood and wood products, rubber, cement, gem mining

Agriculture: accounts for 50% of GDP; mainly subsistence farming except for rubber plantations; main crops—rice, rubber, corn; food shortages—rice, meat, vegetables, dairy products, sugar, flour

Illicit drugs: secondary transshipment country for heroin produced in the Golden Triangle

Economic aid:
recipient: US commitments, including Ex-Im (FY70-89), $725 million; Western (non-US countries) (1970-89), $300 million; Communist countries (1970-89), $1.8 billion donor countries and multilateral institutions pledged $880 million in assistance in 1992

Currency: 1 new riel (CR) = 100 sen

Exchange rates: riels (CR) per US$1—2,390 (December 1993), 2,800 (September 1992), 500 (December 1991), 560 (1990), 159.00 (1988), 100.00 (1987)

Fiscal year: calendar year

Communications

Railroads: 612 km 1.000-meter gauge, government owned
Highways:
total: 13,351 km (some roads in serious disrepair)
paved: bituminous 2,622 km
unpaved: crushed stone, gravel, or improved earth 7,105 km; unimproved earth 3,624 km
Inland waterways: 3,700 km navigable all year to craft drawing 0.6 meters; 282 km navigable to craft drawing 1.8 meters
Ports: Kampong Saom, Phnom Penh
Airports:
total: 20
usable: 13
with permanent-surface runways: 6
with runways over 3,659 m: 0
with runways 2,440-3,659 m: 2
with runways 1,220-2,439 m: 8
Telecommunications: service barely adequate for government requirements and virtually nonexistent for general public; international service limited to Vietnam and other adjacent countries; broadcast stations—1 AM, no FM, 1 TV

Defense Forces

Branches:
Khmer Royal Armed Forces (KRAF): created in 1993 by the merger of the Cambodian People's Armed Forces and the two non-Communist resistance armies; note—the KRAF is also known as the Royal Cambodian Armed Forces (RCAF)
Resistance forces: National Army of Democratic Kampuchea (Khmer Rouge)
Manpower availability: males age 15-49 2,182,912; fit for military service 1,217,357; reach military age (18) annually 67,463 (1994 est.)
Defense expenditures: exchange rate conversion—$NA, NA% of GDP

Geography

Location: Southeastern Asia, bordering the Gulf of Thailand, between Thailand and Vietnam

Map references: Asia, Southeast Asia, Standard Time Zones of the World
Area:
total area: 181,040 sq km
land area: 176,520 sq km
comparative area: slightly smaller than Oklahoma
Land boundaries: total 2,572 km, Laos 541 km, Thailand 803 km, Vietnam 1,228 km
Coastline: 443 km
Maritime claims:
contiguous zone: 24 nm
continental shelf: 200 nm
exclusive economic zone: 200 nm
territorial sea: 12 nm
International disputes: offshore islands and sections of the boundary with Vietnam are in dispute; maritime boundary with Vietnam not defined; parts of border with Thailand in dispute; maritime boundary with Thailand not clearly defined
Climate: tropical; rainy, monsoon season (May to October); dry season (December to March); little seasonal temperature variation
Terrain: mostly low, flat plains; mountains in southwest and north
Natural resources: timber, gemstones, some iron ore, manganese, phosphates, hydropower potential
Land use:
arable land: 16%
permanent crops: 1%
meadows and pastures: 3%
forest and woodland: 76%
other: 4%
Irrigated land: 920 sq km (1989 est.)
Environment:
current issues: deforestation resulting in habitat loss and declining biodiversity (in particular, destruction of mangrove swamps threatens natural fisheries)
natural hazards: monsoonal rains (June to November)
international agreements: party to—Marine Life Conservation; signed, but not ratified—Endangered Species, Law of the Sea, Marine Dumping
Note: a land of paddies and forests dominated by the Mekong River and Tonle Sap

People

Population: 10,264,628 (July 1994 est.)
Population growth rate: 2.87% (1994 est.)
Birth rate: 45.09 births/1,000 population (1994 est.)
Death rate: 16.36 deaths/1,000 population (1994 est.)
Net migration rate: 0 migrant(s)/1,000 population (1994 est.)
Infant mortality rate: 110.6 deaths/1,000 live births (1994 est.)
Life expectancy at birth:
total population: 49.26 years
male: 47.8 years
female: 50.8 years (1994 est.)
Total fertility rate: 5.81 children born/woman (1994 est.)
Nationality:
noun: Cambodian(s)
adjective: Cambodian
Ethnic divisions: Khmer 90%, Vietnamese 5%, Chinese 1%, other 4%
Religions: Theravada Buddhism 95%, other 5%
Languages: Khmer (official), French
Literacy: age 15 and over can read and write (1990 est.)
total population: 35%
male: 48%
female: 22%
Labor force: 2,500,000 to 3,000,000
by occupation: agriculture 80% (1988 est.)

Government

Names:
conventional long form: Kingdom of Cambodia
conventional short form: Cambodia
Digraph: CB
Type: multiparty liberal democracy under a constitutional monarchy established in September 1993
Capital: Phnom Penh
Administrative divisions: 20 provinces (khet, singular and plural); Banteay Meanchey, Batdambang, Kampong Cham, Kampong Chhnang, Kampong Spoe, Kampong Thum, Kampot, Kandal, Kaoh Kong, Kracheh, Mondol Kiri, Phnum Penh, Pouthisat, Preah Vihear, Prey Veng, Rotanokiri, Siemreab-Otdar Meanchey, Stoeng Treng, Svay Rieng, Takev
Independence: 9 November 1949 (from France)
National holiday: Independence Day, 9 November 1949
Constitution: promulgated September 1993
Legal system: currently being defined
Suffrage: 18 years of age; universal
Executive branch:
chief of state: King Norodom SIHANOUK (reinstated NA September 1993)
head of government: power shared between First Prime Minister Prince Norodom RANARIDDH and Second Prime Minister HUN SEN
cabinet: Council of Ministers; elected by the National Assembly
Legislative branch: unicameral; a 120-member constituent assembly based on proportional representation within each province was establised following the UN-supervised election in May 1993; the constituent assembly was transformed into a legislature in September 1993 after delegates promulgated the constitution
Judicial branch: Supreme Court established under the constitution has not yet been established and the future judicial system is yet to be defined by law
Political parties and leaders: National United Front for an Independent, Neutral, Peaceful, and Cooperative Cambodia (FUNCINPEC) under Prince NORODOM RANARIDDH; Cambodian Pracheachon Party or Cambodian People's Party (CPP) under CHEA SIM; Buddhist Liberal Democratic Party under SON SANN; Democratic Kampuchea (DK, also known as the Khmer Rouge) under KHIEU SAMPHAN
Member of: ACCT (observer), AsDB, CP, ESCAP, FAO, G-77, IAEA, IBRD, ICAO, IDA, IFAD, ILO, IMF, IMO, INTELSAT (nonsignatory user), INTERPOL, ITU, LORCS, NAM, PCA, UN, UNCTAD, UNESCO, UPU, WFTU, WHO, WMO, WTO
Diplomatic representation in US:
Ambassador SISOWATH SIRIRATH

represents Cambodia at the United Nations
US diplomatic representation:
chief of mission: Ambassador Charles H.
TWINING
embassy: 27 EO Street 240, Phnom Penh
mailing address: Box P, APO AP 96546
telephone: (855) 23-26436 or (855) 23-26438
FAX: (855) 23-26437
Flag: horizontal band of red separates two
equal horizontal bands of blue with a white
three-towered temple representing Angkor
Wat in the center

U.S. Government Contacts:

U.S. Trade Desk: (202) 482-3877

CHINA

1200 km

Boundary representation is not necessarily authoritative.

Economy

Overview: Beginning in late 1978 the Chinese leadership has been trying to move the economy from the sluggish Soviet-style centrally planned economy to a more productive and flexible economy with market elements, but still within the framework of monolithic Communist control. To this end the authorities switched to a system of household responsibility in agriculture in place of the old collectivization, increased the authority of local officials and plant managers in industry, permitted a wide variety of small-scale enterprise in services and light manufacturing, and opened the economy to increased foreign trade and investment. The result has been a strong surge in production, particularly in agriculture in the early 1980s. Industry also has posted major gains, especially in coastal areas near Hong Kong and opposite Taiwan, where foreign investment and modern production methods have helped spur production of both domestic and export goods. Aggregate output has more than doubled since 1978. On the darker side, the leadership has often experienced in its hybrid system the worst results of socialism (bureaucracy, lassitude, corruption) and of capitalism (windfall gains and stepped-up inflation). Beijing thus has periodically backtracked, retightening central controls at intervals. In 1992-93 annual growth of GDP has accelerated, particularly in the coastal areas—to more than 10% annually according to official claims. In late 1993 China's leadership approved additional reforms aimed at giving more play to market-oriented institutions and at strengthening the center's control over the financial system. Popular resistance, changes in central policy, and loss of authority by rural cadres have weakened China's population control program, which is essential to the nation's long-term economic viability.

National product: GDP—purchasing power equivalent—$2.61 trillion (1993 estimate based on a 1990 figure from the UN International Comparison Program, as extended to 1991 and published in the World Bank's World Development Report 1993; and as extrapolated by use of official Chinese growth statistics for 1992 and 1993)

National product real growth rate: 13.4% (1993)

National product per capita: $2,200 (1993 est.)

Inflation rate (consumer prices): 17.6% (December 1993 over December 1992)

Unemployment rate: 2.3% in urban areas (1992); substantial underemployment

Budget: deficit $15.6 billion (1993)

Exports: $92 billion (f.o.b., 1993)
commodities: textiles, garments, footwear, toys, crude oil
partners: Hong Kong, US, Japan, Germany, South Korea, Russia (1993)

Imports: $104 billion (c.i.f., 1993)
commodities: rolled steel, motor vehicles, textile machinery, oil products
partners: Japan, Taiwan, US, Hong Kong, Germany, South Korea (1993)

External debt: $80 billion (1993 est.)

Industrial production: growth rate 20.8% (1992)
Electricity:
capacity: 158,690,000 kW
production: 740 billion kWh
consumption per capita: 630 kWh (1992)
Industries: iron and steel, coal, machine building, armaments, textiles, petroleum, cement, chemical fertilizers, consumer durables, food processing
Agriculture: accounts for 26% of GNP; among the world's largest producers of rice, potatoes, sorghum, peanuts, tea, millet, barley, and pork; commercial crops include cotton, other fibers, and oilseeds; produces variety of livestock products; basically self-sufficient in food; fish catch of 13.35 million metric tons (including fresh water and pond raised) (1991)
Illicit drugs: illicit producer of opium; bulk of production is in Yunnan Province; transshipment point for heroin produced in the Golden Triangle
Economic aid:
donor: to less developed countries (1970-89) $7 billion
recipient: US commitments, including Ex-Im (FY70-87), $220.7 million; Western (non-US) countries, ODA and OOF bilateral commitments (1970-87), $13.5 billion
Currency: 1 yuan (¥) = 10 jiao
Exchange rates: yuan (¥) per US$1—8.7000 (January 1994), 5.7620 (1993), 5.5146 (1992), 5.3234 (1991), 4.7832 (1990), 3.7651 (1989)
note: beginning 1 January 1994, the People's Bank of China quotes the midpoint rate against the US dollar based on the previous day's prevailing rate in the interbank foreign exchange market
Fiscal year: calendar year

Communications

Railroads: total about 64,000 km; 54,000 km of common carrier lines, of which 53,400 km are 1.435-meter gauge (standard) and 600 km are 1.000-meter gauge (narrow); 11,200 km of standard gauge common carrier route are double tracked and 6,900 km are electrified (1990); an additional 10,000 km of varying gauges (0.762 to 1.067-meter) are dedicated industrial lines
Highways:
total: 1.029 million km
paved: 170,000 km
unpaved: gravel/improved earth 648,000 km; unimproved earth 211,000 km (1990)
Inland waterways: 138,600 km; about 109,800 km navigable
Pipelines: crude oil 9,700 km (1990); petroleum products 1,100 km; natural gas 6,200 km
Ports: Dalian, Guangzhou, Huangpu, Qingdao, Qinhuangdao, Shanghai, Xingang, Zhanjiang, Ningbo, Xiamen, Tanggu, Shantou
Merchant marine: 1,541 ships (1,000 GRT or over) totaling 14,884,756 GRT/22,475,985 DWT, passenger 24, short-sea passenger 43, passenger-cargo 25, cargo 819, refrigerated cargo 17, container 85, roll-on/roll-off cargo 21, multifunction/barge carrier 1, oil tanker 192, chemical tanker 13, bulk 285, liquefied gas 4, vehicle carrier 2, combination bulk 9, barge carrier 1
note: China beneficially owns an additional 227 ships (1,000 GRT or over) totaling approximately 6,187,117 DWT that operate under Panamanian, British, Hong Kong, Maltese, Liberian, Vanuatu, Cypriot, Saint Vincent, Bahamian, and Romanian registry
Airports:
total: 330
usable: 330
with permanent-surface runways: 260
with runways over 3,659 m: fewer than 10
with runways 2,440-3,659 m: 90
with runways 1,220-2,439 m: 200
Telecommunications: domestic and international services are increasingly available for private use; unevenly distributed internal system serves principal cities, industrial centers, and most townships; 11,000,000 telephones (December 1989); broadcast stations—274 AM, unknown FM, 202 (2,050 repeaters) TV; more than 215 million radio receivers; 75 million TVs; satellite earth stations—4 Pacific Ocean INTELSAT, 1 Indian Ocean INTELSAT, 1 INMARSAT, and 55 domestic

Defense Forces

Branches: People's Liberation Army (PLA), PLA Navy (including Marines), PLA Air Force, Second Artillery Corps (the strategic missile force), People's Armed Police (internal security troops, nominally subordinate to Ministry of Public Security, but included by the Chinese as part of the "armed forces" and considered to be an adjunct to the PLA in war time)

Manpower availability: males age 15-49 347,458,052; fit for military service 192,546,413; reach military age (18) annually 10,256,181 (1994 est.)

Defense expenditures: defense budget— 52.04 billion yuan, NA% of GDP (1994 est.); note - conversion of the defense budget into US dollars using the current exchange rate could produce misleading results

Geography

Location: Eastern Asia, between India and Mongolia

Map references: Asia, Southeast Asia, Standard Time Zones of the World

Area:
total area: 9,596,960 sq km
land area: 9,326,410 sq km
comparative area: slightly larger than the US

Land boundaries: total 22,143.34 km, Afghanistan 76 km, Bhutan 470 km, Burma 2,185 km, Hong Kong 30 km, India 3,380 km, Kazakhstan 1,533 km, North Korea 1,416 km, Kyrgyzstan 858 km, Laos 423 km, Macau 0.34 km, Mongolia 4,673 km, Nepal 1,236 km, Pakistan 523 km, Russia (northeast) 3,605 km, Russia (northwest) 40 km, Tajikistan 414 km, Vietnam 1,281 km

Coastline: 14,500 km

Maritime claims:
continental shelf: claim to shallow areas of East China Sea and Yellow Sea
territorial sea: 12 nm

International disputes: boundary with India; bilateral negotiations are under way to resolve disputed sections of the boundary with Russia; boundary with Tajikistan in dispute; a short section of the boundary with North Korea is indefinite; involved in a complex dispute over the Spratly Islands with Malaysia, Philippines, Taiwan, Vietnam, and possibly Brunei; maritime boundary dispute with Vietnam in the Gulf of Tonkin; Paracel Islands occupied by China, but claimed by Vietnam and Taiwan; claims Japanese-administered Senkaku-shoto (Senkaku Islands/Diaoyu Tai), as does Taiwan

Climate: extremely diverse; tropical in south to subarctic in north

Terrain: mostly mountains, high plateaus, deserts in west; plains, deltas, and hills in east

Natural resources: coal, iron ore, petroleum, mercury, tin, tungsten, antimony, manganese, molybdenum, vanadium, magnetite, aluminum, lead, zinc, uranium, hydropower potential (world's largest)

Land use:
arable land: 10%
permanent crops: 0%
meadows and pastures: 31%
forest and woodland: 14%
other: 45%

Irrigated land: 478,220 sq km (1991— Chinese statistic)

Environment:
current issues: air pollution from the overwhelming use of coal as a fuel, produces acid rain which is damaging forests; water pollution from industrial effluents; many people do not have access to safe drinking water; less than 10% of sewage receives treatment; deforestation; estimated loss of one-third of agricultural land since 1957 to soil erosion and economic development; desertification
natural hazards: frequent typhoons (about five per year along southern and eastern coasts); damaging floods; tsunamis; earthquakes
international agreements: party to—Antarctic Treaty, Biodiversity, Climate Change, Endangered Species, Hazardous Wastes, Marine Dumping, Nuclear Test Ban, Ozone Layer Protection, Ship Pollution, Tropical Timber, Whaling; signed, but not ratified— Antarctic-Environmental Protocol, Law of the Sea

Note: world's third-largest country (after Russia and Canada)

People

Population: 1,190,431,106 (July 1994 est.)
Population growth rate: 1.08% (1994 est.)
Birth rate: 18.1 births/1,000 population (1994 est.)
Death rate: 7.35 deaths/1,000 population (1994 est.)
Net migration rate: 0 migrant(s)/1,000 population (1994 est.)
Infant mortality rate: 52.1 deaths/1,000 live births (1994 est.)
Life expectancy at birth:
total population: 67.91 years
male: 66.93 years
female: 68.99 years (1994 est.)
Total fertility rate: 1.84 children born/woman (1994 est.)
Nationality:
noun: Chinese (singular and plural)
adjective: Chinese
Ethnic divisions: Han Chinese 91.9%, Zhuang, Uygur, Hui, Yi, Tibetan, Miao, Manchu, Mongol, Buyi, Korean, and other nationalities 8.1%
Religions: Daoism (Taoism), Buddhism, Muslim 2-3%, Christian 1% (est.)
note: officially atheist, but traditionally pragmatic and eclectic
Languages: Standard Chinese or Mandarin (Putonghua, based on the Beijing dialect), Yue (Cantonese), Wu (Shanghainese), Minbei (Fuzhou), Minnan (Hokkien-Taiwanese), Xiang, Gan, Hakka dialects, minority languages (see Ethnic divisions entry)
Literacy: age 15 and over can read and write (1990)
total population: 78%
male: 87%
female: 68%
Labor force: 567.4 million
by occupation: agriculture and forestry 60%, industry and commerce 25%, construction and mining 5%, social services 5%, other 5% (1990 est.)

Government

Names:
conventional long form: People's Republic of China
conventional short form: China
local long form: Zhonghua Renmin Gongheguo
local short form: Zhong Guo
Abbreviation: PRC
Digraph: CH
Type: Communist state
Capital: Beijing
Administrative divisions: 23 provinces (sheng, singular and plural), 5 autonomous regions* (zizhiqu, singular and plural), and 3 municipalities** (shi, singular and plural); Anhui, Beijing Shi**, Fujian, Gansu, Guangdong, Guangxi*, Guizhou, Hainan, Hebei, Heilongjiang, Henan, Hubei, Hunan, Jiangsu, Jiangxi, Jilin, Liaoning, Nei Mongol*, Ningxia*, Qinghai, Shaanxi, Shandong, Shanghai Shi**, Shanxi, Sichuan, Tianjin Shi**, Xinjiang*, Xizang* (Tibet), Yunnan, Zhejiang
note: China considers Taiwan its 23rd province
Independence: 221 BC (unification under the Qin or Ch'in Dynasty 221 BC; Qing or Ch'ing Dynasty replaced by the Republic on 12 February 1912; People's Republic established 1 October 1949)
National holiday: National Day, 1 October (1949)
Constitution: most recent promulgated 4 December 1982
Legal system: a complex amalgam of custom and statute, largely criminal law; rudimentary civil code in effect since 1 January 1987; new legal codes in effect since 1 January 1980; continuing efforts are being made to improve civil, administrative, criminal, and commercial law
Suffrage: 18 years of age; universal
Executive branch:
chief of state: President JIANG Zemin (since 27 March 1993); Vice President RONG Yiren (since 27 March 1993); election last held 27 March 1993 (next to be held NA 1998);

results—JIANG Zemin was nominally elected by the Eighth National People's Congress
chief of state and head of government (de facto): DENG Xiaoping (since NA 1977)
head of government: Premier LI Peng (Acting Premier since 24 November 1987, Premier since 9 April 1988) Vice Premier ZHU Rongji (since 8 April 1991); Vice Premier ZOU Jiahua (since 8 April 1991); Vice Premier QIAN Qichen (since 29 March 1993); Vice Premier LI Lanqing (29 March 1993)
cabinet: State Council; containing 28 ministers and 8 state commissions and appointed by the National People's Congress (March 1993)
Legislative branch: unicameral
National People's Congress: (Quanguo Renmin Daibiao Dahui) elections last held March 1993 (next to be held March 1998); results—CCP is the only party but there are also independents; seats—(2,977 total) (elected at county or xian level)
Judicial branch: Supreme People's Court
Political parties and leaders: Chinese Communist Party (CCP), JIANG Zemin, general secretary of the Central Committee (since 24 June 1989); eight registered small parties controlled by CCP
Other political or pressure groups: such meaningful opposition as exists consists of loose coalitions, usually within the party and government organization, that vary by issue
Member of: AfDB, APEC, AsDB, CCC, ESCAP, FAO, IAEA, IBRD, ICAO, ICFTU, IDA, IFAD, IFC, ILO, IMF, IMO, INMARSAT, INTELSAT, INTERPOL, IOC, ISO, ITU, LORCS, MINURSO, NAM (observer), PCA, UN, UNCTAD, UNESCO, UNHCR, UNIDO, UNIKOM, UN Security Council, UNTAC, UNTSO, UN Trusteeship Council, UPU, WHO, WIPO, WMO, WTO
Diplomatic representation in US:
chief of mission: Ambassador LI Daoyu
chancery: 2300 Connecticut Avenue NW, Washington, DC 20008
telephone: (202) 328-2500 through 2502
consulate(s) general: Chicago, Houston, Los Angeles, New York, and San Francisco
US diplomatic representation:
chief of mission: Ambassador J. Stapleton ROY

embassy: Xiu Shui Bei Jie 3, Beijing
mailing address: 100600, PSC 461, Box 50, Beijing or FPO AP 96521-0002
telephone: [86] (1) 532-3831
FAX: [86] (1) 532-3178
consulate(s) general: Chengdu, Guangzhou, Shanghai, Shenyang
Flag: red with a large yellow five-pointed star and four smaller yellow five-pointed stars (arranged in a vertical arc toward the middle of the flag) in the upper hoist-side corner

---

U.S. Government Contacts:

U.S. Trade Desk: (202) 482-3932
(202) 482-3583

American Embassy Commercial Section
Guang Hua Lu 17
Beijing, China
FPO AP 96521
Tel: 86-1-532-3831 x490
Fax: 86-1-532-3297

American Consulate General - Guangzou Commercial Section
Dong Fang Hotel
Box 100, FPO AP 96522
Tel: 86-20-677-842
Fax: 86-20-666-409

American Consulate General - Shanghai Commercial Section
1469 Huai Hai Middle Road
Box 200
FPO AP 96522
Tel: 86-21-433-2492
Fax: 86-21-433-1576

American Consulate General - Shenyang Commercial Section
40 Lane 4, SEction 5
Sanjing St., Heping District
Box 45
FPO AP 96522-0002
Tel: 86-24-222-000
Fax: 86-24-290-074

China Government Contacts:

Embassy of the People's Republic of China
Commercial Section
2300 Connecticut Avenue, N.W.
Washington, DC 20008
Tel: (202) 328-2520

Chambers of Commerce & Organizations:

American Chamber of Commerce in China
Jian Guo Hotel
Jian Guo Men Wai
Beijing, People's Republic of China
Tel: 86-1-59-5261

Legal Services:

C & M Law Office
Suite 422 Main Building
Jing Xin Mansion
A2 Dongsanhuan Bei Road
Beijing (peking) 100027, People's Republic of
China
Tel: 861 4662682; 861 4663366 Ext. 3422,
3425
Fax: 861 4662683
*Entitled to practice before all courts in China
including the Supreme People's Court of
China, Technology Transfer, Foreign
Economic and Trade.*

Travel:

International Airlines to Country:
Northwest, United

International Hotels in Country:
Beijing:
Beijing Hilton, Tel: 86 01 466-2288, Fax: 01
465 3052

FIJI

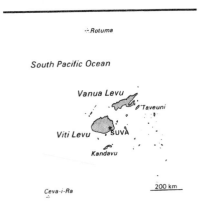

Rotuma

South Pacific Ocean

Vanua Levu
Taveuni
Viti Levu SUVA
Kandavu

Ceva-i-Ra

200 km

Economy

Overview: Fiji's economy is primarily agricultural, with a large subsistence sector. Sugar exports and tourism are the major sources of foreign exchange. Industry contributes 13% to GDP, with sugar processing accounting for one-third of industrial activity. Roughly 250,000 tourists visit each year. Political uncertainty and drought, however, contribute to substantial fluctuations in earnings from tourism and sugar. In 1992, growth was approximately 3%, based on growth in tourism and a lessening of labor-management disputes in the sugar and gold-mining sectors. In 1993, the government's budgeted growth rate of 3% was not achieved because of a decline in non-sugar agricultural output and damage from Cyclone Kina.

National product: GDP—purchasing power equivalent—$3 billion (1993 est.)

National product real growth rate: 1% (1993 est.)

National product per capita: $4,000 (1993 est.)

Inflation rate (consumer prices): 5.6% (1993 est.)

Unemployment rate: 5.9% (1991 est.)

Budget:
revenues: $455 million
expenditures: $546 million, including capital expenditures of $NA (1993 est.)

Exports: $417 million (f.o.b., 1992)
commodities: sugar 40%, clothing, processed fish, gold, lumber
partners: EC 26%, Australia 15%, Pacific Islands 11%, Japan 6%

Imports: $517 million (c.i.f., 1992 est)
commodities: machinery and transport equipment, petroleum products, food, consumer goods, chemicals
partners: Australia 30%, NZ 17%, Japan 13%, EC 6%, US 6%

External debt: $670 million (1994 est.)

Industrial production: growth rate 7.5% (1992 est.); accounts for 13% of GDP

Electricity:
capacity: 215,000 kW
production: 420 million kWh
consumption per capita: 560 kWh (1992)

Industries: sugar, tourism, copra, gold, silver, clothing, lumber, small cottage industries

Agriculture: accounts for 23% of GDP; principal cash crop is sugarcane; coconuts, cassava, rice, sweet potatoes, bananas; small livestock sector includes cattle, pigs, horses, and goats; fish catch nearly 33,000 tons (1989)

Economic aid:
recipient: Western (non-US) countries, ODA and OOF bilateral commitments (1980-89), $815 million

Currency: 1 Fijian dollar (F$) = 100 cents

Exchange rates: Fijian dollars (F$) per US$1—1.5239 (January 1994), 1.5418 (1993), 1.5030 (1992), 1.4756 (1991), 1.4809 (1990), 1.4833 (1989)

Fiscal year: calendar year

Communications

Railroads: 644 km 0.610-meter narrow gauge, belonging to the government-owned Fiji Sugar Corporation

Highways:
total: 3,300 km
paved: 1,590 km
unpaved: gravel, crushed stone, stabilized earth 1,290 km; unimproved earth 420 km (1984)
Inland waterways: 203 km; 122 km navigable by motorized craft and 200-metric-ton barges
Ports: Labasa, Lautoka, Savusavu, Suva
Merchant marine: 8 ships (1,000 GRT or over) totaling 44,911 GRT/54,490 DWT, roll-on/roll-off cargo 2, container 2, oil tanker 1, chemical tanker 2, cargo 1
Airports:
total: 25
usable: 22
with permanent-surface runways: 3
with runways over 3,659 m: 0
with runways 2,440-3,659 m: 1
with runways 1,220-2,439 m: 2
Telecommunications: modern local, interisland, and international (wire/radio integrated) public and special-purpose telephone, telegraph, and teleprinter facilities; regional radio center; important COMPAC cable link between US-Canada and NZ-Australia; 53,228 telephones (71 telephones per 1,000 persons); broadcast stations—7 AM, 1 FM, no TV; 1 Pacific Ocean INTELSAT earth station

Defense Forces

Branches: Republic of Fiji Military Forces (RFMF; including a naval division, police)
Manpower availability: males age 15-49 197,767; fit for military service 109,026; reach military age (18) annually 8,154 (1994 est.)
Defense expenditures: exchange rate conversion—$22.4 million, about 2% of GDP (FY91/92)

Geography

Location: Oceania, Melanesia, 2,500 km north of New Zealand in the South Pacific Ocean

Map references: Oceania, Standard Time Zones of the World
Area:
total area: 18,270 sq km
land area: 18,270 sq km
comparative area: slightly smaller than New Jersey
Land boundaries: 0 km
Coastline: 1,129 km
Maritime claims: measured from claimed archipelagic baselines
continental shelf: 200-m depth or to depth of exploitation; rectilinear shelf claim added
exclusive economic zone: 200 nm
territorial sea: 12 nm
International disputes: none
Climate: tropical marine; only slight seasonal temperature variation
Terrain: mostly mountains of volcanic origin
Natural resources: timber, fish, gold, copper, offshore oil potential
Land use:
arable land: 8%
permanent crops: 5%
meadows and pastures: 3%
forest and woodland: 65%
other: 19%
Irrigated land: 10 sq km (1989 est.)
Environment:
current issues: deforestation; soil erosion
natural hazards: cyclonic storms can occur from November to January
international agreements: party to— Biodiversity, Climate Change, Law of the Sea, Marine Life Conservation, Nuclear Test Ban, Ozone Layer Protection
Note: includes 332 islands of which approximately 110 are inhabited

People

Population: 764,382 (July 1994 est.)
Population growth rate: 1.05% (1994 est.)
Birth rate: 24.18 births/1,000 population (1994 est.)
Death rate: 6.5 deaths/1,000 population (1994 est.)
Net migration rate: -7.15 migrant(s)/1,000 population (1994 est.)

Infant mortality rate: 18.1 deaths/1,000 live births (1994 est.)
Life expectancy at birth:
total population: 65.14 years
male: 62.88 years
female: 67.51 years (1994 est.)
Total fertility rate: 2.92 children born/ woman (1994 est.)
Nationality:
noun: Fijian(s)
adjective: Fijian
Ethnic divisions: Fijian 49%, Indian 46%, European, other Pacific Islanders, overseas Chinese, and other 5%
Religions: Christian 52% (Methodist 37%, Roman Catholic 9%), Hindu 38%, Muslim 8%, other 2%
note: Fijians are mainly Christian, Indians are Hindu, and there is a Muslim minority (1986)
Languages: English (official), Fijian, Hindustani
Literacy: age 15 and over can read and write (1985 est.)
total population: 86%
male: 90%
female: 81%
Labor force: 235,000
by occupation: subsistence agriculture 67%, wage earners 18%, salary earners 15% (1987)

Government

Names:
conventional long form: Republic of Fiji
conventional short form: Fiji
Digraph: FJ
Type: republic
note: military coup leader Maj. Gen. Sitiveni RABUKA formally declared Fiji a republic on 6 October 1987
Capital: Suva
Administrative divisions: 4 divisions and 1 dependency*; Central, Eastern, Northern, Rotuma*, Western
Independence: 10 October 1970 (from UK)
National holiday: Independence Day, 10 October (1970)
Constitution: 10 October 1970 (suspended 1 October 1987); a new Constitution was proposed on 23 September 1988 and promulgated on 25 July 1990; the 1990 Constitution is under review; the review will be complete by 1997
Legal system: based on British system
Suffrage: none
Executive branch:
chief of state: President Ratu Sir Kamisese MARA (since 12 January 1994); First Vice President Ratu Sir Josaia TAIVAIQIA (since 12 January 1994); Second Vice President Ratu Inoke TAKIVEIKATA (since 12 January 1994); note—President GANILAU died on 15 December 1993 and Vice President MARA became acting president; MARA was elected president by the Great Council of Chiefs on 12 January 1994
head of government: Prime Minister Sitiveni RABUKA (since 2 June 1992)
Presidential Council: appointed by the governor general
Great Council of Chiefs: (highest ranking members of the traditional chiefly system)
cabinet: Cabinet; appointed by prime minister from members of Parliament and responsible to Parliament
Legislative branch: the bicameral Parliament was dissolved following the coup of 14 May 1987
Senate: nonelective body containing 34 seats, 24 reserved for Melanesians, 9 for Indians and others, 1 for the island of Rotuma
House of Representatives: elections last held 18-25 February 1994 (next to be held NA 1997); results—percent of vote by party NA; seats—(70 total, with ethnic Fijians allocated 37 seats, ethnic Indians 27 seats, and independents and other 6 seats) number of seats by party SVT 31, NFP 20, FLP 7, FA 5, GVP 4, independents 2, ANC 1
Judicial branch: Supreme Court
Political parties and leaders: Fijian Political Party (SVT—primarily Fijian), leader Maj. Gen. Sitivini RABUKA; National Federation Party (NFP; primarily Indian), Jai Ram REDDY; Christian Fijian Nationalist Party (CFNP), Sakeasi BUTADROKA; Fiji Labor Party (FLP), Mahendra CHAUDHRY; All National Congress (ANC), Apisai TORA; General Voters Party (GVP), Max OLSSON;

Fiji Conservative Party (FCP), Isireli
VUIBAU; Conservative Party of Fiji (CPF),
Jolale ULUDOLE and Viliame SAVU; Fiji
Indian Liberal Party, Swami MAHARAJ; Fiji
Indian Congress Party, Ishwari BAJPAI; Fiji
Independent Labor (Muslim), leader NA; Four
Corners Party, David TULVANUAVOU;
Fijian Association (FA), Josevata
KAMIKAMICA

Member of: ACP, AsDB, CP, ESCAP, FAO,
G-77, GATT, IBRD, ICAO, ICFTU, IDA,
IFAD, IFC, ILO, IMF, IMO, INTELSAT,
INTERPOL, IOC, ITU, LORCS, PCA,
SPARTECA, SPC, SPF, UN, UNCTAD,
UNESCO, UNIDO, UNIFIL, UNIKOM,
UNOMUR, UNTAC, UPU, WHO, WIPO,
WMO

Diplomatic representation in US:
chief of mission: Ambassador Pita Kewa
NACUVA
chancery: Suite 240, 2233 Wisconsin Avenue
NW, Washington, DC 20007
telephone: (202) 337-8320
FAX: (202) 337-1996
consulate(s): New York

US diplomatic representation:
chief of mission: (vacant); Charge d'Affaires
William ROPE
embassy: 31 Loftus Street, Suva
mailing address: P. O. Box 218, Suva
telephone: [679] 314-466
FAX: [679] 300-081

Flag: light blue with the flag of the UK in the
upper hoist-side quadrant and the Fijian shield
centered on the outer half of the flag; the shield
depicts a yellow lion above a white field
quartered by the cross of Saint George
featuring stalks of sugarcane, a palm tree,
bananas, and a white dove

GUAM

10 km

reefs

reefs

Cabras Island
Apra Harbor

★AGANA

North

Pacific

Ocean

reefs

Cocos Island

Economy

Overview: The economy depends mainly on US military spending and on revenues from tourism. Over the past 20 years the tourist industry has grown rapidly, creating a construction boom for new hotels and the expansion of older ones. Visitors numbered about 900,000 in 1992. The slowdown in Japanese economic growth has been reflected in less vigorous growth in the tourism sector. About 60% of the labor force works for the private sector and the rest for government. Most food and industrial goods are imported, with about 75% from the US. In early 1994, Guam faces the problem of building up the civilian economic sector to offset the impact of military downsizing.

National product: GNP—purchasing power equivalent—$2 billion (1991 est.)

National product real growth rate: NA%

National product per capita: $14,000 (1991 est.)

Inflation rate (consumer prices): 4% (1992 est.)

Unemployment rate: 2% (1992 est.)

Budget:

revenues: $525 million

expenditures: $395 million, including capital expenditures of $NA (1991)

Exports: $34 million (f.o.b., 1984)

commodities: mostly transshipments of refined petroleum products, construction materials, fish, food and beverage products

partners: US 25%, Trust Territory of the Pacific Islands 63%, other 12%

Imports: $493 million (c.i.f., 1984)

commodities: petroleum and petroleum products, food, manufactured goods

partners: US 23%, Japan 19%, other 58%

External debt: $NA

Industrial production: growth rate NA%

Electricity:

capacity: 500,000 kW

production: 2.3 billion kWh

consumption per capita: 16,300 kWh (1990)

Industries: US military, tourism, construction, transshipment services, concrete products, printing and publishing, food processing, textiles

Agriculture: relatively undeveloped with most food imported; fruits, vegetables, eggs, pork, poultry, beef, copra

Economic aid: although Guam receives no foreign aid, it does receive large transfer payments from the general revenues of the US Federal Treasury into which Guamanians pay no income or excise taxes; under the provisions of a special law of Congress, the Guamanian Treasury, rather than the US Treasury, receives federal income taxes paid by military and civilian Federal employees stationed in Guam

Currency: 1 United States dollar (US$) = 100 cents

Exchange rates: US currency is used

Fiscal year: 1 October—30 September

Communications

Highways:

total: 674 km (all-weather roads)
paved: NA
unpaved: NA
Ports: Apra Harbor
Airports:
total: 5
usable: 4
with permanent-surface runways: 3
with runways over 3,659 m: 0
with runways 2,440-3,659 m: 3
with runways 1,200-2,439 m: 0
Telecommunications: 26,317 telephones
(1989); broadcast stations—3 AM, 3 FM, 3
TV; 2 Pacific Ocean INTELSAT ground
stations

Defense Forces

Note: defense is the responsibility of the US

Geography

Location: Oceania, Micronesia, in the North
Pacific Ocean, 5,955 km west-southwest of
Honolulu, about three-quarters of the way
between Hawaii and the Philippines
Map references: Oceania
Area:
total area: 541.3 sq km
land area: 541.3 sq km
comparative area: slightly more than three
times the size of Washington, DC
Land boundaries: 0 km
Coastline: 125.5 km
Maritime claims:
contiguous zone: 24 nm
continental shelf: 200-m depth or to depth of
exploitation
exclusive economic zone: 200 nm
territorial sea: 12 nm
International disputes: none
Climate: tropical marine; generally warm and
humid, moderated by northeast trade winds;
dry season from January to June, rainy season
from July to December; little seasonal
temperature variation
Terrain: volcanic origin, surrounded by coral
reefs; relatively flat coraline limestone plateau
(source of most fresh water) with steep coastal
cliffs and narrow coastal plains in north, low-
rising hills in center, mountains in south
Natural resources: fishing (largely
undeveloped), tourism (especially from Japan)
Land use:
arable land: 11%
permanent crops: 11%
meadows and pastures: 15%
forest and woodland: 18%
other: 45%
Irrigated land: NA sq km
Environment:
current issues: NA
natural hazards: frequent squalls during rainy
season; subject to relatively rare, but
potentially very destructive typhoons
(especially in August)
international agreements: NA
Note: largest and southernmost island in the
Mariana Islands archipelago; strategic location
in western North Pacific Ocean

People

Population: 149,620 (July 1994 est.)
Population growth rate: 2.48% (1994 est.)
Birth rate: 25.66 births/1,000 population
(1994 est.)
Death rate: 3.86 deaths/1,000 population
(1994 est.)
Net migration rate: 3 migrant(s)/1,000
population (1994 est.)
Infant mortality rate: 15.17 deaths/1,000
live births (1994 est.)
Life expectancy at birth:
total population: 74.29 years
male: 72.42 years
female: 76.13 years (1994 est.)
Total fertility rate: 2.39 children born/
woman (1994 est.)
Nationality:
noun: Guamanian(s)
adjective: Guamanian
Ethnic divisions: Chamorro 47%, Filipino
25%, Caucasian 10%, Chinese, Japanese,
Korean, and other 18%
Religions: Roman Catholic 98%, other 2%
Languages: English, Chamorro, Japanese
Literacy: age 15 and over can read and write
(1980)

total population: 96%
male: 96%
female: 96%
Labor force: 46,930 (1990)
by occupation: federal and territorial
government 40%, private 60% (trade 18%,
services 15.6%, construction 13.8%, other
12.6%) (1990)

Government

Names:
conventional long form: Territory of Guam
conventional short form: Guam
Digraph: GQ
Type: organized, unincorporated territory of
the US with policy relations between Guam
and the US under the jurisdiction of the Office
of Territorial and International Affairs, US
Department of the Interior
Capital: Agana
Administrative divisions: none (territory of
the US)
Independence: none (territory of the US)
National holiday: Guam Discovery Day (first
Monday in March) (1521); Liberation Day, 21
July
Constitution: Organic Act of 1 August 1950
Legal system: modeled on US; federal laws
apply
Suffrage: 18 years of age; universal; US
citizens, but do not vote in US presidential
elections
Executive branch:
chief of state: President William Jefferson
CLINTON (since 20 January 1993); Vice
President Albert GORE, Jr. (since 20 January
1993)
head of government: Governor Joseph A.
ADA (since November 1986); Lieutenant
Governor Frank F. BLAS (since NA); election
last held on 6 November 1990 (next to be held
NA November 1994); results—Joseph F. ADA
reelected
cabinet: executive departments; heads
appointed by the governor with the consent of
the Guam legislature
Legislative branch: unicameral
Legislature: elections last held on 9 November
1992 (next to be held NA November 1994);

results—percent of vote by party NA; seats—
(21 total) Democratic 14, Republican 7
US House of Representatives: elections last
held 9 November 1992 (next to be held NA
November 1994); Guam elects one delegate;
results—Robert UNDERWOOD was elected
as delegate; seats—(1 total) Democrat 1
Judicial branch: Federal District Court,
Territorial Superior Court
Political parties and leaders: Democratic
Party (controls the legislature); Republican
Party (party of the Governor)
Member of: ESCAP (associate), IOC, SPC
Diplomatic representation in US: none
(territory of the US)
US diplomatic representation: none
(territory of the US)
Flag: territorial flag is dark blue with a narrow
red border on all four sides; centered is a red-
bordered, pointed, vertical ellipse containing a
beach scene, outrigger canoe with sail, and a
palm tree with the word GUAM superimposed
in bold red letters; US flag is the national flag

**Chambers of Commerce &
Organizations:**

Guam Chamber of Commerce
102 Ada Plaza Center
PO Box 283
Agana, Guam 96910
Tel: (671) 472-6311/800

Travel:

International Airlines to Country:
Continental, Northwest, United

International Hotels in Country:
Guam Hilton, Tel: 671 646 1835, Fax: 646
6038

HONG KONG

Lema Channel

Economy

Overview: Hong Kong has a bustling free market economy with few tariffs or nontariff barriers. Natural resources are limited, and food and raw materials must be imported. Manufacturing accounts for about 17% of GDP. Goods and services exports account for about 50% of GDP. Real GDP growth averaged a remarkable 8% in 1987-88, slowed to 3.0% in 1989-90, and picked up to 4.2% in 1991, 5.0% in 1992, and 5.2% in 1993. Unemployment, which has been declining since the mid-1980s, is now about 2%. A shortage of labor continues to put upward pressure on prices and the cost of living. Short-term prospects remain bright so long as major trading partners continue to be reasonably prosperous.

National product: GDP—purchasing power equivalent—$119 billion (1993 est.)

National product real growth rate: 5.2% (1993)

National product per capita: $21,500 (1993 est.)

Inflation rate (consumer prices): 9.5% (1993)

Unemployment rate: 2.3% (1993 est.)

Budget:
revenues: $19.2 billion
expenditures: $19.7 billion, including capital expenditures of $NA (FY94)

Exports: $145.1 billion (including re-exports of $104.2 billion; f.o.b., 1993 est.)
commodities: clothing, textiles, yarn and fabric, footwear, electrical appliances, watches and clocks, toys
partners: China 32%, US 23%, Germany 5%, Japan 5%, UK 3% (1993 est.)

Imports: $149.6 billion (c.i.f., 1993 est.)
commodities: foodstuffs, transport equipment, raw materials, semimanufactures, petroleum
partners: China 36%, Japan 19%, Taiwan 9%, US 7% (1993 est.)

External debt: none (1993)

Industrial production: growth rate 2% (1993 est.)

Electricity:
capacity: 9,566,000 kW
production: 29.4 billion kWh
consumption per capita: 4,980 kWh (1992)

Industries: textiles, clothing, tourism, electronics, plastics, toys, watches, clocks

Agriculture: minor role in the economy; local farmers produce 26% fresh vegetables, 27% live poultry; 8% of land area suitable for farming

Illicit drugs: a hub for Southeast Asian heroin trade; transshipment and major financial and money-laundering center

Economic aid:
recipient: US commitments, including Ex-Im (FY70-87), $152 million; Western (non-US) countries, ODA and OOF bilateral commitments (1970-89), $923 million

Currency: 1 Hong Kong dollar (HK$) = 100 cents

Exchange rates: Hong Kong dollars (HK$) per US$—7.800 (1993), 7.741 (1992), 7.771 (1991), 7.790 (1990), 7.800 (1989); note—linked to the US dollar at the rate of about 7.8 HK$ per 1 US$ since 1985

Fiscal year: 1 April—31 March

Communications

Railroads: 35 km 1.435-meter standard gauge, government owned

Highways:
total: 1,100 km
paved: 794 km
unpaved: gravel, crushed stone, earth 306 km

Ports: Hong Kong

Merchant marine: 201 ships (1,000 GRT or over), totaling 6,972,233 GRT/11,965,809 DWT, short-sea passenger 1, cargo 23, refrigerated cargo 7, container 29, vehicle carrier 2, oil tanker 16, chemical tanker 3, combination ore/oil 6, liquefied gas 7, bulk 105, combination bulk 2
note: a flag of convenience registry; ships registered in Hong Kong fly the UK flag, and an estimated 500 Hong Kong-owned ships are registered elsewhere

Airports:
total: 2
usable: 2
with permanent-surface runways: 2
with runways over 3,659 m: 0
with runways 2,440-3,659 m: 1
with runways 1,220-2,439 m: 0

Telecommunications: modern facilities provide excellent domestic and international services; 3,000,000 telephones; microwave transmission links and extensive optical fiber transmission network; broadcast stations—6 AM, 6 FM, 4 TV; 1 British Broadcasting Corporation (BBC) repeater station and 1 British Forces Broadcasting Service repeater station; 2,500,000 radio receivers; 1,312,000 TV sets (1,224,000 color TV sets); satellite earth stations—1 Pacific Ocean INTELSAT and 2 Indian Ocean INTELSAT; coaxial cable to Guangzhou, China; links to 5 international submarine cables providing access to ASEAN member nations, Japan, Taiwan, Australia, Middle East, and Western Europe

Defense Forces

Branches: Headquarters of British Forces, Royal Navy, Royal Air Force, Royal Hong Kong Auxiliary Air Force, Royal Hong Kong Police Force

Manpower availability: males age 15-49 1,636,397; fit for military service 1,251,901; reach military age (18) annually 42,044 (1994 est.)

Defense expenditures: exchange rate conversion—$300 million, 0.5% of GDP (1989 est.); this represents one-fourth of the total cost of defending itself, the remainder being paid by the UK

Note: defense is the responsibility of the UK

Geography

Location: Eastern Asia, on the southeast coast of China bordering the South China Sea

Map references: Asia, Southeast Asia, Standard Time Zones of the World

Area:
total area: 1,040 sq km
land area: 990 sq km
comparative area: slightly less than six times the size of Washington, DC

Land boundaries: total 30 km, China 30 km

Coastline: 733 km

Maritime claims:
exclusive fishing zone: 3 nm
territorial sea: 3 nm

International disputes: none

Climate: tropical monsoon; cool and humid in winter, hot and rainy from spring through summer, warm and sunny in fall

Terrain: hilly to mountainous with steep slopes; lowlands in north

Natural resources: outstanding deepwater harbor, feldspar

Land use:
arable land: 7%
permanent crops: 1%
meadows and pastures: 1%
forest and woodland: 12%
other: 79%

Irrigated land: 20 sq km (1989)

Environment:
current issues: air and water pollution from rapid urbanization
natural hazards: occasional typhoons
international agreements: NA

Note: more than 200 islands

People

Population: 5,548,754 (July 1994 est.)
Population growth rate: -0.09% (1994 est.)
Birth rate: 12.16 births/1,000 population (1994 est.)
Death rate: 5.85 deaths/1,000 population (1994 est.)
Net migration rate: -7.21 migrant(s)/1,000 population (1994 est.)
Infant mortality rate: 5.8 deaths/1,000 live births (1994 est.)
Life expectancy at birth:
total population: 80.09 years
male: 76.67 years
female: 83.71 years (1994 est.)
Total fertility rate: 1.37 children born/woman (1994 est.)
Nationality:
noun: Chinese
adjective: Chinese
Ethnic divisions: Chinese 95%, other 5%
Religions: eclectic mixture of local religions 90%, Christian 10%
Languages: Chinese (Cantonese), English
Literacy: age 15 and over having ever attended school (1971)
total population: 77%
male: 90%
female: 64%
Labor force: 2.8 million (1990)
by occupation: manufacturing 28.5%, wholesale and retail trade, restaurants, and hotels 27.9%, services 17.7%, financing, insurance, and real estate 9.2%, transport and communications 4.5%, construction 2.5%, other 9.7% (1989)

Government

Names:
conventional long form: none
conventional short form: Hong Kong
Abbreviation: HK
Digraph: HK
Type: dependent territory of the UK scheduled to revert to China in 1997
Capital: Victoria
Administrative divisions: none (dependent territory of the UK)

Independence: none (dependent territory of the UK; the UK signed an agreement with China on 19 December 1984 to return Hong Kong to China on 1 July 1997; in the joint declaration, China promises to respect Hong Kong's existing social and economic systems and lifestyle)
National holiday: Liberation Day, 29 August (1945)
Constitution: unwritten; partly statutes, partly common law and practice; new Basic Law approved in March 1990 in preparation for 1997
Legal system: based on English common law
Suffrage: direct election 21 years of age; universal for permanent residents living in the territory of Hong Kong for the past seven years; indirect election limited to about 100,000 professionals of electoral college and functional constituencies
Executive branch:
chief of state: Queen ELIZABETH II (since 6 February 1952)
head of government: Governor Chris PATTEN (since 9 July 1992); Chief Secretary Anson CHAN Fang On-Sang (since 29 November 1993)
cabinet: Executive Council; appointed by the governor
Legislative branch: unicameral
Legislative Council: indirect elections last held 12 September 1991 and direct elections were held for the first time 15 September 1991 (next to be held in September 1995 when the number of directly-elected seats increases to 20); results—percent of vote by party NA; seats—(60 total; 21 indirectly elected by functional constituencies, 18 directly elected, 18 appointed by governor, 3 ex officio members); indirect elections—number of seats by functional constituency NA; direct elections—UDHK 12, Meeting Point 3, ADPL 1, other 2
Judicial branch: Supreme Court
Political parties and leaders: United Democrats of Hong Kong, Martin LEE, chairman; Democratic Alliance for the Betterment of Hong Kong, TSANG Yuk-shing, chairman; Hong Kong Democratic Foundation, Dr. Patrick SHIU Kin-ying, chairman

note: in April 1994, the United Democrats of Hong Kong and Meeting Point merged to form the "Democratic Party;" the merger becomes effective in October 1994

Other political or pressure groups: Liberal Party, Allen LEE, chairman; Meeting Point, Anthony CHEUNG Bing-leung, chairman; Association for Democracy and People's Livelihood, Frederick FUNG Kin Kee, chairman; Liberal Democratic Federation, HU Fa-kuang, chairman; Federation of Trade Unions (pro-China), LEE Chark-tim, president; Hong Kong and Kowloon Trade Union Council (pro-Taiwan); Confederation of Trade Unions (pro-democracy), LAU Chin-shek, chairman; Hong Kong General Chamber of Commerce; Chinese General Chamber of Commerce (pro-China); Federation of Hong Kong Industries; Chinese Manufacturers' Association of Hong Kong; Hong Kong Professional Teachers' Union, CHEUNG Man-kwong, president; Hong Kong Alliance in Support of the Patriotic Democratic Movement in China, Szeto WAH, chairman *note:* in April 1994, the United Democrats of Hong Kong and Meeting Point merged to form the "Democratic Party;" the merger becomes effective in October 1994

Member of: COCOM (cooperating), APEC, AsDB, CCC, ESCAP (associate), GATT, ICFTU, IMO (associate), INTERPOL (subbureau), IOC, ISO (correspondent), WCL, WMO

Diplomatic representation in US: none (dependent territory of the UK)

US diplomatic representation:
chief of mission: Consul General Richard MUELLER
consulate general: 26 Garden Road, Hong Kong
mailing address: PSC 464, Box 30, Hong Kong, or FPO AP 96522-0002
telephone: [852] 523-9011
FAX: [852] 845-1598

Flag: blue with the flag of the UK in the upper hoist-side quadrant with the Hong Kong coat of arms on a white disk centered on the outer half of the flag; the coat of arms contains a shield (bearing two junks below a crown) held by a lion (representing the UK) and a dragon (representing China) with another lion above the shield and a banner bearing the words HONG KONG below the shield

U.S. Government Contacts:

U.S. Trade Desk: (202) 482-3932

American Consulate General - Commercial Section
26 Garden Road
Hong Kong
FPO AP 96522
Tel: 852-521-1467
Fax: 852-845-9800

Hong Kong Government Contacts:

Hong Kong Office/British Embassy
3100 Massachusetts Avenue, N.W.
Washington, DC 20008
Tel: (202) 898-4591

Chambers of Commerce & Organizations:

American Chamber of Commerce in Hong Kong
1030 Swire Road, Central P.O. Box 355
Hong Kong
Tel: 852-526-0165
Fax: 852-810-1289

Travel:

International Airlines to Country:
Continental, Northwest, United

International Hotels in Country:
Hong Kong Island:
Grand Hyatt, Tel: 852 588-1234, Fax: 852 802-0677
The Hong Kong Hilton International, Tel: 852 523-3111, Fax: 852 845-2590
Mandarin Oriental, Tel: 852 522-0111, Fax: 852 529-7978.

INDIA

Economy

Overview: India's economy is a mixture of traditional village farming, modern agriculture, handicrafts, a wide range of modern industries, and a multitude of support services. Faster economic growth in the 1980s permitted a significant increase in real per capita private consumption. A large share of the population, perhaps as much as 40%, remains too poor to afford an adequate diet. Financial strains in 1990 and 1991 prompted government austerity measures that slowed industrial growth but permitted India to meet its international payment obligations without rescheduling its debt. Policy reforms since 1991 have extended earlier economic liberalization and greatly reduced government controls on production, trade, and investment. US and other foreign firms are increasing their investment in India. In January 1994, international financial reserves were comfortably high.
National product: GDP—purchasing power equivalent—$1.17 trillion (FY94 est.)
National product real growth rate: 3.8% (FY94 est.)
National product per capita: $1,300 (FY94 est.)

Inflation rate (consumer prices): 8% (1993 est.)
Unemployment rate: NA%
Budget:
revenues: $29.6 billion
expenditures: $45.1 billion, including capital expenditures of $11.2 billion (FY93)
Exports: $21.4 billion (f.o.b., 1993)
commodities: gems and jewelry, clothing, engineering goods, chemicals, leather manufactures, cotton yarn, and fabric
partners: US 18.9%, Germany 7.8%, Italy 7.8%, (FY93)
Imports: $22 billion (c.i.f., 1993)
commodities: crude oil and petroleum products, gems, fertilizer, chemicals, machinery
partners: US 9.8%, Belgium 8.4%, Germany 7.6% (FY93)
External debt: $90.1 billion (March 1993)
Industrial production: growth rate 2% (1993 est.); accounts for about 25% of GDP
Electricity:
capacity: 82,000,000 kW
production: 310 billion kWh
consumption per capita: 340 kWh (1992)
Industries: textiles, chemicals, food processing, steel, transportation equipment, cement, mining, petroleum, machinery
Agriculture: accounts for about 40% of GDP and employs 65% of labor force; principal crops—rice, wheat, oilseeds, cotton, jute, tea, sugarcane, potatoes; livestock—cattle, buffaloes, sheep, goats, poultry; fish catch of about 3 million metric tons ranks India among the world's top 10 fishing nations
Illicit drugs: licit producer of opium poppy for the pharmaceutical trade, but some opium is diverted to illicit international drug markets; major transit country for illicit narcotics produced in neighboring countries; illicit producer of hashish; minor production of illicit opium

Economic aid:
recipient: US commitments, including Ex-Im (FY70-89), $4.4 billion; Western (non-US) countries, ODA and OOF bilateral commitments (1980-89), $31.7 billion; OPEC bilateral aid (1979-89), $315 million; USSR (1970-89), $11.6 billion; Eastern Europe (1970-89), $105 million
Currency: 1 Indian rupee (Re) = 100 paise
Exchange rates: Indian rupees (Rs) per US$1—31.370 (January 1994), 30.493 (1993), 25.918 (1992), 22.742 (1991), 17.504 (1990), 16.226 (1989)
Fiscal year: 1 April—31 March

Communications

Railroads: 61,850 km total (1986); 33,553 km 1.676-meter broad gauge, 24,051 km 1.000-meter gauge, 4,246 km narrow gauge (0.762 meter and 0.610 meter); 12,617 km is double track; 6,500 km is electrified
Highways:
total: 1.97 million km
paved: 960,000 km
unpaved: gravel, crushed stone, earth 1.01 million km (1989)
Inland waterways: 16,180 km; 3,631 km navigable by large vessels
Pipelines: crude oil 3,497 km; petroleum products 1,703 km; natural gas 902 km (1989)
Ports: Bombay, Calcutta, Cochin, Kandla, Madras, New Mangalore, Port Blair (Andaman Islands)
Merchant marine: 297 ships (1,000 GRT or over) totaling 6,236,902 GRT/10,369,948 DWT, short-sea passenger 1, passenger-cargo 6, cargo 81, roll-on/roll-off cargo 1, container 7, oil tanker 66, chemical tanker 9, combination ore/oil 7, bulk 111, combination bulk 2, liquefied gas 6
Airports:
total: 337
usable: 288
with permanent-surface runways: 208
with runways over 3,659 m: 2
with runways 2,440-3,659 m: 59
with runways 1,220-2,439 m: 92
Telecommunications: domestic telephone system is poor providing only one telephone for about 200 persons on average; long distance telephoning has been improved by a domestic satellite system which also carries TV; international service is provided by 3 Indian Ocean INTELSAT earth stations and by submarine cables to Malaysia and the United Arab Emirates; broadcast stations—96 AM, 4 FM, 274 TV (government controlled)

Defense Forces

Branches: Army, Navy, Air Force, Security or Paramilitary Forces (including Border Security Force, Assam Rifles, and Coast Guard)
Manpower availability: males age 15-49 247,948,906; fit for military service 145,881,705; reach military age (17) annually 9,408,586 (1994 est.)
Defense expenditures: exchange rate conversion—$5.8 billion, 2.4% of GDP (FY93/94)

Geography

Location: Southern Asia, bordering the Arabian Sea and the Bay of Bengal, between Bangladesh and Pakistan
Map references: Asia, Standard Time Zones of the World
Area:
total area: 3,287,590 km2
land area: 2,973,190 km2
comparative area: slightly more than one-third the size of the US
Land boundaries: total 14,103 km, Bangladesh 4,053 km, Bhutan 605 km, Burma 1,463 km, China 3,380 km, Nepal 1,690 km, Pakistan 2,912 km
Coastline: 7,000 km
Maritime claims:
contiguous zone: 24 nm
continental shelf: 200 nm or the edge of continental margin
exclusive economic zone: 200 nm
territorial sea: 12 nm
International disputes: boundaries with Bangladesh and China; status of Kashmir with

Pakistan; water-sharing problems with downstream riparians, Bangladesh over the Ganges and Pakistan over the Indus
Climate: varies from tropical monsoon in south to temperate in north
Terrain: upland plain (Deccan Plateau) in south, flat to rolling plain along the Ganges, deserts in west, Himalayas in north
Natural resources: coal (fourth-largest reserves in the world), iron ore, manganese, mica, bauxite, titanium ore, chromite, natural gas, diamonds, petroleum, limestone
Land use:
arable land: 55%
permanent crops: 1%
meadows and pastures: 4%
forest and woodland: 23%
other: 17%
Irrigated land: 430,390 sq km (1989)
Environment:
current issues: deforestation; soil erosion; overgrazing; desertification; air pollution from industrial effluents and vehicle emissions; water pollution from raw sewage and runoff of agricultural pesticides; huge and rapidly growing population is overstraining natural resources
natural hazards: droughts, flash floods, severe thunderstorms common; subject to earthquakes (a quake measuring 6.4 on the Richter scale occurred near Hyderabad killing several thousand people and causing extensive damage in late September 1993)
international agreements: party to—Antarctic Treaty, Biodiversity, Climate Change, Endangered Species, Environmental Modification, Hazardous Wastes, Nuclear Test Ban, Ozone Layer Protection, Ship Pollution, Tropical Timber, Wetlands, Whaling; signed, but not ratified—Antarctic-Environmental Protocol, Law of the Sea
Note: dominates South Asian subcontinent; near important Indian Ocean trade routes

People

Population: 919,903,056 (July 1994 est.)
Population growth rate: 1.82% (1994 est.)
Birth rate: 28.45 births/1,000 population (1994 est.)

Death rate: 10.29 deaths/1,000 population (1994 est.)
Net migration rate: 0 migrant(s)/1,000 population (1994 est.)
Infant mortality rate: 78.4 deaths/1,000 live births (1994 est.)
Life expectancy at birth:
total population: 58.58 years
male: 58.09 years
female: 59.09 years (1994 est.)
Total fertility rate: 3.48 children born/ woman (1994 est.)
Nationality:
noun: Indian(s)
adjective: Indian
Ethnic divisions: Indo-Aryan 72%, Dravidian 25%, Mongoloid and other 3%
Religions: Hindu 80%, Muslim 14%, Christian 2.4%, Sikh 2%, Buddhist 0.7%, Jains 0.5%, other 0.4%
Languages: English enjoys associate status but is the most important language for national, political, and commercial communication, Hindi the national language and primary tongue of 30% of the people, Bengali (official), Telugu (official), Marathi (official), Tamil (official), Urdu (official), Gujarati (official), Malayalam (official), Kannada (official), Oriya (official), Punjabi (official), Assamese (official), Kashmiri (official), Sindhi (official), Sanskrit (official), Hindustani a popular variant of Hindu/Urdu, is spoken widely throughout northern India
note: 24 languages each spoken by a million or more persons; numerous other languages and dialects, for the most part mutually unintelligible
Literacy: age 7 and over can read and write (1991 est.)
total population: 52.11%
male: 63.86%
female: 39.42%
Labor force: 314.751 million (1990)
by occupation: agriculture 65% (1993 est.)

Government

Names:
conventional long form: Republic of India
conventional short form: India

Digraph: IN
Type: federal republic
Capital: New Delhi
Administrative divisions: 25 states and 7 union territories*; Andaman and Nicobar Islands*, Andhra Pradesh, Arunachal Pradesh, Assam, Bihar, Chandigarh*, Dadra and Nagar Haveli*, Daman and Diu*, Delhi*, Goa, Gujarat, Haryana, Himachal Pradesh, Jammu and Kashmir, Karnataka, Kerala, Lakshadweep*, Madhya Pradesh, Maharashtra, Manipur, Meghalaya, Mizoram, Nagaland, Orissa, Pondicherry*, Punjab, Rajasthan, Sikkim, Tamil Nadu, Tripura, Uttar Pradesh, West Bengal
Independence: 15 August 1947 (from UK)
National holiday: Anniversary of the Proclamation of the Republic, 26 January (1950)
Constitution: 26 January 1950
Legal system: based on English common law; limited judicial review of legislative acts; accepts compulsory ICJ jurisdiction, with reservations
Suffrage: 18 years of age; universal
Executive branch:
chief of state: President Shankar Dayal SHARMA (since 25 July 1992); Vice President Kicheril Raman NARAYANAN (since 21 August 1992)
head of government: Prime Minister P. V. Narasimha RAO (since 21 June 1991)
cabinet: Council of Ministers; appointed by the president on recommendation of the prime minister
Legislative branch: bicameral Parliament (Sansad)
Council of States (Rajya Sabha): body consisting of not more than 250 members, up to 12 appointed by the president, the remainder chosen by the elected members of the state and territorial assemblies
People's Assembly (Lok Sabha): elections last held 21 May, 12 and 15 June 1991 (next to be held by November 1996); results—percent of vote by party NA; seats—(545 total, 543 elected, 2 appointed) Congress (I) Party 245, Bharatiya Janata Party 119, Janata Dal Party 39, Janata Dal (Ajit Singh) 20, CPI/M 35, CPI 14, Telugu Desam 13, AIADMK 11, Samajwadi Janata Party 5, Shiv Sena 4, RSP 4, BSP 1, Congress (S) Party 1, other 23, vacant 9
Judicial branch: Supreme Court
Political parties and leaders: Congress (I) Party, P. V. Narasimha RAO, president; Bharatiya Janata Party (BJP), L.K. ADVANI; Janata Dal Party, Chandra SHEKHAR; Janata Dal (Ajit Singh), Ajit SINGH; Communist Party of India/Marxist (CPI/M), Harkishan Singh SURJEET; Communist Party of India (CPI), Indrajit GUPTA; Telugu Desam (a regional party in Andhra Pradesh), N. T. Rama RAO; All-India Anna Dravida Munnetra Kazagham (AIADMK; a regional party in Tamil Nadu), Jayaram JAYALALITHA; Samajwadi Party (SP, formerly Samajwadi Janata Party), Mulayam Singh YADAV (President), Om Prakash CHAUTALA, Devi LAL; Shiv Sena, Bal THACKERAY; Revolutionary Socialist Party (RSP), Tridip CHOWDHURY; Bahujana Samaj Party (BSP), Kanshi RAM; Congress (S) Party, leader NA; Communist Party of India/Marxist-Leninist (CPI/ML), Vinod MISHRA; Dravida Munnetra Kazagham (a regional party in Tamil Nadu), M. KARUNANIDHI; Akali Dal factions representing Sikh religious community in the Punjab; National Conference (NC; a regional party in Jammu and Kashmir), Farooq ABDULLAH
Other political or pressure groups: various separatist groups seeking greater communal and/or regional autonomy; numerous religious or militant/chauvinistic organizations, including Adam Sena, Ananda Marg, Vishwa Hindu Parishad, and Rashtriya Swayamsevak Sangh
Member of: AG (observer), AsDB, C, CCC, CP, ESCAP, FAO, G-6, G-15, G-19, AfDB, G-24, G-77, GATT, IAEA, IBRD, ICAO, ICC, ICFTU, IDA, IFAD, IFC, ILO, IMF, IMO, INMARSAT, INTELSAT, INTERPOL, IOC, IOM (observer), ISO, ITU, LORCS, NAM, OAS (observer), ONUSAL, PCA, SAARC, UN, UNAVEM II, UNCTAD, UNESCO, UNIDO, UNIKOM, UNOMOZ, UNOSOM, UNPROFOR, UNTAC, UPU, WFTU, WHO, WIPO, WMO, WTO

Diplomatic representation in US:
chief of mission: Ambassador Siddhartha Shankar RAY
chancery: 2107 Massachusetts Avenue NW, Washington, DC 20008
telephone: (202) 939-7000
consulate(s) general: Chicago, New York, and San Francisco
US diplomatic representation:
chief of mission: Ambassador-designate Frank WISNER
embassy: Shanti Path, Chanakyapuri 110021, New Delhi
mailing address: use embassy street address
telephone: [91] (11) 600651
FAX: [91] (11) 687-2028
consulate(s) general: Bombay, Calcutta, Madras
Flag: three equal horizontal bands of orange (top), white, and green with a blue chakra (24-spoked wheel) centered in the white band; similar to the flag of Niger, which has a small orange disk centered in the white band

---

U.S. Government Contacts:

U.S. Trade Desk: (202) 482-2954

American Embassy Commercial Section
Shanti Path, Chanahyapuri
110021 New Delhi, India
c/o U.S. Department of State (New Delhi)
Washington, DC 20521-9000
Tel: 91-11-600-651
Fax: 91-11-687-2391

**American Consulate General - Bombay
Commercial Section**
Lincoln House
78 Bhulabhai Desai Road
Bombay 400026, India
c/o U.S. Department of State (Bombay)
Washington, DC 20521-6240
Tel: 91-022-822-3611/8
Fax: 91-22-822-0350

**American Consulate General - Calcutta
Commercial Section**
5/1 Ho Chi Minh Sarani
Calcutta 700071, India

c/o U.S. Department of State (Calcutta)
Washington, DC 20521-6250
Tel: 91-033-44-3611/6
Fax: 91-033-283-823

**American Consulate General - Madras
Commercial Section**
Mount Road - 6
Madras 600006, India
c/o U.S. Department of State (Madras)
Washington, DC 20521-6260
Tel: 91-44-477-542
Fax: 91-44-825-0240

India Government Contacts:

Embassy of India Commercial Section
2107 Massachusetts Avenue, N.W.
Washington, DC 20008
Tel: (202) 939-7000

**Chambers of Commerce &
Organizations:**

American Business Council - India
Mohan Dey Building, 11th Floor
13, Tolstoy Marg
New Delhi 110 001, India
Tel: (91) 11 332-2723
Fax: (91) 11 371-2827

**Dr. Abhijit Sen
President
Indo-American Chamber of Commerce**
1-C, Vulcan Insurance Building
Veer Nariman Road,
Churchgate,
Bombay 400020
Tel: 91-22-221413/221485

Legal Services:

**Amarchand & Mangaldas & Hiralal
Shroff & Co.**
Lentin Chambers, Dalal Street
Bombay 400 023, India
Tel: 9122 2654866
Fax: 9122 2653891
International Loan and Financial Documentation, Monopolies Control, Franchising, Energy Law, Joint Ventures and Foreign Collaborations.

Bhasin and Bhasin
Advocates & Legal Consultants
C- 14 South Extension Part II
New Delhi 110049
Tel: 91-11-6443280, 6451705
Fax: 91-11-6464498

J.B. Dadachanji & Co.
Solicitors and Advocates
3, Parliament Street
New Delhi 11001
Tel: 91-11-311013, 312573
Fax: 91-11-352505, 3746029

Mahojoan & Associates
Solicitors & Advocates
E- 185, Geater kailash Part I
New Delhi 110048
Tel: 91-11-6417669
Fax: 91-11-6472013

Jai Mangharam Mukhi
A-27 Neeti Bagh
New Delhi 110 049, India
Tel: 9111 66 8900
Fax: 9111 686 4679
*Monopolies and Restrictive Trade Practices
Commission, Anti-Trust Law, International
Law and Public International Law, Contracts.*

Rajinder Narain & Co.
14-F, Connaught Place
New Delhi 110 001, India
9111 331 32 32
Fax: 9111 332 83 19
*Intellectual Property Law, Industrial Labor
Law, Constitutional Law in the Supreme Court
and High Courts, Sale of Goods, Technology
Transfers.*

Singhania & Co.
Solicitors & Advocates
B-92 Himalaya House,
23 Kasturbha Gandhi Marg
New Delhi 110001
Tel: 91-11-3318300
Fax: 91-11-3314413
*Branch offices in Bombay, Calcutta, Madras,
Bangalore, Hyderabad, London and New York.*

Travel:

International Hotels in Country:
New Delhi:
Hyatt Regency Delhi, Tel: 91 11 6881234, Fax:
91 11 6886833

INDONESIA

Strait of Malacca

Medan

Borneo

Celebes

Sumatra

JAKARTA

Java

Timor

North Pacific Ocean

New Guinea

Indian Ocean

Economy

Overview: Indonesia is a mixed economy with some socialist institutions and central planning but with a recent emphasis on deregulation and private enterprise. Indonesia has extensive natural wealth, yet, with a large and rapidly increasing population, it remains a poor country. Real GDP growth in 1985-93 averaged about 6%, quite impressive, but not sufficient to both slash underemployment and absorb the 2.3 million workers annually entering the labor force. Agriculture, including forestry and fishing, is an important sector, accounting for 21% of GDP and over 50% of the labor force. The staple crop is rice. Once the world's largest rice importer, Indonesia is now nearly self-sufficient. Plantation crops—rubber and palm oil—and textiles and plywood are being encouraged for both export and job generation. Industrial output now accounts for almost 40% of GDP and is based on a supply of diverse natural resources, including crude oil, natural gas, timber, metals, and coal. Foreign investment has also boosted manufacturing output and exports in recent years. Indeed, the economy's growth is highly dependent on the continuing expansion of nonoil exports. Japan remains Indonesia's most important customer

and supplier of aid. Rapid growth in the money supply in 1989-90 prompted Jakarta to implement a tight monetary policy in 1991, forcing the private sector to go to foreign banks for investment financing. Real interest rates remained above 10% and off-shore commercial debt grew. The growth in off-shore debt prompted Jakarta to limit foreign borrowing beginning in late 1991. Despite the continued problems in moving toward a more open financial system and the persistence of a fairly tight credit situation, GDP growth in 1992 and 1993 has matched the government target of 6%-7% annual growth.

National product: GDP—purchasing power equivalent—$571 billion (1993 est.)

National product real growth rate: 6.5% (1993 est.)

National product per capita: $2,900 (1993 est.)

Inflation rate (consumer prices): 10% (1993 est.)

Unemployment rate: 3% official rate; underemployment 45% (1993 est.)

Budget:
revenues: $32.8 billion
expenditures: $32.8 billion, including capital expenditures of $12.9 billion (FY95)

Exports: $38.2 billion (f.o.b., 1993 est.)
commodities: petroleum and gas 28%, clothing and fabrics 15%, plywood 11%, footwear 4% (1992)
partners: Japan 32%, US 13%, Singapore 9%, South Korea 6% (1992)

Imports: $28.3 billion (f.o.b., 1993 est.)
commodities: machinery 37%, semi-finished goods 16%, chemicals 14%, raw materials 10%, transport equipment 7%, foodstuffs 6%, petroleum products 4%, consumer goods 3% (1992)
partners: Japan 22%, US 14%, Germany 8%, South Korea 7%, Singapore 6%, Australia 5%, Taiwan 5% (1992)

External debt: $100 billion (1994 est.)

Industrial production: growth rate 11.6%

(1989 est.); accounts 35% of GDP

Electricity:
capacity: 11,600,000 kW
production: 38 billion kWh
consumption per capita: 200 kWh (1990)

Industries: petroleum and natural gas, textiles, mining, cement, chemical fertilizers, plywood, food, rubber

Agriculture: accounts for 21% of GDP; subsistence food production; small-holder and plantation production for export; main products are rice, cassava, peanuts, rubber, cocoa, coffee, palm oil, copra, other tropical products, poultry, beef, pork, eggs

Illicit drugs: illicit producer of cannabis for the international drug trade, but not a major player; government actively eradicating plantings and prosecuting traffickers

Economic aid:
recipient: US commitments, including Ex-Im (FY70-89), $4.4 billion; Western (non-US) countries, ODA and OOF bilateral commitments (1970-89), $25.9 billion; OPEC bilateral aid (1979-89), $213 million; Communist countries (1970-89), $175 million

Currency: 1 Indonesian rupiah (Rp) = 100 sen (sen no longer used)

Exchange rates: Indonesian rupiahs (Rp) per US$1—2,116.9 (January 1994), 2,087.1 (1993), 2,029.9 (1992), 1,950.3 (1991), 1,842.8 (1990), 1,770.1 (1989)

Fiscal year: 1 April—31 March

Communications

Railroads: 6,964 km total; 6,389 km 1.067-meter gauge, 497 km 0.750-meter gauge, 78 km 0.600-meter gauge; 211 km double track; 101 km electrified; all government owned

Highways:
total: 119,500 km
paved: NA
unpaved: NA
undifferentiated: provincial 34,180 km; district 73,508 km; state 11,812 km

Inland waterways: 21,579 km total; Sumatra 5,471 km, Java and Madura 820 km, Kalimantan 10,460 km, Sulawesi 241 km, Irian Jaya 4,587 km

Pipelines: crude oil 2,505 km; petroleum products 456 km; natural gas 1,703 km (1989)

Ports: Cilacap, Cirebon, Jakarta, Kupang, Palembang, Ujungpandang, Semarang, Surabaya

Merchant marine: 430 ships (1,000 GRT or over) totaling 1,893,830 GRT/2,768,294 DWT, short-sea passenger 7, passenger-cargo 13, cargo 256, container 11, roll-on/roll-off cargo 5, vehicle carrier 4, oil tanker 83, chemical tanker 7, liquefied gas 6, specialized tanker 7, livestock carrier 1, bulk 26, passenger 4

Airports:
total: 444
usable: 414
with permanent-surface runways: 122
with runways over 3,659 m: 1
with runways 2,440-3,659 m: 11
with runways 1,220-2,439 m: 68

Telecommunications: interisland microwave system and HF police net; domestic service fair, international service good; radiobroadcast coverage good; 763,000 telephones (1986); broadcast stations—618 AM, 38 FM, 9 TV; satellite earth stations—1 Indian Ocean INTELSAT earth station and 1 Pacific Ocean INTELSAT earth station; and 1 domestic satellite communications system

Defense Forces

Branches: Army, Navy, Air Force, National Police

Manpower availability: males age 15-49 54,518,490; fit for military service 32,175,853; reach military age (18) annually 2,201,295 (1994 est.)

Defense expenditures: exchange rate conversion—$2.1 billion, 1.5% of GNP (FY93/94 est.)

Geography

Location: Southeastern Asia, between Malaysia and Australia

Map references: Oceania, Southeast Asia, Standard Time Zones of the World

The Internationalist

Area:
total area: 1,919,440 sq km
land area: 1,826,440 sq km
comparative area: slightly less than three times the size of Texas
Land boundaries: total 2,602 km, Malaysia 1,782 km, Papua New Guinea 820 km
Coastline: 54,716 km
Maritime claims: measured from claimed archipelagic baselines
exclusive economic zone: 200 nm
territorial sea: 12 nm
International disputes: sovereignty over Timor Timur (East Timor Province) disputed with Portugal and not recognized by the UN; two islands in dispute with Malaysia
Climate: tropical; hot, humid; more moderate in highlands
Terrain: mostly coastal lowlands; larger islands have interior mountains
Natural resources: petroleum, tin, natural gas, nickel, timber, bauxite, copper, fertile soils, coal, gold, silver
Land use:
arable land: 8%
permanent crops: 3%
meadows and pastures: 7%
forest and woodland: 67%
other: 15%
Irrigated land: 75,500 sq km (1989 est.)
Environment:
current issues: deforestation; water pollution from industrial wastes, sewage; air pollution in urban areas
natural hazards: occasional floods, severe droughts, and tsunamis
international agreements: party to—Endangered Species, Hazardous Wastes, Law of the Sea, Nuclear Test Ban, Ozone Layer Protection, Ship Pollution, Tropical Timber; signed, but not ratified—Biodiversity, Climate Change, Marine Life Conservation
Note: archipelago of 13,500 islands (6,000 inhabited); straddles Equator; strategic location astride or along major sea lanes from Indian Ocean to Pacific Ocean

People

Population: 200,409,741 (July 1994 est.)

Population growth rate: 1.59% (1994 est.)
Birth rate: 24.45 births/1,000 population (1994 est.)
Death rate: 8.6 deaths/1,000 population (1994 est.)
Net migration rate: 0 migrant(s)/1,000 population (1994 est.)
Infant mortality rate: 67.3 deaths/1,000 live births (1994 est.)
Life expectancy at birth:
total population: 60.74 years
male: 58.7 years
female: 62.88 years (1994 est.)
Total fertility rate: 2.8 children born/woman (1994 est.)
Nationality:
noun: Indonesian(s)
adjective: Indonesian
Ethnic divisions: Javanese 45%, Sundanese 14%, Madurese 7.5%, coastal Malays 7.5%, other 26%
Religions: Muslim 87%, Protestant 6%, Roman Catholic 3%, Hindu 2%, Buddhist 1%, other 1% (1985)
Languages: Bahasa Indonesia (modified form of Malay; official), English, Dutch, local dialects the most widely spoken of which is Javanese
Literacy: age 15 and over can read and write (1990 est.)
total population: 77%
male: 84%
female: 68%
Labor force: 67 million
by occupation: agriculture 55%, manufacturing 10%, construction 4%, transport and communications 3% (1985 est.)

Government

Names:
conventional long form: Republic of Indonesia
conventional short form: Indonesia
local long form: Republik Indonesia
local short form: Indonesia
former name: Netherlands East Indies; Dutch East Indies
Digraph: ID
Type: republic

Capital: Jakarta

Administrative divisions: 24 provinces (propinsi-propinsi, singular—propinsi), 2 special regions* (daerah-daerah istimewa, singular—daerah istimewa), and 1 special capital city district** (daerah khusus ibukota); Aceh*, Bali, Bengkulu, Irian Jaya, Jakarta Raya**, Jambi, Jawa Barat, Jawa Tengah, Jawa Timur, Kalimantan Barat, Kalimantan Selatan, Kalimantan Tengah, Kalimantan Timur, Lampung, Maluku, Nusa Tenggara Barat, Nusa Tenggara Timur, Riau, Sulawesi Selatan, Sulawesi Tengah, Sulawesi Tenggara, Sulawesi Utara, Sumatera Barat, Sumatera Selatan, Sumatera Utara, Timor Timur, Yogyakarta*

Independence: 17 August 1945 (proclaimed independence; on 27 December 1949, Indonesia became legally independent from the Netherlands)

National holiday: Independence Day, 17 August (1945)

Constitution: August 1945, abrogated by Federal Constitution of 1949 and Provisional Constitution of 1950, restored 5 July 1959

Legal system: based on Roman-Dutch law, substantially modified by indigenous concepts and by new criminal procedures code; has not accepted compulsory ICJ jurisdiction

Suffrage: 17 years of age; universal and married persons regardless of age

Executive branch:
chief of state and head of government: President Gen. (Ret.) SOEHARTO (since 27 March 1968); Vice President Gen. (Ret.) Try SUTRISNO (since 11 March 1993)
cabinet: Cabinet

Legislative branch: unicameral
House of Representatives: (Dewan Perwakilan Rakyat or DPR) elections last held on 8 June 1992 (next to be held NA 1997); results— GOLKAR 68%, PPP 17%, PDI 15%; seats— (500 total, 400 elected, 100 military representatives appointed) GOLKAR 282, PPP 62, PDI 56
note: the People's Consultative Assembly (Majelis Permusyawaratan Rakyat or MPR) includes the DPR plus 500 indirectly elected members who meet every five years to elect the president and vice president and, theoretically, to determine national policy

Judicial branch: Supreme Court (Mahkamah Agung)

Political parties and leaders: GOLKAR (quasi-official party based on functional groups), Lt. Gen. (Ret.) HARMOKO, general chairman; Indonesia Democracy Party (PDI— federation of former Nationalist and Christian Parties), Megawati SUKARNOPUTRI, chairman; Development Unity Party (PPP, federation of former Islamic parties), Ismail Hasan METAREUM, chairman

Member of: APEC, AsDB, ASEAN, CCC, CP, ESCAP, FAO, G-15, G-19, G-77, GATT, IAEA, IBRD, ICAO, ICC, ICFTU, IDA, IDB, IFAD, IFC, ILO, IMF, IMO, INMARSAT, INTELSAT, INTERPOL, IOC, IOM (observer), ISO, ITU, LORCS, NAM, OIC, OPEC, UN, UNCTAD, UNESCO, UNIDO, UNIKOM, UNOSOM, UNTAC, UPU, WCL, WFTU, WHO, WIPO, WMO, WTO

Diplomatic representation in US:
chief of mission: Ambassador Arifin SIREGAR
chancery: 2020 Massachusetts Avenue NW, Washington, DC 20036
telephone: (202) 775-5200
FAX: (202) 775-5365
consulate(s) general: Chicago, Houston, New York, and Los Angeles
consulate(s): San Francisco

US diplomatic representation:
chief of mission: Ambassador Robert L. BARRY
embassy: Medan Merdeka Selatan 5, Box 1, Jakarta
mailing address: APO AP 96520
telephone: [62] (21) 360-360
FAX: [62] (21) 386-2259
consulate(s): Medan, Surabaya

Flag: two equal horizontal bands of red (top) and white; similar to the flag of Monaco, which is shorter; also similar to the flag of Poland, which is white (top) and red

---

U.S. Government Contacts:

U.S. Trade Desk: (202) 482-3877

American Embassy Commercial Section
Medan Merdeka Selatan 5
Jakarta, Indonesia
APO AP 96520
Tel: 62-21-360-360
Fax: 62-21-360-644

American Consulate - Medan Commercial Section
Jalan Imam Bonjol 13
Medan, Indonesia
APO AP 96520
Tel: 62-61-322-200

Indonesia Government Contacts:

Embassy of Indonesia Commercial Section
2020 Massachusetts Avenue, N.W.
Washington, DC 20036
Tel: (202) 775-5200

Chambers of Commerce& Organizations:

American Chamber of Commerce in Indonesia
The Landmark Centre, 22nd Floor
Jalan Jendral Sudirman I
Jakarta, Indonesia
Tel: 62-21-578-065

Legal Services:

Lubis, Ganie & Surowidjojo
Bumi Daya Plaza, 28th & 29th Floor
Jalan Imam, Bonjol No. 61
Jakarta 10310, Indonesia
Tel: 6221 335101
General Corporate and Commercial Law Practice. Commercial Litigation, Maritime/Shipping. Mininig. Real Estate.

Suria Nataadmadja & Associates
Jalan Malaka 19-D, 3rd Floor
Jakarta, 11230, Indonesia
Tel: 6221 6904403
Fax: 6221 6902792
Solves difficult problems between foreign investors and its local partners.

Travel:

International Airlines to Country:
Continental

International Hotels in Country:
Jakarta:
Grand Hyatt, Tel: 6221 /390-1234, Fax: 6221/334321
Hotel Borobudur Intercontinental, Tel: 6221/370108, Fax: 6221/359741
Mandarin Oriental, Tel: 6221/321307, Fax: 6221/324669.

JAPAN

500 km
Hokkaido
Sapporo
Occupied by the Soviet Union in 1945, administered by Russia, claimed by Japan.
Sea of Japan
Sendai
Honshu
TOKYO
Korea Strait
Kitakyūshū
Ōsaka
North Pacific Ocean
Shikoku
East China Sea
Kyushu
Philippine Sea
Okinawa

Economy

Overview: Government-industry cooperation, a strong work ethic, mastery of high technology, and a comparatively small defense allocation have helped Japan advance with extraordinary rapidity to the rank of second most powerful economy in the world. Industry, the most important sector of the economy, is heavily dependent on imported raw materials and fuels. Self-sufficient in rice, Japan must import about 50% of its requirements of other grain and fodder crops. Japan maintains one of the world's largest fishing fleets and accounts for nearly 15% of the global catch. Overall economic growth has been spectacular: a 10% average in the 1960s, a 5% average in the 1970s and 1980s. Economic growth came to a halt in 1992-93 largely because of contractionary domestic policies intended to wring speculative excesses from the stock and real estate markets. At the same time, the stronger yen and slower global growth are containing export growth. Unemployment and inflation remain remarkably low in comparison with the other industrialized nations. Japan continues to run a huge trade surplus—$120 billion in 1993, up more than 10% from the year earlier—which

supports extensive investment in foreign assets. The new prime minister HATA in early 1994 reiterated previous governments' vows of administrative and economic reform, including reduction in the trade surplus, but his weak coalition government faces strong resistance from traditional interest groups. The crowding of the habitable land area and the aging of the population are two major long-run problems.

National product: GDP—purchasing power equivalent—$2.549 trillion (1993)

National product real growth rate: 0% (1993)

National product per capita: $20,400 (1993)

Inflation rate (consumer prices): 1.3% (1993)

Unemployment rate: 2.5% (1993)

Budget:
revenues: $490 billion
expenditures: $579 billion, including capital expenditures (public works only) of about $68 billion (FY93)

Exports: $360.9 billion (f.o.b., 1993)
commodities: manufactures 97% (including machinery 46%, motor vehicles 20%, consumer electronics 10%)
partners: Southeast Asia 33%, US 29%, Western Europe 18%, China 5%

Imports: $240.7 billion (c.i.f., 1993)
commodities: manufactures 52%, fossil fuels 20%, foodstuffs and raw materials 28%
partners: Southeast Asia 25%, US 23%, Western Europe 15%, China 9%

External debt: $NA

Industrial production: growth rate -4.0% (1993); accounts for 30% of GDP

Electricity:
capacity: 196,000,000 kW
production: 835 billion kWh
consumption per capita: 6,700 kWh (1992)

Industries: steel and non-ferrous metallurgy, heavy electrical equipment, construction and mining equipment, motor vehicles and parts, electronic and telecommunication equipment and components, machine tools and automated production systems, locomotives and railroad rolling stock, shipbuilding, chemicals, textiles, food processing

Agriculture: accounts for only 2% of GDP; highly subsidized and protected sector, with crop yields among highest in world; principal crops—rice, sugar beets, vegetables, fruit; animal products include pork, poultry, dairy and eggs; about 50% self-sufficient in food production; shortages of wheat, corn, soybeans; world's largest fish catch of 10 million metric tons in 1991

Economic aid:
donor: ODA and OOF commitments (1970-93), $123 billion
note: ODA outlay of $9.9 billion in 1994 (est.)

Currency: yen (¥)

Exchange rates: yen (¥) per US$1—111.51 (January 1994), 111.20 (1993), 126.65 (1992), 134.71 (1991), 144.79 (1990), 137.96 (1989)

Fiscal year: 1 April—31 March

Communications

Railroads: 27,327 km total; 2,012 km 1.435-meter standard gauge and 25,315 km predominantly 1.067-meter narrow gauge; 5,724 km doubletrack and multitrack sections, 9,038 km 1.067-meter narrow-gauge electrified, 2,012 km 1.435-meter standard-gauge electrified (1987)

Highways:
total: 1,115,609 km
paved: 782,042 km (including 4,869 km of national expressways)
unpaved: gravel, crushed stone, or earth 333,567 km (1991)

Inland waterways: about 1,770 km; seagoing craft ply all coastal inland seas

Pipelines: crude oil 84 km; petroleum products 322 km; natural gas 1,800 km

Ports: Chiba, Muroran, Kitakyushu, Kobe, Tomakomai, Nagoya, Osaka, Tokyo, Yokkaichi, Yokohama, Kawasaki, Niigata, Fushiki-Toyama, Shimizu, Himeji, Wakayama-Shimozu, Shimonoseki, Tokuyama-Shimomatsu

Merchant marine: 926 ships (1,000 GRT or over) totaling 20,383,101 GRT/31,007,515

DWT, passenger 10, short-sea passenger 36, passenger cargo 3, cargo 76, container 44, roll-on/roll-off cargo 44, refrigerated cargo 66, vehicle carrier 94, oil tanker 265, chemical tanker 9, liquefied gas 42, combination ore/oil 9, specialized tanker 2, bulk 225, multi-function large load carrier 1
note: Japan also owns a large flag of convenience fleet, including up to 38% of the total number of ships under the Panamanian flag

Airports:
total: 167
usable: 165
with permanent-surface runways: 137
with runways over 3,659 m: 2
with runways 2,440-3,659 m: 34
with runways 1,220-2,439 m: 52

Telecommunications: excellent domestic and international service; 64,000,000 telephones; broadcast stations—318 AM, 58 FM, 12,350 TV (196 major—1 kw or greater); satellite earth stations—4 Pacific Ocean INTELSAT and 1 Indian Ocean INTELSAT; submarine cables to US (via Guam), Philippines, China, and Russia

Defense Forces

Branches: Japan Ground Self-Defense Force (Army), Japan Maritime Self-Defense Force (Navy), Japan Air Self-Defense Force (Air Force), Maritime Safety Agency (Coast Guard)

Manpower availability: males age 15-49 32,044,032; fit for military service 27,597,444; reach military age (18) annually 953,928 (1994 est.)

Defense expenditures: exchange rate conversion—$37 billion, 0.94% of GDP (FY93/94 est.)

Geography

Location: Eastern Asia, off the southeast coast of Russia and east of the Korean peninsula

Map references: Asia, Standard Time Zones of the World

Area:

total area: 377,835 sq km
land area: 374,744 sq km
comparative area: slightly smaller than California
note: includes Bonin Islands (Ogasawara-gunto), Daito-shoto, Minami-jima, Okinotori-shima, Ryukyu Islands (Nansei-shoto), and Volcano Islands (Kazan-retto)

Land boundaries: 0 km
Coastline: 29,751 km
Maritime claims:
exclusive fishing zone: 200 nm
territorial sea: 12 nm; 3 nm in the international straits—La Perouse or Soya, Tsugaru, Osumi, and Eastern and Western Channels of the Korea or Tsushima Strait

International disputes: islands of Etorofu, Kunashiri, Shikotau, and the Habomai group occupied by the Soviet Union in 1945, now administered by Russia, claimed by Japan; Liancourt Rocks disputed with South Korea; Senkaku-shoto (Senkaku Islands) claimed by China and Taiwan

Climate: varies from tropical in south to cool temperate in north
Terrain: mostly rugged and mountainous
Natural resources: negligible mineral resources, fish
Land use:
arable land: 13%
permanent crops: 1%
meadows and pastures: 1%
forest and woodland: 67%
other: 18%

Irrigated land: 28,680 sq km (1989)
Environment:
current issues: air pollution from power plant emissions results in acid rain; acidification of lakes and reservoirs degrading water quality and threatening aquatic life
natural hazards: many dormant and some active volcanoes; about 1,500 seismic occurrences (mostly tremors) every year; subject to tsunamis
international agreements: party to—Antarctic Treaty, Biodiversity, Climate Change, Endangered Species, Environmental Modification, Hazardous Wastes, Marine Dumping, Nuclear Test Ban, Ozone Layer Protection, Ship Pollution, Tropical Timber, Wetlands, Whaling; signed, but not ratified—Antarctic-Environmental Protocol, Law of the Sea

Note: strategic location in northeast Asia

People

Population: 125,106,937 (July 1994 est.)
Population growth rate: 0.32% (1994 est.)
Birth rate: 10.49 births/1,000 population (1994 est.)
Death rate: 7.31 deaths/1,000 population (1994 est.)
Net migration rate: 0 migrant(s)/1,000 population (1994 est.)
Infant mortality rate: 4.3 deaths/1,000 live births (1994 est.)
Life expectancy at birth:
total population: 79.31 years
male: 76.47 years
female: 82.28 years (1994 est.)
Total fertility rate: 1.55 children born/ woman (1994 est.)
Nationality:
noun: Japanese (singular and plural)
adjective: Japanese
Ethnic divisions: Japanese 99.4%, other 0.6% (mostly Korean)
Religions: observe both Shinto and Buddhist 84%, other 16% (including 0.7% Christian)
Languages: Japanese
Literacy: age 15 and over can read and write (1970 est.)
total population: 99%
male: NA%
female: NA%
Labor force: 63.33 million
by occupation: trade and services 54%, manufacturing, mining, and construction 33%, agriculture, forestry, and fishing 7%, government 3% (1988)

Government

Names:
conventional long form: none

conventional short form: Japan
Digraph: JA
Type: constitutional monarchy
Capital: Tokyo
Administrative divisions: 47 prefectures; Aichi, Akita, Aomori, Chiba, Ehime, Fukui, Fukuoka, Fukushima, Gifu, Gumma, Hiroshima, Hokkaido, Hyogo, Ibaraki, Ishikawa, Iwate, Kagawa, Kagoshima, Kanagawa, Kochi, Kumamoto, Kyoto, Mie, Miyagi, Miyazaki, Nagano, Nagasaki, Nara, Niigata, Oita, Okayama, Okinawa, Osaka, Saga, Saitama, Shiga, Shimane, Shizuoka, Tochigi, Tokushima, Tokyo, Tottori, Toyama, Wakayama, Yamagata, Yamaguchi, Yamanashi
Independence: 660 BC (traditional founding by Emperor Jimmu)
National holiday: Birthday of the Emperor, 23 December (1933)
Constitution: 3 May 1947
Legal system: modeled after European civil law system with English-American influence; judicial review of legislative acts in the Supreme Court; accepts compulsory ICJ jurisdiction, with reservations
Suffrage: 20 years of age; universal
Executive branch:
chief of state: Emperor AKIHITO (since 7 January 1989)
head of government: Prime Minister Tsutomu HATA (since 25 April 1994); Deputy Prime Minister (vacant)
cabinet: Cabinet; appointed by the prime minister
Legislative branch: bicameral Diet (Kokkai)
House of Councillors (Sangi-in): elections last held on 26 July 1992 (next to be held NA July 1995); results—percent of vote by party NA; seats—(252 total) LDP 95, SDPJ 68, Shin Ryoku fu-Kai 37, CGP 24, JCP 11, other 17
House of Representatives (Shugi-in): elections last held on 18 July 1993 (next to be held by NA); results—percent of vote by party NA; seats—(511 total) LDP 206, SDPJ 74, Shinseito 62, CGP 52, JNP 37, DSP 19, JCP 15, Sakigake 15, others 19, independents 10, vacant 2
Judicial branch: Supreme Court
Political parties and leaders: Liberal Democratic Party (LDP), Yohei KONO, president; Yoshiro MORI, secretary general; Social Democratic Party of Japan (SDPJ), Tomiichi MURAYAMA; Democratic Socialist Party (DSP), Keigo OUCHI, chairman; Japan Communist Party (JCP), Tetsuzo FUWA, Presidium chairman; Komeito (Clean Government Party, CGP), Koshiro ISHIDA, chairman; Japan New Party (JNP), Morihiro HOSOKAWA, chairman; Shinseito (Japan Renewal Party, JRP), Tsutomu HATA, chairman; Ichiro OZAWA, secretary general; Sakigake (Harbinger), Masayoshi TAKEMURA, chairman; Mirai (Future Party), Michihiko KANO, chairman; The Liberal Party, Koji KAKIZAWA, chairman
note: Shin Ryoku fu-Kai is a new, upper house only, parliamentary alliance which includes the JRP, JNP, DSP, and a minor labor group
Member of: AfDB, AG (observer), Australia Group, APEC, AsDB, BIS, CCC, COCOM, CP, CSCE (observer), EBRD, ESCAP, FAO, G-2, G-5, G-7, G-8, G-10, GATT, IADB, IAEA, IBRD, ICAO, ICC, ICFTU, IDA, IEA, IFAD, IFC, ILO, IMF, IMO, INMARSAT, INTELSAT, INTERPOL, IOC, IOM (observer), ISO, ITU, LORCS, MTCR, NEA, NSG, OAS (observer), OECD, PCA, UN, UNCTAD, UNESCO, UNHCR, UNIDO, UNRWA, UNTAC, UPU, WFTU, WHO, WIPO, WMO, WTO, ZC
Diplomatic representation in US:
chief of mission: Ambassador Takakazu KURIYAMA
chancery: 2520 Massachusetts Avenue NW, Washington, DC 20008
telephone: (202) 939-6700
FAX: (202) 328-2187
consulate(s) general: Agana (Guam), Anchorage, Atlanta, Boston, Chicago, Detroit, Honolulu, Houston, Kansas City (Missouri), Los Angeles, Miami, New Orleans, New York, Portland (Oregon), San Francisco, and Seattle
consulate(s): Saipan (Northern Mariana Islands)
US diplomatic representation:
chief of mission: Ambassador Walter F. MONDALE
embassy: 10-5, Akasaka 1-chome, Minato-ku

The Internationalist

(107), Tokyo
mailing address: Unit 45004, Box 258, Tokyo;
APO AP 96337-0001
telephone: [81] (3) 3224-5000
FAX: [81] (3) 3505-1862
consulate(s) general: Naha (Okinawa), Osaka-Kobe, Sapporo
consulate(s): Fukuoka
Flag: white with a large red disk (representing the sun without rays) in the center

U.S. Government Contacts:

U.S. Trade Desk: (202) 482-2425

American Embassy Commercial Section
10-5 Akasaka, 1-chome
Minato-ku (107)
Tokyo, Japan
APO AP 96337
Tel: 81-3-3224-5050
Fax: 81-3-3589-4235

American Consulate General - Osaka Commercial Section
11-15, Nishitenma 2-chome
Kita-ku
Osaka (530), Japan
APO AP 96337
Tel: 81-6-315-5953
Fax: 81-6-361-5978

American Consulate - Fukuoka Commercial Section
5-26 Ohori 2-chome
Chuo-ku
Fukuoka (810), Japan
Box 10
FPO AP 96322
Fax: 81-92-71-3922

Japan Government Contacts:

Embassy of Japan Commercial Section
2520 Massachusetts Avenue, N.W.
Washington, DC 20008
Tel: (202) 939-6700

Chambers of Commerce & Organizations:

American Chamber of Commerce in Japan - Tokyo
Fukide Building, No.2
4-1-21 Toranomon
Minatu-ku
Tokyo (105), Japan
Tel: 81-3-436-1446

American Chamber of Commerce in Japan - Okinawa
P.O. Box 235
Okinawa City (904), Japan
Tel: 81-989-352-684

American Electronics Association
Nambu Building, 3F, 3-3, Kiochio
Chiyoda-ku
Tokyo (105), Japan
Tel: 81-3-237-7195
Fax: 81-3-237-1237

Semiconductor Industry Association, Japan Office
Nambu Building, 3f, 3-3, Kiochio
Chiyoda-ku
Tokyo, (105), Japan
Tel: 81-3-237-7683
Fax: 81-3-237-1237

U.S. Automotive Parts Industry, Japan Office
Towa Horidomecho Building, 3F, 2-1-1
Nihonbashi-Horidomecho
Chuo-ku
Tokyo (103), Japan
Tel: 81-3-663-8484
Fax: 81-3-663-8483

Japan Extrernal Trade Organization (JETRO)
2-2-5 Toranomon
Minato-ku
Tokyo (105), Japan
Tel: 81-3-582-5511

Japan External Trade Organization
Machinery and Technology Dept.
2-5 Toranomon 2-chome
Minato-ku
Tokyo 105 Japan

JETRO, New York
1221 Avenue of the Americas
New York, NY 10020-1079 U.S.A.
Tel: (212) 997-0400

Legal Servies:

Oh-Ebashi Law Office
Suite 803, Umedashinmichi Building
1-5, Dojima 1-Chome, Kita-Ku
Osaka 530, Japan
Tel: 816-341-0461
Fax: 816-347-0688
*Intellectual Property, Domestic Civil and
Commercial Law, Real Estate and Taxation,
International Business Transactions.*

Shimada, Seno, Amitani & Hirata
Kanda Chuo Building 2 F
3-20, Kanda Nishiki-Cho, Chiyoda-Ku
Tokyo 101, Japan
Tel: 813 3291-2971
Fax: 813 3291-2888
*Ship Finance, Intellectual Property, Aircraft
Finance, Mergers and Acquisitions,
Competition and Trade Regulations.*

Yamagami & Yamagami
5th Floor, Seyama Building
1-1 Nishi-Tenma, 5-Chome, Kita-Ku
Osaka 530, Japan
Tel: 816 365-1800
Fax: 816 365-1801
*General Practice, Corporation, Patent,
Trademark and Licensing Law.*

Travel:

International Airlines to Country:
American, Continental, Northwest, United

International Hotels in Country:
Tokyo:
Capital Tokyo Hotel, Tel: 81-3-3581-4511
Four Seasons Hotel Chinzan-so, Tel: 81-3-
3943-2222, Fax: 81-3-3943-2300
Hotel Okura, Tel: 81-3-3582-0111
Palace Hotel, Tel: 81-3-3211-5211.

LAOS

Economy

Overview: Laos has had a Communist centrally planned economy with government ownership and control of major productive enterprises. Since 1986, however, the government has been decentralizing control and encouraging private enterprise. Laos is a landlocked country with a primitive infrastructure; it has no railroads, a rudimentary road system, limited external and internal telecommunications, and electricity available in only a limited area. Subsistence agriculture is the main occupation, accounting for over 60% of GDP and providing about 85-90% of total employment. The predominant crop is rice. For the foreseeable future the economy will continue to depend for its survival on foreign aid from the IMF and other international sources; aid from the former USSR and Eastern Europe has been cut sharply.

National product: GDP—purchasing power equivalent—$4.1 billion (1993 est.)

National product real growth rate: 7% (1992 est.)

National product per capita: $900 (1993 est.)

Inflation rate (consumer prices): 9.8% (1992 est.)

Unemployment rate: 21% (1989 est.)

Budget:
revenues: $83 million
expenditures: $188.5 million, including capital expenditures of $94 million (1990 est.)
Exports: $133 million (f.o.b., 1992 est.)
commodities: electricity, wood products, coffee, tin
partners: Thailand, Malaysia, Vietnam, FSU, US, China
Imports: $266 million (c.i.f., 1992 est.)
commodities: food, fuel oil, consumer goods, manufactures
partners: Thailand, FSU, Japan, France, Vietnam, China
External debt: $1.1 billion (1990 est.)
Industrial production: growth rate 12% (1991 est.); accounts for about 18% of GDP (1991 est.)
Electricity:
capacity: 226,000 kW
production: 990 million kWh
consumption per capita: 220 kWh (1992)
Industries: tin and gypsum mining, timber, electric power, agricultural processing, construction
Agriculture: accounts for 60% of GDP and employs most of the work force; subsistence farming predominates; normally self-sufficient in nondrought years; principal crops—rice (80% of cultivated land), sweet potatoes, vegetables, corn, coffee, sugarcane, cotton; livestock—buffaloes, hogs, cattle, poultry
Illicit drugs: illicit producer of cannabis, opium poppy for the international drug trade, third-largest opium producer (180 metric tons in 1993)
Economic aid:
recipient: US commitments, including Ex-Im (FY70-79), $276 million; Western (non-US) countries, ODA and OOF bilateral commitments (1970-89), $605 million; Communist countries (1970-89), $995 million
Currency: 1 new kip (NK) = 100 at
Exchange rates: new kips (NK) per US$1— 720 (July 1993). 710 (May 1992), 710 (December 1991), 700 (September 1990), 576 (1989)
Fiscal year: 1 July—30 June

Communications

Railroads: none
Highways:
total: 27,527 km
paved: bituminous 1,856 km
unpaved: gravel, crushed stone, improved earth 7,451 km; unimproved earth 18,220 km (often impassable during rainy season mid-May to mid-September)
Inland waterways: about 4,587 km, primarily Mekong and tributaries; 2,897 additional kilometers are sectionally navigable by craft drawing less than 0.5 m
Pipelines: petroleum products 136 km
Ports: none
Merchant marine: 1 cargo ship (1,000 GRT or over) totaling 2,370 GRT/3,000 DWT
Airports:
total: 53
usable: 41
with permanent-surface runways: 8
with runways over 3,659 m: 0
with runways 2,440-3,659 m: 1
with runways 1,220-2,439 m: 15
Telecommunications: service to general public practically non-existant; radio communications network provides generally erratic service to government users; 7,390 telephones (1986); broadcast stations—10 AM, no FM, 1 TV; 1 satellite earth station

Defense Forces

Branches: Lao People's Army (LPA; including naval, aviation, and militia elements), Air Force, National Police Department
Manpower availability: males age 15-49 1,015,357; fit for military service 547,566; reach military age (18) annually 49,348 (1994 est.)
Defense expenditures: exchange rate conversion—$NA, NA% of GDP

Geography

Location: Southeastern Asia, between Vietnam and Thailand

Map references: Southeast Asia, Standard Time Zones of the World
Area:
total area: 236,800 sq km
land area: 230,800 sq km
comparative area: slightly larger than Utah
Land boundaries: total 5,083 km, Burma 235 km, Cambodia 541 km, China 423 km, Thailand 1,754 km, Vietnam 2,130 km
Coastline: 0 km (landlocked)
Maritime claims: none; landlocked
International disputes: boundary dispute with Thailand
Climate: tropical monsoon; rainy season (May to November); dry season (December to April)
Terrain: mostly rugged mountains; some plains and plateaus
Natural resources: timber, hydropower, gypsum, tin, gold, gemstones
Land use:
arable land: 4%
permanent crops: 0%
meadows and pastures: 3%
forest and woodland: 58%
other: 35%
Irrigated land: 1,200 sq km (1989 est.)
Environment:
current issues: deforestation; soil erosion
natural hazards: subject to floods, drought, and blight
international agreements: party to— Environmental Modification, Nuclear Test Ban; signed, but not ratified—Law of the Sea
Note: landlocked

People

Population: 4,701,654 (July 1994 est.)
Population growth rate: 2.85% (1994 est.)
Birth rate: 43.23 births/1,000 population (1994 est.)
Death rate: 14.74 deaths/1,000 population (1994 est.)
Net migration rate: 0 migrant(s)/1,000 population (1994 est.)
Infant mortality rate: 101.8 deaths/1,000 live births (1994 est.)
Life expectancy at birth:
total population: 51.68 years

male: 50.16 years
female: 53.28 years (1994 est.)
Total fertility rate: 6.07 children born/
woman (1994 est.)
Nationality:
noun: Lao(s) or Laotian(s)
adjective: Lao or Laotian
Ethnic divisions: Lao 50%, Phoutheung
(Kha) 15%, tribal Thai 20%, Meo, Hmong,
Yao, and other 15%
Religions: Buddhist 85%, animist and other
15%
Languages: Lao (official), French, English
Literacy: age 15-45 can read and write (1993)
total population: 64%
male: NA%
female: NA%
Labor force: 1 million-1.5 million
by occupation: agriculture 85-90% (est.)

Government

Names:
conventional long form: Lao People's
Democratic Republic
conventional short form: Laos
local long form: Sathalanalat Paxathipatai
Paxaxon Lao
local short form: none
Digraph: LA
Type: Communist state
Capital: Vientiane
Administrative divisions: 16 provinces
(khoueng, singular and plural) and 1
municipality* (kampheng nakhon, singular and
plural); Attapu, Bokeo, Bolikhamsai,
Champasak, Houaphan, Khammouan, Louang
Namtha, Louangphrabang, Oudomxai,
Phongsali, Saravan, Savannakhet, Xekong,
Vientiane, Viangchan*, Xaignabouri,
Xiangkhoang
Independence: 19 July 1949 (from France)
National holiday: National Day, 2 December
(1975) (proclamation of the Lao People's
Democratic Republic)
Constitution: promulgated 14 August 1991
Legal system: based on civil law system; has
not accepted compulsory ICJ jurisdiction
Suffrage: 18 years of age; universal

Executive branch:
chief of state: President NOUHAK
PHOUMSAVAN (since 25 November 1992)
head of government: Prime Minister Gen.
KHAMTAI SIPHANDON (since 15 August
1991)
cabinet: Council of Ministers; appointed by
the president, approved by the Assembly
Legislative branch: unicameral
Third National Assembly: elections last held
on 20 December 1992 (next to be held NA);
results—percent of vote by party NA; seats—
(85 total) number of seats by party NA
Judicial branch: Supreme People's Court
Political parties and leaders: Lao People's
Revolutionary Party (LPRP), KHAMTAI
Siphandon, party president; includes Lao Front
for National Construction (LFNC); other
parties moribund
Other political or pressure groups:
non-Communist political groups moribund;
most leaders fled the country in 1975
Member of: ACCT, AsDB, ASEAN
(observer), CP, ESCAP, FAO, G-77, IBRD,
ICAO, IDA, IFAD, IFC, ILO, IMF,
INTELSAT (nonsignatory user), INTERPOL,
IOC, ITU, LORCS, NAM, PCA, UN,
UNCTAD, UNESCO, UNIDO, UPU, WFTU,
WHO, WMO, WTO
Diplomatic representation in US:
chief of mission: Ambassador HIEM
PHOMMACHANH
chancery: 2222 S Street NW, Washington, DC
20008
telephone: (202) 332-6416 or 6417
FAX: (202) 332-4923
US diplomatic representation:
chief of mission: Ambassador Victor
TOMSETH
embassy: Rue Bartholonie, Vientiane
mailing address: B. P. 114, Vientiane, or
American Embassy, Box V, APO AP 96546
telephone: [851] 2220, 2357, or 3570, 16-9581
FAX: [851] 4675
Flag: three horizontal bands of red (top), blue
(double width), and red with a large white disk
centered in the blue band

U.S. Government Contacts:

U.S. Trade Desk: (202) 482-3877

MACAU

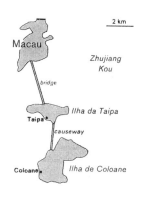

Macau

2 km

Zhujiang Kou

bridge

Ilha da Taipa

Taipa

causeway

Coloane

Ilha de Coloane

Economy

Overview: The economy is based largely on tourism (including gambling) and textile and fireworks manufacturing. Efforts to diversify have spawned other small industries—toys, artificial flowers, and electronics. The tourist sector has accounted for roughly 25% of GDP, and the clothing industry has provided about two-thirds of export earnings; the gambling industry represented well over 40% of GDP in 1992. Macau depends on China for most of its food, fresh water, and energy imports. Japan and Hong Kong are the main suppliers of raw materials and capital goods.

National product: GDP—exchange rate conversion—$3.5 billion (1992 est.)

National product real growth rate: 12% (1992)

National product per capita: $7,300 (1992)

Inflation rate (consumer prices): 7.7% (1992 est.)

Unemployment rate: 2% (1992 est.)

Budget:
revenues: $305 million
expenditures: $298 million, including capital expenditures of $NA (1989 est.)

Exports: $1.8 billion (1992 est.)
commodities: textiles, clothing, toys
partners: US 35%, Hong Kong 12.5%, Germany 12%, China 9.9%, France 8% (1992 est.)

Imports: $2 billion (1992 est.)
commodities: raw materials, foodstuffs, capital goods
partners: Hong Kong 33%, China 20%, Japan 18% (1992 est.)

External debt: $91 million (1985)

Industrial production: NA

Electricity:
capacity: 258,000 kW
production: 855 million kWh
consumption per capita: 1,806 kWh (1992)

Industries: clothing, textiles, toys, plastic products, furniture, tourism

Agriculture: rice, vegetables; food shortages—rice, vegetables, meat; depends mostly on imports for food requirements

Economic aid: none

Currency: 1 pataca (P) = 100 avos

Exchange rates: patacas (P) per US$1— 8.034 (1991-93), 8.024 (1990), 8.030 (1989); note - linked to the Hong Kong dollar at the rate of 1.03 patacas per Hong Kong dollar

Fiscal year: calendar year

Communications

Highways:
total: 42 km
paved: 42 km

Ports: Macau

Airports: none usable, 1 under construction; 1 seaplane station

Telecommunications: fairly modern communication facilities maintained for domestic and international services; 52,000 telephones; broadcast stations—4 AM, 3 FM, no TV (TV programs received from Hong Kong); 115,000 radio receivers (est.); international high-frequency radio communication facility; access to international communications carriers provided via Hong Kong and China; 1 Indian Ocean INTELSAT earth station

Defense Forces

Manpower availability: males age 15-49 139,499; fit for military service 77,887
Note: defense is responsibility of Portugal

Geography

Location: Eastern Asia, 27 km west-southwest of Hong Kong on the southeast coast of China bordering the South China Sea
Map references: Asia, Oceania, Southeast Asia, Standard Time Zones of the World
Area:
total area: 16 sq km
land area: 16 sq km
comparative area: about 0.1 times the size of Washington, DC
Land boundaries: total 0.34 km, China 0.34 km
Coastline: 40 km
Maritime claims: not specified
International disputes: none
Climate: subtropical; marine with cool winters, warm summers
Terrain: generally flat
Natural resources: negligible
Land use:
arable land: 0%
permanent crops: 0%
meadows and pastures: 0%
forest and woodland: 0%
other: 100%
Irrigated land: NA sq km
Environment:
current issues: NA
natural hazards: NA
international agreements: party to—Ozone Layer Protection
Note: essentially urban; one causeway and one bridge connect the two islands to the peninsula on mainland

People

Population: 484,557 (July 1994 est.)
Population growth rate: 1.35% (1994 est.)
Birth rate: 14.78 births/1,000 population (1994 est.)
Death rate: 4.12 deaths/1,000 population (1994 est.)
Net migration rate: 2.83 migrant(s)/1,000 population (1994 est.)
Infant mortality rate: 5.5 deaths/1,000 live births (1994 est.)
Life expectancy at birth:
total population: 79.75 years
male: 77.33 years
female: 82.3 years (1994 est.)
Total fertility rate: 1.46 children born/woman (1994 est.)
Nationality:
noun: Macanese (singular and plural)
adjective: Macau
Ethnic divisions: Chinese 95%, Portuguese 3%, other 2%
Religions: Buddhist 45%, Roman Catholic 7%, Protestant 1%, none 45.8%, other 1.2% (1981)
Languages: Portuguese (official), Cantonese is the language of commerce
Literacy: age 15 and over can read and write (1981)
total population: 90%
male: 93%
female: 86%
Labor force: 180,000 (1986)
by occupation: NA

Government

Names:
conventional long form: none
conventional short form: Macau
local long form: none
local short form: Ilha de Macau
Digraph: MC
Type: overseas territory of Portugal scheduled to revert to China in 1999
Capital: Macau
Administrative divisions: 2 districts (concelhos, singular—concelho); Ilhas, Macau

Independence: none (territory of Portugal; Portugal signed an agreement with China on 13 April 1987 to return Macau to China on 20 December 1999; in the joint declaration, China promises to respect Macau's existing social and economic systems and lifestyle for 50 year after transition)

National holiday: Day of Portugal, 10 June (1580)

Constitution: 17 February 1976, Organic Law of Macau; basic law drafted primarily by Beijing awaiting final approval

Legal system: Portuguese civil law system

Suffrage: 18 years of age; universal

Executive branch:
chief of state: President (of Portugal) Mario Alberto SOARES (since 9 March 1986)
head of government: Governor Gen. Vasco Joachim Rocha VIEIRA (since 20 March 1991)
cabinet: Consultative Council; consists of five members appointed by the governor, two nominated by the governor, five members elected for a four-year term (2 represent administrative bodies, 1 represents moral, cultural, and welfare interests, and 2 economic interests), and three statuatory members

Legislative branch: unicameral
Legislative Assembly: elections last held on 10 March 1991; results—percent of vote by party NA; seats—(23 total; 8 elected by universal suffrage, 8 by indirect suffrage, and 7 appointed by the governor) number of seats by party NA

Judicial branch: Supreme Court

Political parties and leaders: Association to Defend the Interests of Macau; Macau Democratic Center; Group to Study the Development of Macau; Macau Independent Group

Other political or pressure groups: wealthy Macanese and Chinese representing local interests, wealthy pro-Communist merchants representing China's interests; in January 1967 the Macau Government acceded to Chinese demands that gave China veto power over administration

Member of: ESCAP (associate), GATT, IMO (associate), INTERPOL (subbureau), WTO (associate)

Diplomatic representation in US: none (Chinese territory under Portuguese administration)

US diplomatic representation: the US has no offices in Macau, and US interests are monitored by the US Consulate General in Hong Kong

Flag: the flag of Portugal is used

MALAYSIA

Economy

Overview: The Malaysian economy, a mixture of private enterprise and a soundly managed public sector, has posted a remarkable record of 8%-9% average growth in 1987-93. This growth has resulted in a substantial reduction in poverty and a marked rise in real wages. Despite sluggish growth in the major world economies in 1992-93, demand for Malaysian goods remained strong, and foreign investors continued to commit large sums in the economy. The government is aware of the inflationary potential of this rapid development and is closely monitoring fiscal and monetary policies.
National product: GDP—purchasing power equivalent—$141 billion (1993 est.)
National product real growth rate: 8% (1993 est.)
National product per capita: $7,500 (1993 est.)
Inflation rate (consumer prices): 3.6% (1993)
Unemployment rate: 3% (1993)
Budget:
revenues: $19.6 billion

expenditures: $18 billion, including capital expenditures of $5.4 billion (1994 est.)
Exports: $46.8 billion (f.o.b., 1993 est.)
commodities: electronic equipment, petroleum and petroleum products, palm oil, wood and wood products, rubber, textiles
partners: Singapore 23%, US 15%, Japan 13%, UK 4%, Germany 4%, Thailand 4% (1991)
Imports: $40.4 billion (f.o.b., 1993 est.)
commodities: machinery and equipment, chemicals, food, petroleum products
partners: Japan 26%, Singapore 21%, US 16%, Taiwan 6%, Germany 4%, UK 3%, Australia 3% (1991)
External debt: $18.4 billion (1993 est.)
Industrial production: growth rate 13% (1992); accounts for 43% of GDP
Electricity:
capacity: 8,000,000 kW
production: 30 billion kWh
consumption per capita: 1,610 kWh (1992)
Industries:
Peninsular Malaysia: rubber and oil palm processing and manufacturing, light manufacturing industry, electronics, tin mining and smelting, logging and processing timber
Sabah: logging, petroleum production
Sarawak: agriculture processing, petroleum production and refining, logging
Agriculture: accounts for 17% of GDP
Peninsular Malaysia: natural rubber, palm oil, rice
Sabah: mainly subsistence, but also rubber, timber, coconut, rice
Sarawak: rubber, timber, pepper; deficit of rice in all areas
Illicit drugs: transit point for Golden Triangle heroin going to the US, Western Europe, and the Third World despite severe penalties for drug trafficking
Economic aid:
recipient: US commitments, including Ex-Im (FY70-84), $170 million; Western (non-US) countries, ODA and OOF bilateral

commitments (1970-89), $4.7 million; OPEC bilateral aid (1979-89), $42 million
Currency: 1 ringgit (M$) = 100 sen
Exchange rates: ringgits (M$) per US$1— 2.7123 (January 1994), 2.5741 (1993), 2.5474 (1992), 2.7501 (1991), 1.7048 (1990), 2.7088 (1989)
Fiscal year: calendar year

Communications

Railroads:
Peninsular Malaysia: 1,665 km 1.04-meter gauge; 13 km double track, government owned
Sabah: 136 km 1.000-meter gauge
Sarawak: none
Highways:
total: 29,026 km (Peninsular Malaysia 23,600 km, Sabah 3,782 km, Sarawak 1,644 km)
paved: NA (Peninsular Malaysia 19,352 km mostly bituminous treated)
unpaved: NA (Peninsular Malaysia 4,248 km)
Inland waterways:
Peninsular Malaysia: 3,209 km
Sabah: 1,569 km
Sarawak: 2,518 km
Pipelines: crude oil 1,307 km; natural gas 379 km
Ports: Tanjong Kidurong, Kota Kinabalu, Kuching, Pasir Gudang, Penang, Port Kelang, Sandakan, Tawau
Merchant marine: 183 ships (1,000 GRT or over) totaling 1,935,210 GRT/2,913,808 DWT, passenger-cargo 1, short-sea passenger 2, cargo 69, container 26, vehicle carrier 2, roll-on/roll-off cargo 2, livestock carrier 1, oil tanker 39, chemical tanker 6, liquefied gas 6, bulk 29
Airports:
total: 113
usable: 104
with permanent-surface runways: 33
with runways over 3,659 m: 1
with runways 2,440-3,659 m: 7
with runways 1,220-2,439 m: 18
Telecommunications: good intercity service provided on Peninsular Malaysia mainly by microwave radio relay; adequate intercity microwave radio relay network between Sabah and Sarawak via Brunei; international service good; good coverage by radio and television broadcasts; 994,860 telephones (1984); broadcast stations—28 AM, 3 FM, 33 TV; submarine cables extend to India and Sarawak; SEACOM submarine cable links to Hong Kong and Singapore; satellite earth stations—1 Indian Ocean INTELSAT, 1 Pacific Ocean INTELSAT, and 2 domestic

Defense Forces

Branches: Malaysian Army, Royal Malaysian Navy, Royal Malaysian Air Force, Royal Malaysian Police Force, Marine Police, Sarawak Border Scouts
Manpower availability: males age 15-49 4,942,387; fit for military service 3,001,972; reach military age (21) annually 182,850 (1994 est.)
Defense expenditures: exchange rate conversion—$2.4 billion, about 5% of GDP (1992)

Geography

Location: Southeastern Asia, bordering the South China Sea, between Vietnam and Indonesia
Map references: Asia, Oceania, Southeast Asia, Standard Time Zones of the World
Area:
total area: 329,750 sq km
land area: 328,550 sq km
comparative area: slightly larger than New Mexico
Land boundaries: total 2,669 km, Brunei 381 km, Indonesia 1,782 km, Thailand 506 km
Coastline: 4,675 km (Peninsular Malaysia 2,068 km, East Malaysia 2,607 km)
Maritime claims:
continental shelf: 200-m depth or to depth of exploitation; specified boundary in the South China Sea
exclusive fishing zone: 200 nm
exclusive economic zone: 200 nm
territorial sea: 12 nm
International disputes: involved in a complex dispute over the Spratly Islands with

China, Philippines, Taiwan, Vietnam, and possibly Brunei; State of Sabah claimed by the Philippines; Brunei may wish to purchase the Malaysian salient that divides Brunei into two parts; two islands in dispute with Singapore; two islands in dispute with Indonesia
Climate: tropical; annual southwest (April to October) and northeast (October to February) monsoons
Terrain: coastal plains rising to hills and mountains
Natural resources: tin, petroleum, timber, copper, iron ore, natural gas, bauxite
Land use:
arable land: 3%
permanent crops: 10%
meadows and pastures: 0%
forest and woodland: 63%
other: 24%
Irrigated land: 3,420 sq km (1989 est.)
Environment:
current issues: air and water pollution; deforestation
natural hazards: subject to flooding
international agreements: party to—Endangered Species, Hazardous Wastes, Marine Life Conservation, Nuclear Test Ban, Ozone Layer Protection, Tropical Timber; signed, but not ratified—Biodiversity, Climate Change, Law of the Sea
Note: strategic location along Strait of Malacca and southern South China Sea

People

Population: 19,283,157 (July 1994 est.)
Population growth rate: 2.28% (1994 est.)
Birth rate: 28.45 births/1,000 population (1994 est.)
Death rate: 5.67 deaths/1,000 population (1994 est.)
Net migration rate: 0 migrant(s)/1,000 population (1994 est.)
Infant mortality rate: 25.6 deaths/1,000 live births (1994 est.)
Life expectancy at birth:
total population: 69.15 years
male: 66.26 years
female: 72.18 years (1994 est.)

Total fertility rate: 3.51 children born/woman (1994 est.)
Nationality:
noun: Malaysian(s)
adjective: Malaysian
Ethnic divisions: Malay and other indigenous 59%, Chinese 32%, Indian 9%
Religions:
Peninsular Malaysia: Muslim (Malays), Buddhist (Chinese), Hindu (Indians)
Sabah: Muslim 38%, Christian 17%, other 45%
Sarawak: tribal religion 35%, Buddhist and Confucianist 24%, Muslim 20%, Christian 16%, other 5%
Languages:
Peninsular Malaysia: Malay (official), English, Chinese dialects, Tamil
Sabah: English, Malay, numerous tribal dialects, Chinese (Mandarin and Hakka dialects predominate)
Sarawak: English, Malay, Mandarin, numerous tribal languages,
Literacy: age 15 and over can read and write (1990 est.)
total population: 78%
male: 86%
female: 70%
Labor force: 7.258 million (1991 est.)

Government

Names:
conventional long form: none
conventional short form: Malaysia
former: Malayan Union
Digraph: MY
Type: constitutional monarchy
note: Federation of Malaysia formed 9 July 1963; nominally headed by the paramount ruler (king) and a bicameral Parliament; Peninsular Malaysian states—hereditary rulers in all but Melaka, where governors are appointed by
Malaysian Pulau Pinang Government; powers of state governments are limited by federal Constitution; Sabah—self-governing state, holds 20 seats in House of Representatives, with foreign affairs, defense, internal security,

and other powers delegated to federal government; Sarawak—self-governing state, holds 27 seats in House of Representatives, with foreign affairs, defense, internal security, and other powers delegated to federal government
Capital: Kuala Lumpur
Administrative divisions: 13 states (negeri-negeri, singular—negeri) and 2 federal territories* (wilayah-wilayah persekutuan, singular—wilayah persekutuan); Johor, Kedah, Kelantan, Labuan*, Melaka, Negeri Sembilan, Pahang, Perak, Perlis, Pulau Pinang, Sabah, Sarawak, Selangor, Terengganu, Wilayah Persekutuan*
Independence: 31 August 1957 (from UK)
National holiday: National Day, 31 August (1957)
Constitution: 31 August 1957, amended 16 September 1963
Legal system: based on English common law; judicial review of legislative acts in the Supreme Court at request of supreme head of the federation; has not accepted compulsory ICJ jurisdiction
Suffrage: 21 years of age; universal
Executive branch:
chief of state: Paramount Ruler JA'AFAR ibni Abdul Rahman (since 26 April 1994); Deputy Paramount Ruler SALAHUDDIN ibni Hisammuddin Alam Shah (since 26 April 1994)
head of government: Prime Minister Dr. MAHATHIR bin Mohamad (since 16 July 1981); Deputy Prime Minister ANWAR bin Ibrahim (since 1 December 1993)
cabinet: Cabinet; appointed by the Paramount Ruler from members of parliament
Legislative branch: bicameral Parliament (Parlimen)
Senate (Dewan Negara): consists of a 58-member body, 32 appointed by the paramount ruler and 16 elected by the state legislatures
House of Representatives (Dewan Rakyat): elections last held 21 October 1990 (next to be held by August 1995); results—National Front 52%, other 48%; seats—(180 total) National Front 127, DAP 20, PAS 7, independents 4, other 22; note—within the National Front, UMNO got 71 seats and MCA 18 seats

Judicial branch: Supreme Court
Political parties and leaders:
Peninsular Malaysia: National Front, a confederation of 13 political parties dominated by United Malays National Organization Baru (UMNO Baru), MAHATHIR bin Mohamad; Malaysian Chinese Association (MCA), LING Liong Sik; Gerakan Rakyat Malaysia, LIM Keng Yaik; Malaysian Indian Congress (MIC), S. Samy VELLU
Sabah: National Front, Tan Sri SAKARAN, Sabah Chief Minister; United Sabah National Organizaton (USNO), leader NA
Sarawak: coalition Sarawak National Front composed of the Party Pesaka Bumiputra Bersatu (PBB), Datuk Patinggi Amar Haji Abdul TAIB Mahmud; Sarawak United People's Party (SUPP), Datuk Amar James WONG Soon Kai; Sarawak National Party (SNAP), Datuk Amar James WONG; Parti Bansa Dayak Sarawak (PBDS), Datuk Leo MOGGIE; major opposition parties are Democratic Action Party (DAP), LIM Kit Siang and Pan-Malaysian Islamic Party (PAS), Fadzil NOOR
Member of: APEC, AsDB, ASEAN, C, CCC, CP, ESCAP, FAO, G-15, G-77, GATT, IAEA, IBRD, ICAO, ICFTU, IDA, IDB, IFAD, IFC, ILO, IMF, IMO, INMARSAT, INTELSAT, INTERPOL, IOC, ISO, ITU, LORCS, MINURSO, NAM, OIC, UN, UNAVEM II, UNCTAD, UNESCO, UNIDO, UNIKOM, UNOMOZ, UNOSOM, UNTAC, UPU, WCL, WHO, WIPO, WMO, WTO
Diplomatic representation in US:
chief of mission: Ambassador Abdul MAJID bin Mohamed
chancery: 2401 Massachusetts Avenue NW, Washington, DC 20008
telephone: (202) 328-2700
FAX: (202) 483-7661
consulate(s) general: Los Angeles and New York
US diplomatic representation:
chief of mission: Ambassador John S. WOLF
embassy: 376 Jalan Tun Razak, 50400 Kuala Lumpur
mailing address: P. O. Box No. 10035, 50700 Kuala Lumpur; APO AP 96535-5000

telephone: [60] (3) 248-9011
FAX: [60] (3) 242-2207
Flag: fourteen equal horizontal stripes of red (top) alternating with white (bottom); there is a blue rectangle in the upper hoist-side corner bearing a yellow crescent and a yellow fourteen-pointed star; the crescent and the star are traditional symbols of Islam; the design was based on the flag of the US

U.S. Government Contacts:

U.S. Trade Desk: (202) 482-3877

American Embassy Commercial Section
AIA Building 376 Jalan Tun Razah
P.O. Box 10035
50700 Kuala Lumpur, Malaysia
c/o U.S. Department of State (Kuala Lumpur)
Washington, DC 20521-4210
Tel: 60-248-9011
Fax: 60-3-242-1866

Malaysia Government Contacts:

Embassy of Malaysia Commercial Section
2401 Massachusetts Avenue, N.W.
Washington, DC 20008
Tel: (202) 328-2700

Consulate General of Malaysia Commercial Section
630 Third Avenue, 11th Floor
New York, NY 10017
Tel: (212) 682-0232
Fax: (212) 983-1987

Malaysian Industrial Development Authority (MIDA)
Ground, 3-6, & 9th Floor
Wisma Damansara
Jalan Semantan
P.O. Box 10618
50720 Kuala Lumpur
Tel: 03-2553633
Fax: 03-2557970

Malaysian External Trade Development Corp. (MATRADE)
P.O. Box 13509

50812 Kuala Lumpur
Tel: 03-2947259
Fax: 03-2947362

Chambers of Commerce & Organizations:

American Business Council of Malaysia
15 01, 15th Floor, Amoda, Lajan Imbi
55100 Kuala Lumpur, Malaysia
Tel: 60-3-243-7682

Legal Services:

Paul Chong & Kraal
18th Floor, Wisma Bumi Raya
10 Jalan Raja Laut
50350 Kuala Lumpur, Malaysia
Tel: 603 291-1511
Fax: 603 292-9105
Acquisitions, Corporate, Contracts, Insurance, Labor and Industrial Litigation, Joint Ventures.

Travel:

International Hotels in Country:
Kuala Lumpur:
Kuala Lumpur Hilton, Tel: 603 242-2122, Fax: 603 244-2157
P.J. Hilton, Tel: 603/755-9122, Fax: 603/755-3909
Regent, Tel: 603/241-8000, Fax: 603/242-1441.

FEDERATED STATES OF MICRONESIA

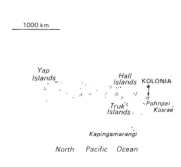

1000 km

Yap
Islands

Hall
Islands   KOLONIA

Truk
Islands   Pohnpei
             Kosrae

Kapingamarangi

North   Pacific   Ocean

Economy

Overview: Economic activity consists primarily of subsistence farming and fishing. The islands have few mineral deposits worth exploiting, except for high-grade phosphate. The potential for a tourist industry exists, but the remoteness of the location and a lack of adequate facilities hinder development. Financial assistance from the US is the primary source of revenue, with the US pledged to spend $1 billion in the islands in the 1990s. Geographical isolation and a poorly developed infrastructure are major impediments to long-term growth.
National product: GNP—purchasing power equivalent—$150 million (1989 est.)
note: GNP numbers reflect US spending
National product real growth rate: NA%
National product per capita: $1,500 (1989 est.)
Inflation rate (consumer prices): NA%
Unemployment rate: 27% (1989)
Budget:
revenues: $165 million
expenditures: $115 million, including capital expenditures of $20 million (1988 est.)
Exports: $2.3 million (f.o.b., 1988)
commodities: copra

partners: NA
Imports: $67.7 million (c.i.f., 1988)
commodities: NA
partners: NA
External debt: $NA
Industrial production: growth rate NA%
Electricity:
capacity: 18,000 kW
production: 40 million kWh
consumption per capita: 380 kWh (1990)
Industries: tourism, construction, fish processing, craft items from shell, wood, and pearls
Agriculture: mainly a subsistence economy; black pepper; tropical fruits and vegetables, coconuts, cassava, sweet potatoes, pigs, chickens
Economic aid:
recipient: under terms of the Compact of Free Association, the US will provide $1.3 billion in grant aid during the period 1986-2001
Currency: 1 United States dollar (US$) = 100 cents
Exchange rates: US currency is used
Fiscal year: 1 October—30 September

Communications

Highways:
total: 226 km
paved: 39 km (on major islands)
unpaved: stone, coral, laterite 187 km
Ports: Colonia (Yap), Truk, Okat and Lelu (Kosrae)
Airports:
total: 6
usable: 5
with permanent-surface runways: 4
with runways over 3,659 m: 0
with runways 2,440-3,659 m: 0
with runways 1,220-2,439 m: 4
Telecommunications: telephone network— 960 telephone lines total at Kolonia and Truk; islands interconnected by shortwave radio (used mostly for government purposes);

16,000 radio receivers, 1,125 TV sets (est. 1987); broadcast stations—5 AM, 1 FM, 6 TV, 1 shortwave; 4 Pacific Ocean INTELSAT earth stations

Defense Forces

Note: defense is the responsibility of the US

Geography

Location: Oceania, Micronesia, in the North Pacific Ocean, about three-quarters of the way between Hawaii and Indonesia
Map references: Oceania, Southeast Asia, Standard Time Zones of the World
Area:
total area: 702 sq km
land area: 702 sq km
comparative area: slightly less than four times the size of Washington, DC
note: includes Pohnpei (Ponape), Truk (Chuuk), Yap, and Kosrae
Land boundaries: 0 km
Coastline: 6,112 km
Maritime claims:
exclusive economic zone: 200 nm
territorial sea: 12 nm
International disputes: none
Climate: tropical; heavy year-round rainfall, especially in the eastern islands; located on southern edge of the typhoon belt with occasional severe damage
Terrain: islands vary geologically from high mountainous islands to low, coral atolls; volcanic outcroppings on Pohnpei, Kosrae, and Truk
Natural resources: forests, marine products, deep-seabed minerals
Land use:
arable land: NA%
permanent crops: NA%
meadows and pastures: NA%
forest and woodland: NA%
other: NA%
Irrigated land: NA sq km
Environment:
current issues: NA
natural hazards: subject to typhoons (June to December)
international agreements: party to—Climate Change, Law of the Sea; signed, but not ratified—Biodiversity
Note: four major island groups totaling 607 islands

People

Population: 120,347 (July 1994 est.)
Population growth rate: 3.36% (1994 est.)
Birth rate: 28.3 births/1,000 population (1994 est.)
Death rate: 6.38 deaths/1,000 population (1994 est.)
Net migration rate: 11.65 migrant(s)/1,000 population (1994 est.)
Infant mortality rate: 37.24 deaths/1,000 live births (1994 est.)
Life expectancy at birth:
total population: 67.63 years
male: 65.67 years
female: 69.62 years (1994 est.)
Total fertility rate: 4.01 children born/woman (1994 est.)
Nationality:
noun: Micronesian(s)
adjective: Micronesian; Kosrae(s), Pohnpeian(s), Trukese, Yapese
Ethnic divisions: nine ethnic Micronesian and Polynesian groups
Religions: Christian (divided between Roman Catholic and Protestant; other churches include Assembly of God, Jehovah's Witnesses, Seventh-Day Adventist, Latter-Day Saints, and the Baha'i Faith)
Languages: English (official and common language), Trukese, Pohnpeian, Yapese, Kosrean
Literacy: age 15 and over can read and write (1980)
total population: 90%
male: 90%
female: 85%
Labor force: NA
by occupation: two-thirds are government employees
note: 45,000 people are between the ages of 15 and 65

Government

Names:
conventional long form: Federated States of Micronesia
conventional short form: none
former: Kosrae, Ponape, Truk, and Yap Districts (Trust Territory of the Pacific Islands)
Abbreviation: FSM
Digraph: FM
Type: constitutional government in free association with the US; the Compact of Free Association entered into force 3 November 1986
Capital: Kolonia (on the island of Pohnpei)
note: a new capital is being built about 10 km southwest in the Palikir valley
Administrative divisions: 4 states; Kosrae, Pohnpei, Chuuk (Truk), Yap
Independence: 3 November 1986 (from the US-administered UN Trusteeship)
National holiday: Proclamation of the Federated States of Micronesia, 10 May (1979)
Constitution: 10 May 1979
Legal system: based on adapted Trust Territory laws, acts of the legislature, municipal, common, and customary laws
Suffrage: 18 years of age; universal
Executive branch:
chief of state and head of government:
President Bailey OLTER (since 21 May 1991); Vice President Jacob NENA (since 21 May 1991); election last held 11 May 1991 (next to be held March 1995); results—President Bailey OLTER elected president; Vice-President Jacob NENA
cabinet: Cabinet
Legislative branch: unicameral
Congress: elections last held on 5 March 1991 (next to be held March 1993); results—percent of vote NA; seats—(14 total)
Judicial branch: Supreme Court
Political parties and leaders: no formal parties
Member of: AsDB, ESCAP, IBRD, ICAO, IDA, IFC, IMF, ITU, SPARTECA, SPC, SPF, UN, UNCTAD, WHO
Diplomatic representation in US:
chief of mission: Ambassador Jesse B.

MAREHALAU
chancery: 1725 N Street NW, Washington, DC 20036
telephone: (202) 223-4383
FAX: (202) 223-4391
consulate(s) general: Honolulu and Tamuning (Guam)
US diplomatic representation:
chief of mission: Ambassador Aurelia E. BRAZEAL
embassy: address NA, Kolonia
mailing address: P. O. Box 1286, Pohnpei, Federated States of Micronesia 96941
telephone: 691-320-2187
FAX: 691-320-2186
Flag: light blue with four white five-pointed stars centered; the stars are arranged in a diamond pattern

Travel:

International Airlines to Country:
Continental

International Hotels in Country:
Saipan:
Hyatt Regency Saipan, Tel: 670 234-1234, Fax: 670 234-7745

MONGOLIA

500 km

Economy

Overview: Mongolia's severe climate, scattered population, and wide expanses of unproductive land have constrained economic development. Economic activity traditionally has been based on agriculture and the breeding of livestock—Mongolia has the highest number of livestock per person in the world. In past years extensive mineral resources had been developed with Soviet support; total Soviet assistance at its height amounted to 30% of GDP. The mining and processing of coal, copper, molybdenum, tin, tungsten, and gold account for a large part of industrial production. Timber and fishing are also important sectors. The Mongolian leadership is trying to make the transition from Soviet-style central planning to a market economy through privatization and price reform, and is soliciting support from international financial agencies and foreign investors. The economy, however, has still not recovered from the loss of Soviet aid, and the country continues to suffer substantial economic hardships.

National product: GDP—purchasing power equivalent—$2.8 billion (1993 est.)

National product real growth rate: -1.3% (1993 est.)

National product per capita: $1,200 (1993 est.)

Inflation rate (consumer prices): 325% (1992 est.)

Unemployment rate: 15% (1991 est.)

Budget:
revenues: $NA
expenditures: $NA, including capital expenditures of $NA (1991 est.)
note: deficit of $67 million

Exports: $355 million (f.o.b., 1992 est.)
commodities: copper, livestock, animal products, cashmere, wool, hides, fluorspar, other nonferrous metals
partners: former CMEA countries 62%, China 17%, EC 8% (1992)

Imports: $501 million (f.o.b., 1991 est.)
commodities: machinery and equipment, fuels, food products, industrial consumer goods, chemicals, building materials, sugar, tea
partners: USSR 75%, Austria 5%, China 5%

External debt: $16.8 billion (yearend 1990); 98.6% with USSR

Industrial production: growth rate -15% (1992 est.); accounts for about 42% of GDP

Electricity:
capacity: 1,248,000 kW
production: 3,740 kWh
consumption per capita: 1,622 kWh (1992)

Industries: copper, processing of animal products, building materials, food and beverage, mining (particularly coal)

Agriculture: accounts for about 35% of GDP and provides livelihood for about 50% of the population; livestock raising predominates (primarily sheep and goats, but also cattle, camels, and horses); crops—wheat, barley, potatoes, forage

Economic aid: NA

Currency: 1 tughrik (Tug) = 100 mongos

Exchange rates: tughriks (Tug) per US$1— 150 (1 January 1993), 40 (1992), 7.1 (1991), 5.63 (1990), 3.00 (1989)
note: the exchange rate 40 tughriks = 1US$ was introduced June 1991 and was in force to the end of 1992

Fiscal year: calendar year

Communications

Railroads: 1,750 km 1.524-meter broad gauge (1988)
Highways:
total: 46,700 km
paved: 1,000 km
unpaved: 45,700 km (1988)
Inland waterways: 397 km of principal routes (1988)
Ports: none; landlocked
Airports:
total: 81
usable: 31
with permanent-surface runways: 11
with runways over 3,659 m: fewer than 5
with runways 2,440-3,659 m: fewer than 20
with runways 1,220-2,439 m: 12
Telecommunications: 63,000 telephones (1989); broadcast stations—12 AM, 1 FM, 1 TV (with 18 provincial repeaters); repeat of Russian TV; 120,000 TVs; 220,000 radios; at least 1 earth station

Defense Forces

Branches: Mongolian People's Army (includes Internal Security Forces and Frontier Guards), Air Force
Manpower availability: males age 15-49 587,113; fit for military service 382,633; reach military age (18) annually 25,261 (1994 est.)
Defense expenditures: exchange rate conversion—$22.8 million of GDP, 1% of GDP (1992)
embassy: address NA, Ulaanbaatar
mailing address: Ulaanbaatar, c/o American Embassy Beijing, Micro Region II, Big Ring Road; PSC 461, Box 300, FPO AP 96521-0002
telephone: [976] (1) 329095 through 329606
FAX: [976] (1) 320-776
Flag: three equal, vertical bands of red (hoist side), blue, and red, centered on the hoist-side red band in yellow is the national emblem ("soyombo"—a columnar arrangement of abstract and geometric representation for fire, sun, moon, earth, water, and the yin-yang symbol)

Geography

Location: Northern Asia, between China and Russia
Map references: Asia, Standard Time Zones of the World
Area:
total area: 1.565 million sq km
land area: 1.565 million sq km
comparative area: slightly larger than Alaska
Land boundaries: total 8,114 km, China 4,673 km, Russia 3,441 km
Coastline: 0 km (landlocked)
Maritime claims: none; landlocked
International disputes: none
Climate: desert; continental (large daily and seasonal temperature ranges)
Terrain: vast semidesert and desert plains; mountains in west and southwest; Gobi Desert in southeast
Natural resources: oil, coal, copper, molybdenum, tungsten, phosphates, tin, nickel, zinc, wolfram, fluorspar, gold
Land use:
arable land: 1%
permanent crops: 0%
meadows and pastures: 79%
forest and woodland: 10%
other: 10%
Irrigated land: 770 sq km (1989)
Environment:
current issues: limited water resources; policies of the former communist regime promoting rapid urbanization and industrial growth have raised concerns about their negative effects on the environment; the burning of soft coal and the concentration of factories in Ulaanbaatar have severely polluted the air; deforestation, overgrazing, the converting of virgin land to agricultural production have increased soil erosion from wind and rain; desertification
natural hazards: NA
international agreements: party to— Biodiversity, Climate Change, Environmental Modification, Nuclear Test Ban; signed, but not ratified—Law of the Sea
Note: landlocked; strategic location between China and Russia

People

Population: 2,429,762 (July 1994 est.)
Population growth rate: 2.61% (1994 est.)
Birth rate: 33.04 births/1,000 population (1994 est.)
Death rate: 6.99 deaths/1,000 population (1994 est.)
Net migration rate: 0 migrant(s)/1,000 population (1994 est.)
Infant mortality rate: 43.4 deaths/1,000 live births (1994 est.)
Life expectancy at birth:
total population: 66.16 years
male: 63.9 years
female: 68.52 years (1994 est.)
Total fertility rate: 4.33 children born/woman (1994 est.)
Nationality:
noun: Mongolian(s)
adjective: Mongolian
Ethnic divisions: Mongol 90%, Kazakh 4%, Chinese 2%, Russian 2%, other 2%
Religions: predominantly Tibetan Buddhist, Muslim 4%
note: previously limited religious activity because of Communist regime
Languages: Khalkha Mongol 90%, Turkic, Russian, Chinese
Literacy:
total population: NA%
male: NA%
female: NA%
Labor force: NA
by occupation: primarily herding/agricultural
note: over half the adult population is in the labor force, including a large percentage of women; shortage of skilled labor

Government

Names:
conventional long form: none
conventional short form: Mongolia
local long form: none
local short form: Mongol Uls
former: Outer Mongolia
Digraph: MG
Type: republic

Capital: Ulaanbaatar
Administrative divisions: 18 provinces (aymguud, singular—aymag) and 3 municipalities* (hotuud, singular—hot); Arhangay, Bayanhongor, Bayan-Olgiy, Bulgan, Darhan*, Dornod, Dornogovi, Dundgovi, Dzavhan, Erdenet*, Govi-Altay, Hentiy, Hovd, Hovsgol, Omnogovi, Ovorhangay, Selenge, Suhbaatar, Tov, Ulaanbaatar*, Uvs
Independence: 13 March 1921 (from China)
National holiday: National Day, 11 July (1921)
Constitution: adopted 13 January 1992
Legal system: blend of Russian, Chinese, and Turkish systems of law; no constitutional provision for judicial review of legislative acts; has not accepted compulsory ICJ jurisdiction
Suffrage: 18 years of age; universal
Executive branch:
chief of state: President Punsalmaagiyn OCHIRBAT (since 3 September 1990); election last held 6 June 1993 (next to be held NA 1997); results—Punsalmaagiyn OCHIRBAT (MNDP and MSDP) elected directly with 57.8% of the vote; other candidate Lodongiyn TUDEV (MPRP)
head of government: Prime Minister Putsagiyn JASRAY (since 3 August 1992); Deputy Prime Ministers Lhamsuren ENEBISH and Choijilsurengiyn PUREVDORJ (since NA)
cabinet: Cabinet; appointed by the Great Hural
Legislative branch: unicameral
State Great Hural: elections first time held 28 June 1992 (next to be held NA); results—percent of vote by party NA; seats—(76 total) MPRP 71, United Party 4, MSDP 1
note: the People's Small Hural no longer exists
Judicial branch: Supreme Court serves as appeals court for people's and provincial courts, but to date rarely overturns verdicts of lower courts
Political parties and leaders: Mongolian People's Revolutionary Party (MPRP), Budragchagiin DASH-YONDON, secretary general; Mongolian Democratic Party (MDP), Erdenijiyn BAT-UUL, general coordinator; National Progress Party (NPP), S. BYAMBAA and Luusandambyn DASHNYAM, leaders; Social Democratic Party (SDP), BATBAYAR

and Tsohiogyyn ADYASUREN, leaders;
Mongolian Independence Party (MIP), D.
ZORIGT, leader; United Party of Mongolia
(made up of the MDP, SDP, and NPP);
Mongolian National Democratic Party
(MNDP), D. GANBOLD, chairman;
Mongolian Social Democratic Party (MSDP),
B. BATBAYAR, chairman; Mongolian
Conservative Party, O. ZOYA; Mongolian
Green Party (MGP), M. GANBAT
note: opposition parties were legalized in May
1990
Member of: AsDB, CCC, ESCAP, FAO,
G-77, IAEA, IBRD, ICAO, IDA, IFC, ILO,
IMF, INTELSAT (nonsignatory user),
INTERPOL, IOC, ISO, ITU, LORCS, NAM
(observer), UN, UNCTAD, UNESCO,
UNIDO, UPU, WFTU, WHO, WIPO, WMO,
WTO
Diplomatic representation in US:
chief of mission: Ambassador Luvsandorj
DAWAGIV
chancery: 2833 M Street NW, Washington,
DC 20007
telephone: (202) 333-7117
FAX: (202) 298-9227
consulate(s) general: New York
US diplomatic representation:
chief of mission: Ambassador Donald C.
JOHNSON

U.S. Government Contacts:

U.S. Trade Desk: (202) 482-3932

NEPAL

Economy

Overview: Nepal is among the poorest and least developed countries in the world. Agriculture is the mainstay of the economy, providing a livelihood for over 90% of the population and accounting for 60% of GDP. Industrial activity is limited, mainly involving the processing of agricultural produce (jute, sugarcane, tobacco, and grain). Production of textiles and carpets has expanded recently and accounted for 85% of foreign exchange earnings in FY94. Apart from agricultural land and forests, exploitable natural resources are mica, hydropower, and tourism. Agricultural production in the late 1980s grew by about 5%, as compared with annual population growth of 2.6%. More than 40% of the population is undernourished. Since May 1991, the government has been encouraging trade and foreign investment, e.g., by eliminating business licenses and registration requirements in order to simplify domestic and foreign investment. The government also has been cutting public expenditures by reducing subsidies, privatizing state industries, and laying off civil servants. Prospects for foreign trade and investment in the 1990s remain poor, however, because of the small size of the economy, its technological backwardness, its remoteness, and susceptibility to natural disaster. Nepal experienced severe flooding in August 1993 which caused at least $50 million in damage to the country's infrastructure.

National product: GDP—purchasing power equivalent—$20.5 billion (1993 est.)

National product real growth rate: 2.9% (FY93)

National product per capita: $1,000 (1993 est.)

Inflation rate (consumer prices): 9% (September 1993)

Unemployment rate: 5% (1987); underemployment estimated at 25-40%

Budget:
revenues: $457 million
expenditures: $725 million, including capital expenditures of $427 million (FY93 est.)

Exports: $369 million (f.o.b., FY93) but does not include unrecorded border trade with India
commodities: carpets, clothing, leather goods, jute goods, grain
partners: US, Germany, India, UK

Imports: $789 million (c.i.f., FY93 est.)
commodities: petroleum products 20%, fertilizer 11%, machinery 10%
partners: India, Singapore, Japan, Germany

External debt: $2 billion (FY93 est.)

Industrial production: growth rate 6% (FY91 est.); accounts for 16% of GDP

Electricity:
capacity: 300,000 kW
production: 1 billion kWh
consumption per capita: 50 kWh (1992)

Industries: small rice, jute, sugar, and oilseed mills; cigarette, textile, carpet, cement, and brick production; tourism

Agriculture: accounts for 60% of GDP and 93% of work force; farm products—rice, corn, wheat, sugarcane, root crops, milk, buffalo meat; not self-sufficient in food, particularly in drought years

Illicit drugs: illicit producer of cannabis for the domestic and international drug markets; transit point for heroin from Southeast Asia to the West

Economic aid:
recipient: US commitments, including Ex-Im (FY70-89), $304 million; Western (non-US) countries, ODA and OOF bilateral commitments (1980-89), $2.23 billion; OPEC bilateral aid (1979-89), $30 million; Communist countries (1970-89), $286 million
Currency: 1 Nepalese rupee (NR) = 100 paisa
Exchange rates: Nepalese rupees (NRs) per US$1—49.240 (January 1994), 48.607 (1993), 42.742 (1992), 37.255 (1991), 29.370 (1990), 27.189 (1989)
Fiscal year: 16 July—15 July

Communications

Railroads: 52 km (1990), all 0.762-meter narrow gauge; all in Terai close to Indian border; 10 km from Raxaul to Birganj is government owned
Highways:
total: 7,080 km
paved: 2,898 km
unpaved: gravel, crushed stone 1,660 km; seasonally motorable tracks 2,522 km (1990)
Airports:
total: 37
usable: 37
with permanent-surface runways: 5
with runways over 3,659 m: 0
with runways 2,440-3,659 m: 1
with runways 1,220-2,439 m: 8
Telecommunications: poor telephone and telegraph service; fair radio communication and broadcast service; international radio communication service is poor; 50,000 telephones (1990); broadcast stations—88 AM, no FM, 1 TV; 1 Indian Ocean INTELSAT earth station

Defense Forces

Branches: Royal Nepalese Army, Royal Nepalese Army Air Service, Nepalese Police Force
Manpower availability: males age 15-49 5,003,661; fit for military service 2,598,507; reach military age (17) annually 241,405 (1994 est.)

Defense expenditures: exchange rate conversion—$34 million, 2% of GDP (FY91/92)

Geography

Location: Southern Asia, in the Himalayas, between China and India
Map references: Asia, Standard Time Zones of the World
Area:
total area: 140,800 sq km
land area: 136,800 sq km
comparative area: slightly larger than Arkansas
Land boundaries: total 2,926 km, China 1,236 km, India 1,690 km
Coastline: 0 km (landlocked)
Maritime claims: none; landlocked
International disputes: none
Climate: varies from cool summers and severe winters in north to subtropical summers and mild winters in south
Terrain: Terai or flat river plain of the Ganges in south, central hill region, rugged Himalayas in north
Natural resources: quartz, water, timber, hydroelectric potential, scenic beauty, small deposits of lignite, copper, cobalt, iron ore
Land use:
arable land: 17%
permanent crops: 0%
meadows and pastures: 13%
forest and woodland: 33%
other: 37%
Irrigated land: 9,430 sq km (1989)
Environment:
current issues: the almost total dependence on wood for fuel and cutting down trees to expand agricultural land without replanting has resulted in widespread deforestation; soil erosion; water pollution (use of contaminated water presents human health risks)
natural hazards: vulnerable to severe thunderstorms, flooding, landslides, drought, and famine depending on the timing, intensity, and duration of the summer monsoons
international agreements: party to—Biodiversity, Endangered Species, Nuclear

Test Ban, Tropical Timber, Wetlands; signed, but not ratified—Climate Change, Law of the Sea, Marine Dumping, Marine Life Conservation

Note: landlocked; strategic location between China and India; contains eight of world's 10 highest peaks

People

Population: 21,041,527 (July 1994 est.)
Population growth rate: 2.44% (1994 est.)
Birth rate: 37.63 births/1,000 population (1994 est.)
Death rate: 13.28 deaths/1,000 population (1994 est.)
Net migration rate: 0 migrant(s)/1,000 population (1994 est.)
Infant mortality rate: 83.5 deaths/1,000 live births (1994 est.)
Life expectancy at birth:
total population: 52.53 years
male: 52.35 years
female: 52.73 years (1994 est.)
Total fertility rate: 5.24 children born/woman (1994 est.)
Nationality:
noun: Nepalese (singular and plural)
adjective: Nepalese
Ethnic divisions: Newars, Indians, Tibetans, Gurungs, Magars, Tamangs, Bhotias, Rais, Limbus, Sherpas
Religions: Hindu 90%, Buddhist 5%, Muslim 3%, other 2% (1981)
note: only official Hindu state in world, although no sharp distinction between many Hindu and Buddhist groups
Languages: Nepali (official), 20 languages divided into numerous dialects
Literacy: age 15 and over can read and write (1990 est.)
total population: 26%
male: 38%
female: 13%
Labor force: 8.5 million (1991 est.)
by occupation: agriculture 93%, services 5%, industry 2%
note: severe lack of skilled labor

Government

Names:
conventional long form: Kingdom of Nepal
conventional short form: Nepal
Digraph: NP
Type: parliamentary democracy as of 12 May 1991
Capital: Kathmandu
Administrative divisions: 14 zones (anchal, singular and plural); Bagmati, Bheri, Dhawalagiri, Gandaki, Janakpur, Karnali, Kosi, Lumbini, Mahakali, Mechi, Narayani, Rapti, Sagarmatha, Seti
Independence: 1768 (unified by Prithvi Narayan Shah)
National holiday: Birthday of His Majesty the King, 28 December (1945)
Constitution: 9 November 1990
Legal system: based on Hindu legal concepts and English common law; has not accepted compulsory ICJ jurisdiction
Suffrage: 18 years of age; universal
Executive branch:
head of government: Prime Minister Girija Prasad KOIRALA (since 29 May 1991)
chief of state: King BIRENDRA Bir Bikram Shah Dev (since 31 January 1972, crowned King 24 February 1985); Heir Apparent Crown Prince DIPENDRA Bir Bikram Shah Dev, son of the King (born 21 June 1971)
cabinet: Cabinet; appointed by the king on recommendation of the prime minister
Legislative branch: bicameral Parliament
National Council: consists of a 60-member body, 50 appointed by House of Representatives and 10 by the King
House of Representatives: elections last held on 12 May 1991 (next to be held May 1996); results—NCP 38%, CPN/UML 28%, NDP/Chand 6%, UPF 5%, NDP/Thapa 5%, Terai Rights Sadbhavana Party 4%, Rohit 2%, CPN (Democratic) 1%, independents 4%, other 7%; seats—(205 total) NCP 110, CPN/UML 69, UPF 9, Terai Rights Sadbhavana Party 6, NDP/Chand 3, Rohit 2, CPN (Democratic) 2, NDP/Thapa 1, independents 3; note—the new Constitution of 9 November 1990 gave Nepal a multiparty democracy system for the first time in 32 years

Judicial branch: Supreme Court (Sarbochha Adalat)

Political parties and leaders: Nepali Congress Party (NCP), president Krishna Prasad BHATTARAI, Prime Minister Girija Prasad KOIRALA, Supreme Leader Ganesh Man SINGH; The Conservative National Democratic Party (NDP/Thapa), Surya Bahadur THAPA; Communist Party of Nepal/ United Marxist and Leninist (CPN/UML), Man Mohan ADHIKARI; Terai Rights Sadbhavana (Goodwill) Party, Gajendra Narayan SINGH; United People's Front (UPF), Lila Mani POKHREL; Nepal Workers and Peasants Party (NWPP), Narayan Man BIJUKCHHE; National Democratic Party/ Chand (NDP/Chand), Lokendra Bahadur CHAND; Rohit Party, N. M. BIJUKCHHE; Communist Party of Nepal (Democratic-Manandhar), B. B. MANANDHAR

Other political or pressure groups: numerous small, left-leaning student groups in the capital; several small, radical Nepalese antimonarchist groups

Member of: AsDB, CCC, CP, ESCAP, FAO, G-77, IBRD, ICAO, IDA, IFAD, IFC, ILO, IMF, IMO, INTELSAT, INTERPOL, IOC, ISO (correspondent), ITU, LORCS, NAM, SAARC, UN, UNCTAD, UNESCO, UNIDO, UNIFIL, UNPROFOR, UNTAC, UPU, WFTU, WHO, WMO, WTO

Diplomatic representation in US:
chief of mission: (vacant)
chancery: 2131 Leroy Place NW, Washington, DC 20008
telephone: (202) 667-4550
consulate(s) general: New York

US diplomatic representation:
chief of mission: Ambassador Sandra VOGELGESANG
embassy: Pani Pokhari, Kathmandu
mailing address: use embassy street address
telephone: [977] (1) 411179 or 412718, 411613, 413890
FAX: [977] (1) 419963

Flag: red with a blue border around the unique shape of two overlapping right triangles; the smaller, upper triangle bears a white stylized moon and the larger, lower triangle bears a white 12-pointed sun

U.S. Government Contacts:

U.S. Trade Desk: (202) 482-2954

NEW CALEDONIA

Islands of Huon and
Chesterfield are not shown.

Economy

Overview: New Caledonia has more than 25% of the world's known nickel resources. In recent years the economy has suffered because of depressed international demand for nickel, the principal source of export earnings. Only a negligible amount of the land is suitable for cultivation, and food accounts for about 25% of imports.

National product: GNP—exchange rate conversion—$1 billion (1991 est.)

National product real growth rate: 2.4% (1988)

National product per capita: $6,000 (1991 est.)

Inflation rate (consumer prices): 1.4% (1990)

Unemployment rate: 16% (1989)

Budget:
revenues: $224 million
expenditures: $211 million, including capital expenditures of $NA (1985 est.)

Exports: $671 million (f.o.b., 1989)
commodities: nickel metal 87%, nickel ore
partners: France 32%, Japan 23.5%, US 3.6%

Imports: $764 million (c.i.f., 1989)
commodities: foods, fuels, minerals, machines, electrical equipment
partners: France 44.0%, US 10%, Australia 9%

External debt: $NA

Industrial production: growth rate NA%

Electricity:
capacity: 400,000 kW
production: 2.2 billion kWh
consumption per capita: 12,790 kWh (1990)

Industries: nickel mining and smelting

Agriculture: large areas devoted to cattle grazing; coffee, corn, wheat, vegetables; 60% self-sufficient in beef

Illicit drugs: illicit cannabis cultivation is becoming a principal source of income for some families

Economic aid:
recipient: Western (non-US) countries, ODA and OOF bilateral commitments (1970-89), $4.185 billion

Currency: 1 CFP franc (CFPF) = 100 centimes

Exchange rates: Comptoirs Francais duPacifique francs (CFPF) per US$1—107.63 (January 1994), 102.96 (1993), 96.24 (1992), 102.57 (1991), 99.00 (1990), 115.99 (1989); note—linked at the rate of 18.18 to the French franc

Fiscal year: calendar year

Communications

Highways:
total: 6,340 km
paved: 634 km
unpaved: 5,706 km (1987)

Ports: Noumea, Nepoui, Poro, Thio

Airports:
total: 30
usable: 28
with permanent-surface runways: 4
with runways over 3,659 m: 0
with runways 2,440-3,659 m: 1

with runways *1,220-2,439 m:* 1
Telecommunications: 32,578 telephones
(1987); broadcast stations—5 AM, 3 FM, 7
TV; 1 Pacific Ocean INTELSAT earth station

Defense Forces

Branches: Gendarmerie, Police Force
Note: defense is the responsibility of France

Geography

Location: Oceania, Melanesia, in the South
Pacific Ocean, 1,750 km east of Australia
Map references: Oceania
Area:
total area: 19,060 sq km
land area: 18,760 sq km
comparative area: slightly smaller than New
Jersey
Land boundaries: 0 km
Coastline: 2,254 km
Maritime claims:
exclusive economic zone: 200 nm
territorial sea: 12 nm
International disputes: none
Climate: tropical; modified by southeast trade
winds; hot, humid
Terrain: coastal plains with interior
mountains
Natural resources: nickel, chrome, iron,
cobalt, manganese, silver, gold, lead, copper
Land use:
arable land: 0%
permanent crops: 0%
meadows and pastures: 14%
forest and woodland: 51%
other: 35%
Irrigated land: NA sq km
Environment:
current issues: NA
natural hazards: typhoons most frequent from
November to March
international agreements: NA

People

Population: 181,309 (July 1994 est.)

Population growth rate: 1.79% (1994 est.)
Birth rate: 22.39 births/1,000 population
(1994 est.)
Death rate: 4.96 deaths/1,000 population
(1994 est.)
Net migration rate: 0.49 migrant(s)/1,000
population (1994 est.)
Infant mortality rate: 15.1 deaths/1,000 live
births (1994 est.)
Life expectancy at birth:
total population: 73.62 years
male: 70.32 years
female: 77.09 years (1994 est.)
Total fertility rate: 2.62 children
born/woman (1994 est.)
Nationality:
noun: New Caledonian(s)
adjective: New Caledonian
Ethnic divisions: Melanesian 42.5%,
European 37.1%, Wallisian 8.4%, Polynesian
3.8%, Indonesian 3.6%, Vietnamese 1.6%,
other 3%
Religions: Roman Catholic 60%, Protestant
30%, other 10%
Languages: French, 28 Melanesian-
Polynesian dialects
Literacy: age 15 and over can read and write
(1976)
total population: 91%
male: 91%
female: 90%
Labor force: 50,469 foreign workers for
plantations and mines from Wallis and Futuna,
Vanuatu, and French Polynesia (1980 est.)
by occupation: NA

Government

Names:
conventional long form: Territory of New
Caledonia and Dependencies
conventional short form: New Caledonia
local long form: Territoire des
Nouvelle-Caledonie et Dependances
local short form: Nouvelle-Caledonie
Digraph: NC
Type: overseas territory of France since 1956
Capital: Noumea
Administrative divisions: none (overseas

territory of France); there are no first-order administrative divisions as defined by the US Government, but there are 3 provinces named Iles Loyaute, Nord, and Sud

Independence: none (overseas territory of France; a referendum on independence will be held in 1998)

National holiday: National Day, Taking of the Bastille, 14 July (1789)

Constitution: 28 September 1958 (French Constitution)

Legal system: the 1988 Matignon Accords grant substantial autonomy to the islands; formerly under French law

Suffrage: 18 years of age; universal

Executive branch:

chief of state: President Francois MITTERRAND (since 21 May 1981)

head of government: High Commissioner and President of the Council of Government Alain CHRISTNACHT (since 15 January 1991; appointed by the French Ministry of the Interior); President of the Territorial Congress Simon LOUECKHOTE (since 26 June 1989)

cabinet: Consultative Committee

Legislative branch: unicameral

Territorial Assembly: elections last held 11 June 1989 (next to be held 1993); results—RPCR 44.5%, FLNKS 28.5%, FN 7%, CD 5%, UO 4%, other 11%; seats—(54 total) RPCR 27, FLNKS 19, FN 3, other 5; note—election boycotted by FULK

French Senate: elections last held 27 September 1992 (next to be held September 2001); results—percent of vote by party NA; seats—(1 total) RPCR 1

French National Assembly: elections last held 21 March 1993 (next to be held 21 and 28 March 1998); results—percent of vote by party NA; seats—(2 total) RPCR 2

Judicial branch: Court of Appeal

Political parties and leaders: white-dominated Rassemblement pour la Caledonie dans la Republique (RPCR), conservative, Jacques LAFLEUR—affiliated to France's Rassemblement pour la Republique (RPR); Melanesian proindependence Kanaka Socialist National Liberation Front (FLNKS), Paul NEAOUTYINE; Melanesian moderate Kanak Socialist Liberation (LKS), Nidoish

NAISSELINE; National Front (FN), extreme right, Guy GEORGE; Caledonie Demain (CD), right-wing, Bernard MARANT; Union Oceanienne (UO), conservative, Michel HEMA; Front Uni de Liberation Kanak (FULK), proindependence, Clarence UREGEI; Union Caledonian (UC), Francois BURCK

Member of: ESCAP (associate), FZ, ICFTU, SPC, WFTU, WMO

Diplomatic representation in US: none (overseas territory of France)

US diplomatic representation: none (overseas territory of France)

Flag: the flag of France is used

NEW ZEALAND

500 km

Kermadec Islands

South Pacific Ocean

Tasman Sea

North Island

Auckland

New Plymouth

Gisborne

WELLINGTON

Greymouth

Christchurch

Chatham Islands

South Island

Invercargill

Dunedin

Economy

Overview: Since 1984 the government has been reorienting an agrarian economy dependent on a guaranteed British market to a more industrialized, open free market economy that can compete on the global scene. The government has hoped that dynamic growth would boost real incomes, broaden and deepen the technological capabilities of the industrial sector, reduce inflationary pressures, and permit the expansion of welfare benefits. The results have been mixed: inflation is down from double-digit levels, but growth was sluggish in 1988-91. In 1992-93, growth picked up to 3% annually, a sign that the new economic approach is beginning to pay off. Business confidence has strengthened, and the inflation remains among the lowest in the industrial world. Unemployment, down from 11% in 1991, remains unacceptably high at 9%.

National product: GDP—purchasing power equivalent—$53 billion (1993)

National product real growth rate: 3% (1993)

National product per capita: $15,700 (1993)

Inflation rate (consumer prices): 2% (1993)

Unemployment rate: 9.1% (September 1993)

Budget:
revenues: $NA
expenditures: $NA, including capital expenditures of $NA
note: deficit $345 million (October 1993)

Exports: $10.3 billion (FY93)
commodities: wool, lamb, mutton, beef, fruit, fish, cheese, manufactures, chemicals, forestry products
partners: Australia 18.9%, Japan 15.1%, US 12.5%, South Korea 4.1%

Imports: $9.4 billion (FY93)
commodities: petroleum, consumer goods, motor vehicles, industrial equipment
partners: Australia 21.1%, US 19.6%, Japan 14.7%, UK 6.3%, Germany 4.2%

External debt: $35.3 billion (March 1993)

Industrial production: growth rate 1.9% (1990); accounts for about 20% of GDP

Electricity:
capacity: 8,000,000 kW
production: 31 billion kWh
consumption per capita: 9,250 kWh (1992)

Industries: food processing, wood and paper products, textiles, machinery, transportation equipment, banking and insurance, tourism, mining

Agriculture: accounts for about 9% of GDP and about 10% of the work force; livestock predominates—wool, meat, dairy products all export earners; crops—wheat, barley, potatoes, pulses, fruits, vegetables; surplus producer of farm products; fish catch reached a record 503,000 metric tons in 1988

Economic aid:
donor: ODA and OOF commitments (1970-89), $526 million

Currency: 1 New Zealand dollar (NZ$) = 100 cents

Exchange rates: New Zealand dollars (NZ$) per US$1—1.7771 (January 1994), 1.8495 (1993), 1.8584 (1992), 1.7265 (1991), 1.6750 (1990), 1.6711 (1989)

Fiscal year: 1 July—30 June

Communications

Railroads: 4,716 km total; all 1.067-meter gauge; 274 km double track; 113 km electrified; over 99% government owned
Highways:
total: 92,648 km
paved: 49,547 km
unpaved: gravel, crushed stone 43,101 km
Inland waterways: 1,609 km; of little importance to transportation
Pipelines: natural gas 1,000 km; petroleum products 160 km; condensate (liquified petroleum gas—LPG) 150 km
Ports: Auckland, Christchurch, Dunedin, Wellington, Tauranga
Merchant marine: 18 ships (1,000 GRT or over) totaling 165,514 GRT/218,699 DWT, cargo 2, roll-on/roll-off cargo 5, railcar carrier 1, oil tanker 3, liquefied gas 1, bulk 6
Airports:
total: 108
usable: 108
with permanent-surface runways: 39
with runways over 3,659 m: 1
with runways 2,440-3,659 m: 2
with runways 1,220-2,439 m: 39
Telecommunications: excellent international and domestic systems; 2,110,000 telephones; broadcast stations—64 AM, 2 FM, 14 TV; submarine cables extend to Australia and Fiji; 2 Pacific Ocean INTELSAT earth stations

Defense Forces

Branches: New Zealand Army, Royal New Zealand Navy, Royal New Zealand Air Force
Manpower availability: males age 15-49 880,576; fit for military service 741,629; reach military age (20) annually 28,242 (1994 est.)
Defense expenditures: exchange rate conversion—$792 million, 2% of GDP (FY90/91)

Geography

Location: Southwestern Oceania, southeast of Australia in the South Pacific Ocean
Map references: Oceania, Standard Time Zones of the World
Area:
total area: 268,680 sq km
land area: 268,670 sq km
comparative area: about the size of Colorado
note: includes Antipodes Islands, Auckland Islands, Bounty Islands, Campbell Island, Chatham Islands, and Kermadec Islands
Land boundaries: 0 km
Coastline: 15,134 km
Maritime claims:
continental shelf: 200 nm or the edge of continental margin
exclusive economic zone: 200 nm
territorial sea: 12 nm
International disputes: territorial claim in Antarctica (Ross Dependency)
Climate: temperate with sharp regional contrasts
Terrain: predominately mountainous with some large coastal plains
Natural resources: natural gas, iron ore, sand, coal, timber, hydropower, gold, limestone
Land use:
arable land: 2%
permanent crops: 0%
meadows and pastures: 53%
forest and woodland: 38%
other: 7%
Irrigated land: 2,800 sq km (1989 est.)
Environment:
current issues: deforestation; soil erosion; native flora and fauna hard-hit by species introduced from outside
natural hazards: earthquakes are common, though usually not severe
international agreements: party to—Antarctic Treaty, Biodiversity, Climate Change, Endangered Species, Environmental Modification, Marine Dumping, Nuclear Test Ban, Ozone Layer Protection, Tropical Timber, Wetlands, Whaling; signed, but not ratified—Antarctic-Environmental Protocol,

Hazardous Wastes, Law of the Sea, Marine Life Conservation
Note: about 80% of the population lives in cities

People

Population: 3,388,737 (July 1994 est.)
Population growth rate: 0.57% (1994 est.)
Birth rate: 15.52 births/1,000 population (1994 est.)
Death rate: 8.06 deaths/1,000 population (1994 est.)
Net migration rate: -1.78 migrant(s)/1,000 population (1994 est.)
Infant mortality rate: 8.9 deaths/1,000 live births (1994 est.)
Life expectancy at birth:
total population: 76.38 years
male: 72.76 years
female: 80.18 years (1994 est.)
Total fertility rate: 2.03 children born/ woman (1994 est.)
Nationality:
noun: New Zealander(s)
adjective: New Zealand
Ethnic divisions: European 88%, Maori 8.9%, Pacific Islander 2.9%, other 0.2%
Religions: Anglican 24%, Presbyterian 18%, Roman Catholic 15%, Methodist 5%, Baptist 2%, other Protestant 3%, unspecified or none 9% (1986)
Languages: English (official), Maori
Literacy: age 15 and over can read and write (1980 est.)
total population: 99%
male: NA%
female: NA%
Labor force: 1,603,500 (June 1991)
by occupation: services 67.4%, manufacturing 19.8%, primary production 9.3% (1987)

Government

Names:
conventional long form: none
conventional short form: New Zealand
Abbreviation: NZ
Digraph: NZ

Type: parliamentary democracy
Capital: Wellington
Administrative divisions: 93 counties, 9 districts*, and 3 town districts**; Akaroa, Amuri, Ashburton, Bay of Islands, Bruce, Buller, Chatham Islands, Cheviot, Clifton, Clutha, Cook, Dannevirke, Egmont, Eketahuna, Ellesmere, Eltham, Eyre, Featherston, Franklin, Golden Bay, Great Barrier Island, Grey, Hauraki Plains, Hawera*, Hawke's Bay, Heathcote, Hikurangi**, Hobson, Hokianga, Horowhenua, Hurunui, Hutt, Inangahua, Inglewood, Kaikoura, Kairanga, Kiwitea, Lake, Mackenzie, Malvern, Manaia**, Manawatu, Mangonui, Maniototo, Marlborough, Masterton, Matamata, Mount Herbert, Ohinemuri, Opotiki, Oroua, Otamatea, Otorohanga*, Oxford, Pahiatua, Paparua, Patea, Piako, Pohangina, Raglan, Rangiora*, Rangitikei, Rodney, Rotorua*, Runanga, Saint Kilda, Silverpeaks, Southland, Stewart Island, Stratford, Strathallan, Taranaki, Taumarunui, Taupo, Tauranga, Thames-Coromandel*, Tuapeka, Vincent, Waiapu, Waiheke, Waihemo, Waikato, Waikohu, Waimairi, Waimarino, Waimate, Waimate West, Waimea, Waipa, Waipawa*, Waipukurau*, Wairarapa South, Wairewa, Wairoa, Waitaki, Waitomo*, Waitotara, Wallace, Wanganui, Waverley**, Westland, Whakatane*, Whangarei, Whangaroa, Woodville
Dependent areas: Cook Islands, Niue, Tokelau
Independence: 26 September 1907 (from UK)
National holiday: Waitangi Day, 6 February (1840) (Treaty of Waitangi established British sovereignty)
Constitution: no formal, written constitution; consists of various documents, including certain acts of the UK and New Zealand Parliaments; Constitution Act 1986 was to have come into force 1 January 1987, but has not been enacted
Legal system: based on English law, with special land legislation and land courts for Maoris; accepts compulsory ICJ jurisdiction, with reservations
Suffrage: 18 years of age; universal

Executive branch:
chief of state: Queen ELIZABETH II (since 6 February 1952), represented by Governor General Dame Catherine TIZARD (since 12 December 1990)
head of government: Prime Minister James BOLGER (since 29 October 1990); Deputy Prime Minister Donald McKINNON (since 2 November 1990)
cabinet: Executive Council; appointed by the governor general on recommendation of the prime minister
Legislative branch: unicameral
House of Representatives: (commonly called Parliament) elections last held on 6 November 1993 (next to be held NA November 1996); results—NP 35.2%, NZLP 34.7%, Alliance 18.3%, New Zealand First 8.3%; seats—(99 total) NP 50, NZLP 45, Alliance 2, New Zealand First Party 2
Judicial branch: High Court, Court of Appeal
Political parties and leaders: National Party (NP; government), James BOLGER; New Zealand Labor Party (NZLP; opposition), Helen CLARK; Alliance, Jim ANDERTON; Democratic Party, Dick RYAN; New Zealand Liberal Party, Hanmish MACINTYRE and Gilbert MYLES; Green Party, no official leader; Mana Motuhake, Martin RATA; Socialist Unity Party (SUP; pro-Soviet), Kenneth DOUGLAS; New Zealand First, Winston PETERS
note: the New Labor, Democratic, and Mana Motuhake parties formed a coalition called the Alliance Party, Jim ANDERTON, president, in September 1991; the Green Party joined the coalition in May 1992
Member of: ANZUS (US suspended security obligations to NZ on 11 August 1986), APEC, AsDB, Australia Group, C, CCC, CP, COCOM (cooperating), EBRD, ESCAP, FAO, GATT, IAEA, IBRD, ICAO, ICFTU, IDA, IEA, IFAD, IFC, ILO, IMF, IMO, INMARSAT, INTELSAT, INTERPOL, IOC, IOM (observer), ISO, ITU, LORCS, MTCR, NAM (guest), OECD, PCA, SPARTECA, SPC, SPF, UN, UNAVEM II, UNCTAD, UNESCO, UNIDO, UNOSOM, UNPROFOR, UNTAC, UNTSO, UPU, WHO, WIPO, WMO

Diplomatic representation in US:
chief of mission: Ambassador Lionel John WOOD
chancery: 37 Observatory Circle NW, Washington, DC 20008
telephone: (202) 328-4800
consulate(s) general: Los Angeles
US diplomatic representation:
chief of mission: Ambassador Josiah BEEMAN
embassy: 29 Fitzherbert Terrace, Thorndon, Wellington
mailing address: P. O. Box 1190, Wellington; PSC 467, Box 1, FPO AP 96531-1001
telephone: [64] (4) 472-2068
FAX: [64] (4) 472-3537
consulate(s) general: Auckland
Flag: blue with the flag of the UK in the upper hoist-side quadrant with four red five-pointed stars edged in white centered in the outer half of the flag; the stars represent the Southern Cross constellation

---

U.S. Government Contacts:

U.S. Trade Desk: (202) 482-3647

American Consulate General
Auckland Commercial Section
4th Floor, Yorkshire General Building
Auckland, New Zealand
FPO AP 96531
Tel: 64-9-3030-2038
Fax: 64-9-366-0870

American Embassy Commercial Section
29 Fitzherbert Terrace
Thorndon
Wellington, New Zealand
FPO AP 96531
Tel: 64-4-722-068
Fax: 64-4-781-701

New Zealand Government Contacts:

Embassy of the New Zealand Commercial Section
37 Observatory Circle, N.W.
Washington, DC 20008
Tel: (202) 328-4800

**Chambers of Commerce &
Organizations:**

**The American Chamber of Commerce in
New Zealand**
P.O. Box 3408
Wellington, New Zealand
Tel: 64-4-727-549

Legal Services:

Buddle Findlay
Floors 14, 17, 18 and 19
Stock Exchange Centre, 191-201 Queen Street
P.O. Box 1433
Auckland, New Zealand
Tel: 649 358-2555
Fax: 649-358-2055
*International Joint Ventures, Overseas
Investment and Trade, Broadcasting and
Energy, Documentation in all Courts and
Tribunals.*

Travel:

International Airlines to Country:
United

International Hotels in Country:
Auckland:
Hotel du Vin, Tel: 649/233-6314, Fax:
649/233-6215
Pan Pacific, Tel: 649/366-3000, Fax: 649/366-
3000, Fax: 649/366-0121
The Regent, Tel: 649/309-8888, Fax: 649/379-
6445.

NORTH KOREA

150 km

Boundary representation is not necessarily authoritative.

Najin
Ch'ŏngjin
Hyesan
Kanggye
Kimch'aek
Sinŭiju
Hamhŭng
Sunch'ŏn
Sea of Japan
P'YŎNGYANG
Wŏnsan
Namp'o
Sariwŏn
Yellow Sea
Kaesŏng
P'anmunjŏm

Economy

Overview: More than 90% of this command economy is socialized; agricultural land is collectivized; and state-owned industry produces 95% of manufactured goods. State control of economic affairs is unusually tight even for a Communist country because of the small size and homogeneity of the society and the strict rule of KIM Il-song and his son, KIM Chong-il. Economic growth during the period 1984-88 averaged 2%-3%, but output declined by 3%-5% annually during 1989-92 because of systemic problems and disruptions in socialist-style economic relations with the former USSR and China. In 1992, output dropped sharply, by perhaps 7%-9%, as the economy felt the cumulative effect of the reduction in outside support. The leadership insisted on maintaining its high level of military outlays from a shrinking economic pie. Moreover, a serious drawdown in inventories and critical shortages in the energy sector have led to increasing interruptions in industrial production. Abundant mineral resources and hydropower have formed the basis of industrial development since WWII. Output of the extractive industries includes coal, iron ore, magnesite, graphite, copper, zinc, lead, and precious metals. Manufacturing is centered on heavy industry, including military industry, with light industry lagging far behind. Despite the use of improved seed varieties, expansion of irrigation, and the heavy use of fertilizers, North Korea has not yet become self-sufficient in food production. Six consecutive years of poor harvests, coupled with distribution problems, have led to chronic food shortages. North Korea remains far behind South Korea in economic development and living standards.
National product: GDP—purchasing power equivalent—$22 billion (1992 est.)
National product real growth rate: -7 to -9% (1992 est.)
National product per capita: $1,000 (1992 est.)
Inflation rate (consumer prices): NA%
Unemployment rate: NA%
Budget:
revenues: $19.3 billion
expenditures: $19.3 billion, including capital expenditures of $NA (1992 est.)
Exports: $1.3 billion (f.o.b., 1992 est.)
commodities: minerals, metallurgical products, agricultural and fishery products, manufactures (including armaments)
partners: China, Japan, Russia, South Korea, Germany, Hong Kong, Mexico
Imports: $1.9 billion (f.o.b., 1992 est.)
commodities: petroleum, grain, coking coal, machinery and equipment, consumer goods
partners: China, Russia, Japan, Hong Kong, Germany, Singapore
External debt: $8 billion (1992 est.)
Industrial production: growth rate -7% to -9% (1992 est.)
Electricity:
capacity: 7,300,000 kW
production: 26 billion kWh
consumption per capita: 1,160 kWh (1992)
Industries: machine building, military products, electric power, chemicals, mining, metallurgy, textiles, food processing

Agriculture: accounts for about 25% of GNP and 36% of work force; principal crops—rice, corn, potatoes, soybeans, pulses; livestock and livestock products—cattle, hogs, pork, eggs; not self-sufficient in grain
Economic aid:
recipient: Communist countries, $1.4 billion a year in the 1980s, but very little now
Currency: 1 North Korean won (Wn) = 100 chon
Exchange rates: North Korean won (Wn) per US$1—2.15 (May 1994), 2.13 (May 1992), 2.14 (September 1991), 2.1 (January 1990), 2.3 (December 1989)
Fiscal year: calendar year

Communications

Railroads: 4,915 km total; 4,250 km 1.435-meter standard gauge, 665 km 0.762-meter narrow gauge; 159 km double track; 3,084 km electrified; government owned (1989)
Highways:
total: 30,000 km
paved: 1,440 km
unpaved: gravel, crushed stone, earth 28,560 km (1991)
Inland waterways: 2,253 km; mostly navigable by small craft only
Pipelines: crude oil 37 km
Ports: primary—Ch'ongjin, Hungnam (Hamhung), Najin, Namp'o, Wonsan; secondary—Haeju, Kimch'aek, Kosong, Sinuiju, Songnim, Sonbong (formerly Unggi), Ungsang
Merchant marine: 83 ships (1,000 GRT and over) totaling 706,497 GRT/1,114,827 DWT, passenger 1, short-sea passenger 1, passenger-cargo 2, cargo 67, oil tanker 2, bulk 9, combination bulk 1
Airports:
total: 55
usable: 55 (est.)
with permanent-surface runways: about 30
with runways over 3,659 m: fewer than 5
with runways 2,440-3,659 m: 20
with runways 1,220-2,439 m: 30
Telecommunications: broadcast stations—18 AM, no FM, 11 TV; 300,000 TV sets (1989); 3,500,000 radio receivers; 1 Indian Ocean INTELSAT earth station

Defense Forces

Branches: Korean People's Army (including the Army, Navy, Air Force), Civil Security Forces
Manpower availability: males age 15-49 6,658,529; fit for military service 4,044,355; reach military age (18) annually 196,763 (1994 est.)
Defense expenditures: exchange rate conversion—about $5 billion, 20%-25% of GNP (1991 est.); note—the officially announced but suspect figure is $2.2 billion (1994), about 12% of total spending

Geography

Location: Eastern Asia, between China and South Korea
Map references: Asia, Standard Time Zones of the World
Area:
total area: 120,540 sq km
land area: 120,410 sq km
comparative area: slightly smaller than Mississippi
Land boundaries: total 1,673 km, China 1,416 km, South Korea 238 km, Russia 19 km
Coastline: 2,495 km
Maritime claims:
territorial sea: 12 nm
exclusive economic zone: 200 nm
military boundary line: 50 nm in the Sea of Japan and the exclusive economic zone limit in the Yellow Sea where all foreign vessels and aircraft without permission are banned
International disputes: short section of boundary with China is indefinite; Demarcation Line with South Korea
Climate: temperate with rainfall concentrated in summer
Terrain: mostly hills and mountains separated by deep, narrow valleys; coastal plains wide in west, discontinuous in east
Natural resources: coal, lead, tungsten, zinc, graphite, magnesite, iron ore, copper, gold, pyrites, salt, fluorspar, hydropower
Land use:
arable land: 18%
permanent crops: 1%

meadows and pastures: 0%
forest and woodland: 74%
other: 7%
Irrigated land: 14,000 sq km (1989)
Environment:
current issues: localized air pollution attributable to inadequate industrial controls
natural hazards: late spring droughts often followed by severe flooding; subject to occasional typhoons which occur during the early fall
international agreements: party to—Antarctic Treaty, Environmental Modification, Ship Pollution; signed, but not ratified— Antarctic-Environmental Protocol, Biodiversity, Climate Change, Law of the Sea
Note: strategic location bordering China, South Korea, and Russia; mountainous interior is isolated, nearly inaccessible, and sparsely populated

People

Population: 23,066,573 (July 1994 est.)
Population growth rate: 1.83% (1994 est.)
Birth rate: 23.75 births/1,000 population (1994 est.)
Death rate: 5.5 deaths/1,000 population (1994 est.)
Net migration rate: 0 migrant(s)/1,000 population (1994 est.)
Infant mortality rate: 27.7 deaths/1,000 live births (1994 est.)
Life expectancy at birth:
total population: 69.78 years
male: 66.69 years
female: 73.02 years (1994 est.)
Total fertility rate: 2.37 children born/ woman (1994 est.)
Nationality:
noun: Korean(s)
adjective: Korean
Ethnic divisions: racially homogeneous
Religions: Buddhism and Confucianism, some Christianity and syncretic Chondogyo
note: autonomous religious activities now almost nonexistent; government-sponsored religious groups exist to provide illusion of religious freedom

Languages: Korean
Literacy: age 15 and over can read and write (1990 est.)
total population: 99%
male: 99%
female: 99%
Labor force: 9.615 million
by occupation: agricultural 36%, nonagricultural 64%
note: shortage of skilled and unskilled labor (mid-1987 est.)

Government

Names:
conventional long form: Democratic People's Republic of Korea
conventional short form: North Korea
local long form: Choson-minjujuui-inmin-konghwaguk
local short form: none
Abbreviation: DPRK
Digraph: KN
Type: Communist state; Stalinist dictatorship
Capital: P'yongyang
Administrative divisions: 9 provinces (do, singular and plural) and 3 special cities* (jikhalsi, singular and plural); Chagang-do (Chagang Province), Hamgyong-bukto (North Hamgyong Province), Hamgyong-namdo (South Hamgyong Province), Hwanghae-bukto (North Hwanghae Province), · Hwanghae-namdo (South Hwanghae Province), Kaesong-si* (Kaesong City), Kangwon-do (Kangwon Province), Namp'o-si* (Namp'o City), P'yongan-bukto (North P'yongan Province), P'yongan-namdo (South P'yongan Province), P'yongyang-si* (P'yongyang City), Yanggang-do (Yanggang Province)
Independence: 9 September 1948
note: 15 August 1945, date of independence from the Japanese and celebrated in North Korea as National Liberation Day
National holiday: DPRK Foundation Day, 9 September (1948)
Constitution: adopted 1948, completely revised 27 December 1972, revised again in April 1992

Legal system: based on German civil law
system with Japanese influences and
Communist legal theory; no judicial review of
legislative acts; has not accepted compulsory
ICJ jurisdiction

Suffrage: 17 years of age; universal

Executive branch:

chief of state: President KIM Il-song (national
leader since 1948, president since 28
December 1972); designated successor KIM
Chong-il (son of president, born 16 February
1942); election last held 24 May 1990 (next to
be held by NA 1995); results—President KIM
Il-song was reelected without opposition

head of government: Premier KANG Song-
san (since December 1992)

cabinet: State Administration Council;
appointed by the Supreme People's Assembly

Legislative branch: unicameral

*Supreme People's Assembly (Ch'oego Inmin
Hoeui):* elections last held on 7-9 April 1993
(next to be held NA); results—percent of vote
by party NA; seats—(687 total) the KWP
approves a single list of candidates who are
elected without opposition; minor parties hold
a few seats

Judicial branch: Central Court

Political parties and leaders: major party—
Korean Workers' Party (KWP), KIM Il-song,
general secretary, and his son, KIM Chong-il,
secretary, Central Committee; Korean Social
Democratic Party, KIM Pyong-sik, chairman;
Chondoist Chongu Party, YU Mi-yong,
chairwoman

Member of: ESCAP, FAO, G-77, IAEA,
ICAO, IFAD, IMF (observer), IMO,
INTELSAT (nonsignatory user), IOC, ISO,
ITU, LORCS, NAM, UN, UNCTAD,
UNESCO, UNIDO, UPU, WFTU, WHO,
WIPO, WMO, WTO

Diplomatic representation in US: none

US diplomatic representation: none

Flag: three horizontal bands of blue (top), red
(triple width), and blue; the red band is edged
in white; on the hoist side of the red band is a
white disk with a red five-pointed star

PAPUA NEW GUINEA

500 km

South Pacific Ocean

New Ireland
Wewak
Madang
New
Britain
Bougainville
Lae
Daru
PORT
MORESBY

Coral Sea

Economy

Overview: Papua New Guinea is richly endowed with natural resources, but exploitation has been hampered by the rugged terrain and the high cost of developing an infrastructure. Agriculture provides a subsistence livelihood for 85% of the population. Mining of numerous deposits, including copper and gold, accounts for about 60% of export earnings. Budgetary support from Australia and development aid under World Bank auspices have helped sustain the economy. Robust growth in 1991-92 was led by the mining sector; the opening of a large new gold mine helped the advance. The economy remained strong in 1993, primarily because of continued growth in the mining and oil sectors.

National product: GDP—purchasing power equivalent—$8.2 billion (1993 est.)

National product real growth rate: 1.2% (1993 est.)

National product per capita: $2,000 (1993 est.)

Inflation rate (consumer prices): 4.5% (1992-93)

Unemployment rate: NA%

Budget:
revenues: $1.33 billion
expenditures: $1.49 billion, including capital expenditures of $225 million (1993 est.)

Exports: $1.3 billion (f.o.b., 1990)
commodities: gold, copper ore, oil, logs, palm oil, coffee, cocoa, lobster
partners: Australia, Japan, South Korea, UK, US

Imports: $1.6 billion (c.i.f., 1990)
commodities: machinery and transport equipment, manufactured goods, food, fuels, chemicals
partners: Australia, Japan, US, Singapore, New Zealand, UK

External debt: $2.2 billion (April 1991)

Industrial production: growth rate 21% (1992); accounts for 31% of GDP

Electricity:
capacity: 400,000 kW
production: 1.6 billion kWh
consumption per capita: 400 kWh (1992)

Industries: copra crushing, palm oil processing, plywood production, wood chip production, mining of gold, silver, and copper, construction, tourism

Agriculture: Accounts for 28% of GDP; livelihood for 85% of population; fertile soils and favorable climate permits cultivating a wide variety of crops; cash crops—coffee, cocoa, coconuts, palm kernels; other products—tea, rubber, sweet potatoes, fruit, vegetables, poultry, pork; net importer of food for urban centers

Economic aid:
recipient: US commitments, including Ex-Im (FY70-89), $40.6 million; Western (non-US) countries, ODA and OOF bilateral commitments (1970-89), $6.5 billion; OPEC bilateral aid (1979-89), $17 million

Currency: 1 kina (K) = 100 toea

Exchange rates: kina (K) per US$1—1.0281 (January 1994), 1.0221 (1993), 1.0367 (1992), 1.0504 (1991), 1.0467 (1990), 1.1685 (1989)

Fiscal year: calendar year

Communications

Railroads: none
Highways:
total: 19,200 km
paved: 640 km
unpaved: gravel, crushed stone, stabilized earth 10,960 km; unimproved earth 7,600 km
Inland waterways: 10,940 km
Ports: Anewa Bay, Lae, Madang, Port Moresby, Rabaul
Merchant marine: 11 ships (1,000 GRT or over) totaling 21,337 GRT/25,669 DWT, cargo 3, combination ore/oil 5, bulk 2, container 1
Airports:
total: 504
usable: 462
with permanent-surface runways: 18
with runways over 3,659 m: 0
with runways 2,440-3,659 m: 1
with runways 1,220-2,439 m: 39
Telecommunications: services are adequate and being improved; facilities provide radiobroadcast, radiotelephone and telegraph, coastal radio, aeronautical radio, and international radiocommunication services; submarine cables extend to Australia and Guam; more than 70,000 telephones (1987); broadcast stations—31 AM, 2 FM, 2 TV (1987); 1 Pacific Ocean INTELSAT earth station

Defense Forces

Branches: Papua New Guinea Defense Force (including Army, Navy, Air Force)
Manpower availability: males age 15-49 1,080,316; fit for military service 601,369
Defense expenditures: exchange rate conversion—$55 million, 1.8% of GDP (1993 est.)

Geography

Location: Southeastern Asia, just north of Australia, between Indonesia and the Solomon Islands
Map references: Oceania, Southeast Asia, Standard Time Zones of the World

Area:
total area: 461,690 sq km
land area: 451,710 sq km
comparative area: slightly larger than California
Land boundaries: total 820 km, Indonesia 820 km
Coastline: 5,152 km
Maritime claims: measured from claimed archipelagic baselines
continental shelf: 200-m depth or to depth of exploitation
exclusive fishing zone: 200 nm
territorial sea: 12 nm
International disputes: none
Climate: tropical; northwest monsoon (December to March), southeast monsoon (May to October); slight seasonal temperature variation
Terrain: mostly mountains with coastal lowlands and rolling foothills
Natural resources: gold, copper, silver, natural gas, timber, oil potential
Land use:
arable land: 0%
permanent crops: 1%
meadows and pastures: 0%
forest and woodland: 71%
other: 28%
Irrigated land: NA sq km
Environment:
current issues: deforestation; pollution from mining projects
natural hazards: some active volcanoes; frequent earthquakes
international agreements: party to—Antarctic Treaty, Biodiversity, Climate Change, Endangered Species, Environmental Modification, Marine Dumping, Nuclear Test Ban, Ozone Layer Protection, Ship Pollution, Tropical Timber; signed, but not ratified—Antarctic-Environmental Protocol, Law of the Sea
Note: shares island of New Guinea with Indonesia; one of world's largest swamps along southwest coast

People

Population: 4,196,806 (July 1994 est.)
Population growth rate: 2.31% (1994 est.)
Birth rate: 33.5 births/1,000 population (1994 est.)
Death rate: 10.38 deaths/1,000 population (1994 est.)
Net migration rate: 0 migrant(s)/1,000 population (1994 est.)
Infant mortality rate: 63.3 deaths/1,000 live births (1994 est.)
Life expectancy at birth:
total population: 56.43 years
male: 55.6 years
female: 57.31 years (1994 est.)
Total fertility rate: 4.65 children born/woman (1994 est.)
Nationality:
noun: Papua New Guinean(s)
adjective: Papua New Guinean
Ethnic divisions: Melanesian, Papuan, Negrito, Micronesian, Polynesian
Religions: Roman Catholic 22%, Lutheran 16%, Presbyterian/Methodist/London Missionary Society 8%, Anglican 5%, Evangelical Alliance 4%, Seventh-Day Adventist 1%, other Protestant sects 10%, indigenous beliefs 34%
Languages: English spoken by 1-2%, pidgin English widespread, Motu spoken in Papua region
note: 715 indigenous languages
Literacy: age 15 and over can read and write (1990 est.)
total population: 52%
male: 65%
female: 38%
Labor force: NA

Government

Names:
conventional long form: Independent State of Papua New Guinea
conventional short form: Papua New Guinea
Digraph: PP
Type: parliamentary democracy
Capital: Port Moresby

Administrative divisions: 20 provinces; Central, Chimbu, Eastern Highlands, East New Britain, East Sepik, Enga, Gulf, Madang, Manus, Milne Bay, Morobe, National Capital, New Ireland, Northern, North Solomons, Sandaun, Southern Highlands, Western, Western Highlands, West New Britain
Independence: 16 September 1975 (from UN trusteeship under Australian administration)
National holiday: Independence Day, 16 September (1975)
Constitution: 16 September 1975
Legal system: based on English common law
Suffrage: 18 years of age; universal
Executive branch:
chief of state: Queen ELIZABETH II (since 6 February 1952), represented by Governor General Wiwa KOROWI (since NA November 1991)
head of government: Prime Minister Paias WINGTI (since 17 July 1992); Deputy Prime Minister Sir Julius CHAN (since July 1992)
cabinet: National Executive Council; appointed by the governor on recommendation of the prime minister
Legislative branch: unicameral
National Parliament: (sometimes referred to as the House of Assembly) elections last held 13-26 June 1992 (next to be held NA 1997); results—percent by party NA; seats—(109 total) Pangu Party 24, PDM 17, PPP 10, PAP 10, independents 30, others 18 (association with political parties is fluid)
Judicial branch: Supreme Court
Political parties and leaders: Papua New Guinea United Party (Pangu Party), Jack GENIA; People's Democratic Movement (PDM), Paias WINGTI; People's Action Party (PAP), Akoka DOI; People's Progress Party (PPP), Sir Julius CHAN; United Party (UP), Paul TORATO; Papua Party (PP), Galeva KWARARA; National Party (NP), Paul PORA; Melanesian Alliance (MA), Fr. John MOMIS
Member of: ACP, APEC, AsDB, ASEAN (observer), C, CP, ESCAP, FAO, G-77, IBRD, ICAO, ICFTU, IDA, IFAD, IFC, ILO, IMF, IMO, INTELSAT, INTERPOL, IOC, ISO (correspondent), ITU, LORCS, NAM, SPARTECA, SPC, SPF, UN, UNCTAD,

UNESCO, UNIDO, UPU, WFTU, WHO, WMO

Diplomatic representation in US:
chief of mission: Ambassador-designate Kepas WATANGIA
chancery: 3rd floor, 1615 New Hampshire Avenue NW, Washington, DC 20009
telephone: (202) 745-3680
FAX: (202) 745-3679

US diplomatic representation:
chief of mission: Ambassador Richard TEARE
embassy: Armit Street, Port Moresby
mailing address: P. O. Box 1492, Port Moresby, or APO AE 96553
telephone: [675] 211-455 or 594, 654
FAX: [675] 213-423

Flag: divided diagonally from upper hoist-side corner; the upper triangle is red with a soaring yellow bird of paradise centered; the lower triangle is black with five white five-pointed stars of the Southern Cross constellation centered

PHILIPPINES

500 km

Aparri
Baguio Luzon
South Angeles Quezon Philippine
China MANILA Sea
Sea Mindoro Legaspi
Panay Samar
Palawan Cebu
Negros
Sulu Sea
Zamboanga Davao Mindanao
Celebes Sea

Economy

Overview: Domestic output in this primarily agricultural economy failed to grow in 1992 and rose only slightly in 1993. Drought and power supply problems hampered production, while inadequate revenues prevented government pump priming. Worker remittances helped to supplement GDP. A marked increase in capital goods imports, particularly power generating equipment, telecommunications equipment, and electronic data processors, contributed to 20% import growth in both 1992 and 1993.

National product: GDP—purchasing power equivalent—$171 billion (1993 est.)

National product real growth rate: 1.4% (1993 est.)

National product per capita: $2,500 (1993 est.)

Inflation rate (consumer prices): 7.6% (1993)

Unemployment rate: 9.2% (1993)

Budget:
revenues: $11.5 billion
expenditures: $13 billion, including capital expenditures of $1.7 billion (1994 est.)

Exports: $11.1 billion (f.o.b., 1993 est.)
commodities: electronics, textiles, coconut products, cooper, fish
partners: US 39%, Japan 18%, Germany 5%, UK 5%, Hong Kong 5% (1992)

Imports: $17.1 billion (f.o.b., 1993 est.)
commodities: raw materials 40%, capital goods 25%, petroleum products 10%
partners: Japan 21%, US 18%, Taiwan 7%, Saudi Arabia 6%, Hong Kong 5%, South Korea 5% (1992)

External debt: $34.1 billion (September 1993)

Industrial production: growth rate -1% (1992 est.); accounts for 34% of GDP

Electricity:
capacity: 7,850,000 kW
production: 28 billion kWh
consumption per capita: 420 kWh (1992)

Industries: textiles, pharmaceuticals, chemicals, wood products, food processing, electronics assembly, petroleum refining, fishing

Agriculture: accounts for about 20% of GDP and about 45% of labor force; major crops—rice, coconuts, corn, sugarcane, bananas, pineapples, mangos; animal products—pork, eggs, beef; net exporter of farm products; fish catch of 2 million metric tons annually

Illicit drugs: illicit producer of cannabis for the international drug trade; growers are producing more and better quality cannabis despite government eradication efforts; transit point for Southwest Asian heroin bound for the US

Economic aid:
recipient: US commitments, including Ex-Im (FY70-89), $3.6 billion; Western (non-US) countries, ODA and OOF bilateral commitments (1970-88), $7.9 billion; OPEC bilateral aid (1979-89), $5 million; Communist countries (1975-89), $123 million

Currency: 1 Philippine peso (P) = 100 centavos

Exchange rates: Philippine pesos (P) per US$1—27.725 (January 1994), 22.120 (1993), 25.512 (1992), 27.479 (1991), 24.311 (1990), 21.737 (1989)
Fiscal year: calendar year

Communications

Railroads: 378 km operable on Luzon, 34% government owned (1982)
Highways:
total: 157,450 km
paved: 22,400 km
unpaved: gravel, crushed stone, stabilized earth 85,050 km; unimproved earth 50,000 km (1988)
Inland waterways: 3,219 km; limited to shallow-draft (less than 1.5 m) vessels
Pipelines: petroleum products 357 km
Ports: Cagayan de Oro, Cebu, Davao, Guimaras, Iloilo, Legaspi, Manila, Subic Bay
Merchant marine: 553 ships (1,000 GRT or over) totaling 8,451,047 GRT/13,934,255 DWT, passenger 1, short-sea passenger 12, passenger-cargo 13, cargo 145, refrigerated cargo 27, vehicle carrier 35, livestock carrier 9, roll-on/roll-off cargo 14, container 8, oil tanker 33, chemical tanker 1, liquefied gas 3, combination ore/oil 1, bulk 241, combination bulk 10
note: many Philippine flag ships are foreign owned and are on the register for the purpose of long-term bare-boat charter back to their original owners who are principally in Japan and Germany
Airports:
total: 270
usable: 238
with permanent-surface runways: 74
with runways over 3,659 m: 0
with runways 2,440-3,659 m: 9
with runways 1,220-2,439 m: 57
Telecommunications: good international radio and submarine cable services; domestic and interisland service adequate; 872,900 telephones; broadcast stations—267 AM (including 6 US), 55 FM, 33 TV (including 4 US); submarine cables extended to Hong Kong, Guam, Singapore, Taiwan, and Japan;

satellite earth stations—1 Indian Ocean INTELSAT, 2 Pacific Ocean INTELSAT, and 11 domestic

Defense Forces

Branches: Army, Navy (including Coast Guard and Marine Corps), Air Force
Manpower availability: males age 15-49 17,668,781; fit for military service 12,479,312; reach military age (20) annually 733,880 (1994 est.)
Defense expenditures: exchange rate conversion—$915 million, 1.9% of GNP (1991)

Geography

Location: Southeastern Asia, between Indonesia and China
Map references: Asia, Oceania, Southeast Asia, Standard Time Zones of the World
Area:
total area: 300,000 sq km
land area: 298,170 sq km
comparative area: slightly larger than Arizona
Land boundaries: 0 km
Coastline: 36,289 km
Maritime claims: measured from claimed archipelagic baselines
continental shelf: to depth of exploitation
exclusive economic zone: 200 nm
territorial sea: irregular polygon extending up to 100 nm from coastline as defined by 1898 treaty; since late 1970s has also claimed polygonal-shaped area in South China Sea up to 285 nm in breadth
International disputes: involved in a complex dispute over the Spratly Islands with China, Malaysia, Taiwan, Vietnam, and possibly Brunei; claims Malaysian state of Sabah
Climate: tropical marine; northeast monsoon (November to April); southwest monsoon (May to October)
Terrain: mostly mountains with narrow to extensive coastal lowlands
Natural resources: timber, petroleum, nickel, cobalt, silver, gold, salt, copper

Land use:
arable land: 26%
permanent crops: 11%
meadows and pastures: 4%
forest and woodland: 40%
other: 19%
Irrigated land: 16,200 sq km (1989 est.)
Environment:
current issues: deforestation; soil erosion; water pollution; air pollution in Manila
natural hazards: astride typhoon belt, usually affected by 15 and struck by five to six cyclonic storms per year; subject to landslides, active volcanoes, destructive earthquakes, tsunamis
international agreements: party to—Biodiversity, Endangered Species, Hazardous Wastes, Law of the Sea, Marine Dumping, Nuclear Test Ban, Ozone Layer Protection, Whaling; signed, but not ratified—Climate Change, Tropical Timber

People

Population: 69,808,930 (July 1994 est.)
Population growth rate: 1.92% (1994 est.)
Birth rate: 27.34 births/1,000 population (1994 est.)
Death rate: 6.94 deaths/1,000 population (1994 est.)
Net migration rate: -1.18 migrant(s)/1,000 population (1994 est.)
Infant mortality rate: 50.8 deaths/1,000 live births (1994 est.)
Life expectancy at birth:
total population: 65.39 years
male: 62.88 years
female: 68.02 years (1994 est.)
Total fertility rate: 3.35 children born/woman (1994 est.)
Nationality:
noun: Filipino(s)
adjective: Philippine
Ethnic divisions: Christian Malay 91.5%, Muslim Malay 4%, Chinese 1.5%, other 3%
Religions: Roman Catholic 83%, Protestant 9%, Muslim 5%, Buddhist and other 3%
Languages: Pilipino (official; based on Tagalog), English (official)

Literacy: age 15 and over can read and write (1990 est.)
total population: 90%
male: 90%
female: 90%
Labor force: 24.12 million
by occupation: agriculture 46%, industry and commerce 16%, services 18.5%, government 10%, other 9.5% (1989)

Government

Names:
conventional long form: Republic of the Philippines
conventional short form: Philippines
local long form: Republika ng Pilipinas
local short form: Pilipinas
Digraph: RP
Type: republic
Capital: Manila
Administrative divisions: 72 provinces and 61 chartered cities*; Abra, Agusan del Norte, Agusan del Sur, Aklan, Albay, Angeles*, Antique, Aurora, Bacolod*, Bago*, Baguio*, Bais*, Basilan, Basilan City*, Bataan, Batanes, Batangas, Batangas City*, Benguet, Bohol, Bukidnon, Bulacan, Butuan*, Cabanatuan*, Cadiz*, Cagayan, Cagayan de Oro*, Calbayog*, Caloocan*, Camarines Norte, Camarines Sur, Camiguin, Canlaon*, Capiz, Catanduanes, Cavite, Cavite City*, Cebu, Cebu City*, Cotabato*, Dagupan*, Danao*, Dapitan*, Davao City* Davao, Davao del Sur, Davao Oriental, Dipolog*, Dumaguete*, Eastern Samar, General Santos*, Gingoog*, Ifugao, Iligan*, Ilocos Norte, Ilocos Sur, Iloilo, Iloilo City*, Iriga*, Isabela, Kalinga-Apayao, La Carlota*, Laguna, Lanao del Norte, Lanao del Sur, Laoag*, Lapu-Lapu*, La Union, Legaspi*, Leyte, Lipa*, Lucena*, Maguindanao, Mandaue*, Manila*, Marawi*, Marinduque, Masbate, Mindoro Occidental, Mindoro Oriental, Misamis Occidental, Misamis Oriental, Mountain, Naga*, Negros Occidental, Negros Oriental, North Cotabato, Northern Samar, Nueva Ecija, Nueva Vizcaya, Olongapo*, Ormoc*, Oroquieta*, Ozamis*, Pagadian*, Palawan, Palayan*, Pampanga,

Pangasinan, Pasay*, Puerto Princesa*, Quezon, Quezon City*, Quirino, Rizal, Romblon, Roxas*, Samar, San Carlos* (in Negros Occidental), San Carlos* (in Pangasinan), San Jose*, San Pablo*, Silay*, Siquijor, Sorsogon, South Cotabato, Southern Leyte, Sultan Kudarat, Sulu, Surigao*, Surigao del Norte, Surigao del Sur, Tacloban*, Tagaytay*, Tagbilaran*, Tangub*, Tarlac, Tawitawi, Toledo*, Trece Martires*, Zambales, Zamboanga*, Zamboanga del Norte, Zamboanga del Sur

Independence: 4 July 1946 (from US)

National holiday: Independence Day, 12 June (1898) (from Spain)

Constitution: 2 February 1987, effective 11 February 1987

Legal system: based on Spanish and Anglo-American law; accepts compulsory ICJ jurisdiction, with reservations

Suffrage: 15 years of age; universal

Executive branch:
chief of state and head of government: President Fidel Valdes RAMOS (since 30 June 1992); Vice President Joseph Ejercito ESTRADA (since 30 June 1992); election last held 11 May 1992 (next election to be held NA May 1998); results—Fidel Valdes RAMOS won 23.6% of votes—a narrow plurality
cabinet: Executive Secretary; appointed by the president with the consent of the Commission of Appointments

Legislative branch: bicameral Congress (Kongreso)
Senate (Senado): elections last held 11 May 1992 (next election to be held NA May 1995); results—LDP 66%, NPC 20%, Lakas-NUCD 8%, Liberal 6%; seats—(24 total) LDP 15, NPC 5, Lakas-NUCD 2, Liberal 1, Independent 1
House of Representatives (Kapulungan Ng Mga Kinatawan): elections last held 11 May 1992 (next election to be held NA May 1995); results—LDP 43.5%; Lakas-NUCD 25%, NPC 23.5%, Liberal 5%, KBL 3%; seats—(200 total) LDP 87, NPC 45, Lakas-NUCD 41, Liberal 15, NP 6, KBL 3, Independent 3

Judicial branch: Supreme Court

Political parties and leaders: Democratic Filipino Struggle (Laban ng Demokratikong Pilipinas, Laban), Edgardo ESPIRITU; People Power-National Union of Christian Democrats (Lakas ng Edsa, NUCD and Partido Lakas Tao, Lakas/NUCD); Fidel V. RAMOS, President of the Republic, Raul MANGLAPUS, Jose de VENECIA, secretary general; Nationalist People's Coalition (NPC), Eduardo COJUANGCO; Liberal Party, Jovito SALONGA; People's Reform Party (PRP), Miriam DEFENSOR-SANTIAGO; New Society Movement (Kilusan Bagong Lipunan; KBL), Imelda MARCOS; Nacionalista Party (NP), Salvador H. LAUREL, president

Member of: APEC, AsDB, ASEAN, CCC, CP, ESCAP, FAO, G-24, G-77, GATT, IAEA, IBRD, ICAO, ICFTU, IDA, IFAD, IFC, ILO, IMF, IMO, INMARSAT, INTELSAT, INTERPOL, IOC, IOM, ISO, ITU, LORCS, NAM, UN, UNCTAD, UNESCO, UNHCR, UNIDO, UNTAC, UPU, WCL, WFTU, WHO, WIPO, WMO, WTO

Diplomatic representation in US:
chief of mission: Ambassador Raul Chaves RABE
chancery: 1617 Massachusetts Avenue NW, Washington, DC 20036
telephone: (202) 483-1414
FAX: (202) 328-7614
consulate(s) general: Agana (Guam), Chicago, Honolulu, Houston, Los Angeles, New York, San Francisco, and Seattle
consulate(s): San Diego and San Jose (Saipan)

US diplomatic representation:
chief of mission: Ambassador John D. NEGROPONTE
embassy: 1201 Roxas Boulevard, Ermita Manila 1000
mailing address: APO AP 96440
telephone: [632] 521-7116
FAX: [632] 522-4361
consulate(s) general: Cebu

Flag: two equal horizontal bands of blue (top) and red with a white equilateral triangle based on the hoist side; in the center of the triangle is a yellow sun with eight primary rays (each containing three individual rays) and in each corner of the triangle is a small yellow five-pointed star

U.S. Government Contacts:

U.S. Trade Desk: (202) 482-3877

American Embassy Commercial Section
395 Buendia Avenue
Extension Makati
Manila, the Philippines
APO AP 96440
Tel: 63-2-818-6674
Fax: 63-2-818-2684

Philippines Government Contacts:
Embassy of the Philippines Commercial Section
1617 Massachusetts Avenue, N.W.
Washington, DC 20036
Tel: (202) 483-1414

Trade Office
The Philippine Center
556 Fifth Avenue, 4th Floor
New York, NY 10036
Roman G. Baltazar
Special Trade Representative
Tel: (212) 575-7925/6
Fax: (212) 575-7759

Chambers of Commerce & Organizations:

American Chamber of Commerce in the Philippines
P.O.Box 1578, MCC
Manila, the Philippines
Tel: 63-2-818-7911
Fax: 63-2-816-6359

Legal Services:

Bito, Lozada, Ortega & Castillo
140 Alfaro Street
Salcedo Village, Makati
Mentro Manila, Republic of the Philippines
Tel: 632 818-23-21
Fax: 632 810-3153
Diverse international practice. Acts as adviser to British and Swedish Embassies in the Philippines.

Poblador, Azada & Associates
7th Floor, State Condominium I
186 Salcedo Street, Legaspi Village
Makati
Metro Manila 1229, Republic of the Philippines
Tel: 632 85-07-86
Fax: 632 818 3858
Patents, Trademarks and Copyrights.

SyCip Salazar Hernandez & Gatmaitan
SyCip Law-All Asia Center
105 Paseo de Roxas
1200 Makati
Metro Manila, Republic of the Philippines
Tel: 632 817-9811
Fax: 632 817-3896
Largest firm in the Philippines and offers a full range of legal services.

Travel:

International Airlines to Country:
Continental, Norhtwest, United

International Hotels in Country:
Manila:
Century Park Sheraton, Tel: 63-2-522-1011, Fax: 63-2-521-3413
Philippine Plaza, Tel: 63-2-832-0701, Fax: 63-2-832-3485
Manila Peninsula, Tel: 63-2-819-3456, Fax: 63-2-815-4825.

SINGAPORE

Selat Johor — Selat Johor — Pulau Ubin — Pulau Tekong Besar
Woodlands — Changi — Jurong — SINGAPORE — Sentosa
Singapore Strait
Main Strait
10 km

Economy

Overview: Singapore has an open
entrepreneurial economy with strong service
and manufacturing sectors and excellent
international trading links derived from its
entrepot history. The economy registered
nearly 10% growth in 1993 while stemming
inflation. The construction and financial
services industries and manufacturers of
computer-related components have led
economic growth. Rising labor costs continue
to be a threat to Singapore's competitiveness,
but there are indications that productivity is
keeping up. In applied technology, per capita
output, investment, and labor discipline,
Singapore has key attributes of a developed
country.
National product: GDP—purchasing power
equivalent—$42.4 billion (1993)
National product real growth rate: 9.9%
(1993)
National product per capita: $15,000 (1993
est.)
Inflation rate (consumer prices): 2.4%
(1993)

Unemployment rate: 2.7% (1993)
Budget:
revenues: $11.9 billion
expenditures: $10.5 billion, including capital
expenditures of $3.9 billion (1994 est.)
Exports: $61.5 billion (f.o.b., 1992)
commodities: computer equipment, rubber and
rubber products, petroleum products,
telecommunications equipment
partners: US 21%, Malaysia 12%, Hong Kong
8%, Japan 8%, Thailand 6% (1992)
Imports: $66.4 billion (f.o.b., 1992)
commodities: aircraft, petroleum, chemicals,
foodstuffs
partners: Japan 21%, US 16%, Malaysia 15%,
Saudi Arabia 5%, Taiwan 4%
External debt: $0; Singapore is a net creditor
Industrial production: growth rate 2.3%
(1992); accounts for 28% of GDP
Electricity:
capacity: 4,860,000 kW
production: 18 billion kWh
consumption per capita: 6,420 kWh (1992)
Industries: petroleum refining, electronics,
oil drilling equipment, rubber processing and
rubber products, processed food and
beverages, ship repair, entrepot trade, financial
services, biotechnology
Agriculture: occupies a position of minor
importance in the economy; self-sufficient in
poultry and eggs; must import much of other
food; major crops—rubber, copra, fruit,
vegetables
Illicit drugs: transit point for Golden Triangle
heroin going to the US, Western Europe, and
the Third World; also a major money-
laundering center
Economic aid:
recipient: US commitments, including Ex-Im
(FY70-83), $590 million; Western (non-US)
countries, ODA and OOF bilateral
commitments (1970-89), $1 billion
Currency: 1 Singapore dollar (S$) = 100
cents

Exchange rates: Singapore dollars (S$) per US$1—1.6032 (January 1994), 1.6158 (1993), 1.6290 (1992), 1.7276 (1991), 1.8125 (1990), 1.9503 (1989)
Fiscal year: 1 April—31 March

Communications

Railroads: 38 km of 1.000-meter gauge
Highways:
total: 2,644 km (1985)
paved: NA
unpaved: NA
Ports: Singapore
Merchant marine: 533 ships (1,000 GRT or over) totaling 10,656,067 GRT/17,009,400 DWT, passenger-cargo 1, cargo 125, container 80, roll-on/roll-off cargo 6, refrigerated cargo 3, vehicle carrier 20, livestock carrier 1, oil tanker 179, chemical tanker 14, combination ore/oil 8, specialized tanker 2, liquefied gas 4, bulk 87, combination bulk 3
note: many Singapore flag ships are foreign owned
Airports:
total: 10
usable: 10
with permanent-surface runways: 10
with runways over 3,659 m: 2
with runways 2,440-3,659 m: 4
with runways 1,220-2,439 m: 3
Telecommunications: good domestic facilities; good international service; good radio and television broadcast coverage; 1,110,000 telephones; broadcast stations—13 AM, 4 FM, 2 TV; submarine cables extend to Malaysia (Sabah and Peninsular Malaysia), Indonesia, and the Philippines; satellite earth stations—1 Indian Ocean INTELSAT and 1 Pacific Ocean INTELSAT

Defense Forces

Branches: Army, Navy, Air Force, People's Defense Force, Police Force
Manpower availability: males age 15-49 857,824; fit for military service 630,055
Defense expenditures: exchange rate conversion—$2.7 billion, 6% of GDP (1993 est.)

Geography

Location: Southeastern Asia, between Malaysia and Indonesia
Map references: Asia, Southeast Asia, Standard Time Zones of the World
Area:
total area: 632.6 sq km
land area: 622.6 sq km
comparative area: slightly less than 3.5 times the size of Washington, DC
Land boundaries: 0 km
Coastline: 193 km
Maritime claims:
exclusive fishing zone: 12 nm
territorial sea: 3 nm
International disputes: two islands in dispute with Malaysia
Climate: tropical; hot, humid, rainy; no pronounced rainy or dry seasons; thunderstorms occur on 40% of all days (67% of days in April)
Terrain: lowland; gently undulating central plateau contains water catchment area and nature preserve
Natural resources: fish, deepwater ports
Land use:
arable land: 4%
permanent crops: 7%
meadows and pastures: 0%
forest and woodland: 5%
other: 84%
Irrigated land: NA sq km
Environment:
current issues: industrial pollution; limited water supply; limited land availability presents waste disposal problems
natural hazards: NA
international agreements: party to— Endangered Species, Nuclear Test Ban, Ozone Layer Protection, Ship Pollution; signed, but not ratified—Biodiversity, Climate Change, Law of the Sea
Note: focal point for Southeast Asian sea routes

People

Population: 2,859,142 (July 1994 est.)

Population growth rate: 1.12% (1994 est.)
Birth rate: 16.52 births/1,000 population (1994 est.)
Death rate: 5.3 deaths/1,000 population (1994 est.)
Net migration rate: 0 migrant(s)/1,000 population (1994 est.)
Infant mortality rate: 5.7 deaths/1,000 live births (1994 est.)
Life expectancy at birth:
total population: 75.95 years
male: 73.17 years
female: 78.94 years (1994 est.)
Total fertility rate: 1.88 children born/woman (1994 est.)
Nationality:
noun: Singaporean(s)
adjective: Singapore
Ethnic divisions: Chinese 76.4%, Malay 14.9%, Indian 6.4%, other 2.3%
Religions: Buddhist (Chinese), Muslim (Malays), Christian, Hindu, Sikh, Taoist, Confucianist
Languages: Chinese (official), Malay (official and national), Tamil (official), English (official)
Literacy: age 15 and over can read and write (1990 est.)
total population: 88%
male: 93%
female: 84%
Labor force: 1,485,800
by occupation: financial, business, and other services 30.2%, manufacturing 28.4%, commerce 22.0%, construction 9.0%, other 10.4% (1990)

Government

Names:
conventional long form: Republic of Singapore
conventional short form: Singapore
Digraph: SN
Type: republic within Commonwealth
Capital: Singapore
Administrative divisions: none
Independence: 9 August 1965 (from Malaysia)

National holiday: National Day, 9 August (1965)
Constitution: 3 June 1959, amended 1965; based on preindependence State of Singapore Constitution
Legal system: based on English common law; has not accepted compulsory ICJ jurisdiction
Suffrage: 20 years of age; universal and compulsory
Executive branch:
chief of state: President ONG Teng Cheong (since 1 September 1993) election last held 28 August 1993 (next to be held NA August 1997); results—President ONG was elected with 59% of the vote in the country's first popular election for president
head of government: Prime Minister GOH Chok Tong (since 28 November 1990); Deputy Prime Minister LEE Hsien Loong (since 28 November 1990)
cabinet: Cabinet; appointed by the president, responsible to parliament
Legislative branch: unicameral
Parliament: elections last held 31 August 1991 (next to be held 31 August 1996); results—percent of vote by party NA; seats—(81 total) PAP 77, SDP 3, WP 1
Judicial branch: Supreme Court
Political parties and leaders:
government: People's Action Party (PAP), GOH Chok Tong, secretary general
opposition: Workers' Party (WP), J. B. JEYARETNAM; Singapore Democratic Party (SDP), CHIAM See Tong; National Solidarity Party (NSP), leader NA; Barisan Sosialis (BS, Socialist Front), leader NA
Member of: APEC, AsDB, ASEAN, C, CCC, COCOM (cooperating), CP, ESCAP, G-77, GATT, IAEA, IBRD, ICAO, ICC, ICFTU, IFC, ILO, IMF, IMO, INMARSAT, INTELSAT, INTERPOL, IOC, ISO, ITU, LORCS, NAM, UN, UNAVEM II, UNCTAD, UNIKOM, UNTAC, UPU, WHO, WIPO, WMO
Diplomatic representation in US:
chief of mission: Ambassador Sellapan Rama NATHAN
chancery: 1824 R Street NW, Washington, DC 20009

telephone: (202) 667-7555
FAX: (202) 265-7915
US diplomatic representation:
chief of mission: (vacant)
embassy: 30 Hill Street, Singapore 0617
mailing address: FPO AP 96534
telephone: [65] 338-0251
FAX: [65] 338-5010
Flag: two equal horizontal bands of red (top) and white; near the hoist side of the red band, there is a vertical, white crescent (closed portion is toward the hoist side) partially enclosing five white five-pointed stars arranged in a circle

---

U.S. Government Contacts:

U.S. Trade Desk: (202) 482-3877

American Embassy Commercial Section
One Colombo Court #05-12
Singapore 0617
FPO AP 96534
Tel: 65-338-9722
Fax: 65-338-5010

Singapore Government Contacts:

Embassy of Singapore Commercial Section
1824 R Street, N.W.
Washington, DC 20009
Tel: (202) 667-7555

Chambers of Commerce & Organizations:

American Business Council of Singapore
354 Orchard Road, #10-12 Shaw House
Singapore 0923
Tel: 65-235-0077
Fax: 65-732-5917

Legal Services:

Khattar Wong & Partners
80 Raffles Place #25-01
UOB Plaza 1
Singapore 0104
Tel: 65 535 6844

Fax: 65 534 4892
Leisure and Entertainment Industry, Joint Venture and Investments, Intellectual Property, Shipping Admiralty and Ship Financing.

Travel:

International Airlines to Country:
Northwest, United

International Hotels in Country:
Singapore:
Goodwood Park, Tel: 65-737-7411, Fax: 65-732-8558
Shangi-La, Tel: 65-737-3644, Fax: 65-733-7220
Sharaton Towers, Tel: 65-737-6888, Fax: 65-737-1072.

SOLOMON ISLANDS

South
Pacific
Ocean

400 km

Choiseul

Santa Isabel

Gizo

Malaita

HONIARA

Guadalcanal

San
Cristobal

Santa
Cruz
Islands

Coral Sea

Economy

Overview: The bulk of the population depend on subsistence agriculture, fishing, and forestry for at least part of their livelihood. Most manufactured goods and petroleum products must be imported. The islands are rich in undeveloped mineral resources such as lead, zinc, nickel, and gold. The economy suffered from a severe cyclone in mid-1986 that caused widespread damage to the infrastructure. In 1993, the government was working with the IMF to develop a structural adjustment program to address the country's fiscal deficit.
National product: GDP—purchasing power equivalent—$900 million (1991 est.)
National product real growth rate: 1.8% (1991 est.)
National product per capita: $2,500 (1991 est.)
Inflation rate (consumer prices): 13% (1992 est.)
Unemployment rate: NA%
Budget:
revenues: $48 million
expenditures: $107 million, including capital expenditures of $45 million (1991 est.)

Exports: $84 million (f.o.b., 1991)
commodities: fish 46%, timber 31%, palm oil 5%, cocoa, copra
partners: Japan 39%, UK 23%, Thailand 9%, Australia 5%, US 2% (1991)
Imports: $110 million (c.i.f., 1991)
commodities: plant and machinery manufactured goods, food and live animals, fuel
partners: Australia 34%, Japan 16%, Singapore 14%, NZ 9%
External debt: $128 million (1988 est.)
Industrial production: growth rate -3.8% (1991 est.); accounts for 5% of GDP
Electricity:
capacity: 21,000 kW
production: 39 million kWh
consumption per capita: 115 kWh (1990)
Industries: copra, fish (tuna)
Agriculture: including fishing and forestry, accounts for 31% of GDP; mostly subsistence farming; cash crops—cocoa, beans, coconuts, palm kernels, timber; other products—rice, potatoes, vegetables, fruit, cattle, pigs; not self-sufficient in food grains; 90% of the total fish catch of 44,500 metric tons was exported (1988)
Economic aid:
recipient: Western (non-US) countries, ODA and OOF bilateral commitments (1980-89), $250 million
Currency: 1 Solomon Islands dollar (SI$) = 100 cents
Exchange rates: Solomon Islands dollars (SI$) per US$1—3.2383 (November 1993), 2.9281 (1992), 2.7148 (1991), 2.5288 (1990), 2.2932 (1989)
Fiscal year: calendar year

Communications

Highways:
total: 1,300 km
paved: 30 km
unpaved: gravel 290 km; earth 980 km

note: in addition, there are 800 km of private logging and plantation roads of varied construction (1982)

Ports: Honiara, Ringi Cove

Airports:

total: 31

usable: 30

with permanent-surface runways: 2

with runways over 3,659 m: 0

with runways 2,440-3,659 m: 0

with runways 1,220-2,439 m: 4

Telecommunications: 3,000 telephones; broadcast stations—4 AM, no FM, no TV; 1 Pacific Ocean INTELSAT earth station

---

Defense Forces

Branches: Police Force

Defense expenditures: exchange rate conversion—$NA, NA% of GDP

Geography

Location: Oceania, Melanesia, just east of Papua New Guinea in the South Pacific Ocean

Map references: Oceania, Standard Time Zones of the World

Area:

total area: 28,450 sq km

land area: 27,540 sq km

comparative area: slightly larger than Maryland

Land boundaries: 0 km

Coastline: 5,313 km

Maritime claims: measured from claimed archipelagic baselines

exclusive economic zone: 200 nm

territorial sea: 12 nm

International disputes: none

Climate: tropical monsoon; few extremes of temperature and weather

Terrain: mostly rugged mountains with some low coral atolls

Natural resources: fish, forests, gold, bauxite, phosphates, lead, zinc, nickel

Land use:

arable land: 1%

permanent crops: 1%

meadows and pastures: 1%

forest and woodland: 93%

other: 4%

Irrigated land: NA sq km

Environment:

current issues: deforestation; soil erosion; limited arable land

natural hazards: subject to typhoons, but they are rarely destructive; geologically active region with frequent earth tremors

international agreements: party to—Environmental Modification, Marine Dumping, Marine Life Conservation, Ozone Layer Protection, Whaling; signed, but not ratified—Biodiversity, Climate Change, Law of the Sea

Note: located just east of Papua New Guinea in the South Pacific Ocean

---

People

Population: 385,811 (July 1994 est.)

Population growth rate: 3.43% (1994 est.)

Birth rate: 38.93 births/1,000 population (1994 est.)

Death rate: 4.63 deaths/1,000 population (1994 est.)

Net migration rate: 0 migrant(s)/1,000 population (1994 est.)

Infant mortality rate: 27.8 deaths/1,000 live births (1994 est.)

Life expectancy at birth:

total population: 70.48 years

male: 68.05 years

female: 73.03 years (1994 est.)

Total fertility rate: 5.73 children born/woman (1994 est.)

Nationality:

noun: Solomon Islander(s)

adjective: Solomon Islander

Ethnic divisions: Melanesian 93%, Polynesian 4%, Micronesian 1.5%, European 0.8%, Chinese 0.3%, other 0.4%

Religions: Anglican 34%, Roman Catholic 19%, Baptist 17%, United (Methodist/Presbyterian) 11%, Seventh-Day Adventist 10%, other Protestant 5%

Languages: Melanesian pidgin in much of the country is lingua franca, English spoken by 1%-2% of population

note: 120 indigenous languages
Literacy:
total population: NA%
male: NA%
female: NA%
Labor force: 23,448 economically active
by occupation: agriculture, forestry, and
fishing 32.4%, services 25%, construction,
manufacturing, and mining 7.0%, commerce,
transport, and finance 4.7% (1984)

Government

Names:
conventional long form: none
conventional short form: Solomon Islands
former: British Solomon Islands
Digraph: BP
Type: parliamentary democracy
Capital: Honiara
Administrative divisions: 7 provinces and 1
town*; Central, Guadalcanal, Honiara*, Isabel,
Makira, Malaita, Temotu, Western
Independence: 7 July 1978 (from UK)
National holiday: Independence Day, 7 July
(1978)
Constitution: 7 July 1978
Legal system: common law
Suffrage: 21 years of age; universal
Executive branch:
chief of state: Queen ELIZABETH II (since 6
February 1952), represented by Governor
General Sir George LEPPING (since 27 June
1989, previously acted as governor general
since 7 July 1988)
head of government: Prime Minister Francis
Billy HILLY (since June 1993); Deputy Prime
Minister Francis SAEMALA (since June 1993)
cabinet: Cabinet; appointed by the governor
general on advice of the prime minister from
members of parliament
Legislative branch: unicameral
National Parliament: elections last held NA
May 1993 (next to be held NA 1997); results—
percent of vote by party NA; seats—(47 total)
National Unity Group 21, PAP 8, National
Action Party 6, LP 4, UP 3, Christian
Fellowship 2, NFP 1, independents 2
Judicial branch: High Court

Political parties and leaders: People's
Alliance Party (PAP); United Party (UP),
leader NA; Solomon Islands Liberal Party
(SILP), Bartholemew ULUFA'ALU;
Nationalist Front for Progress (NFP), Andrew
NORI; Labor Party (LP), Joses TUHANUKU;
National Action Party, leader NA; Christian
Fellowship, leader NA; National Unity Group,
Solomon MAMALONI
Member of: ACP, AsDB, C, ESCAP, FAO,
G-77, IBRD, ICAO, IDA, IFAD, IFC, ILO,
IMF, IMO, INTELSAT (nonsignatory user),
IOC, ITU, LORCS, SPARTECA, SPC, SPF,
UN, UNCTAD, UNESCO, UPU, WFTU,
WHO, WMO
Diplomatic representation in US:
chief of mission: (vacant); ambassador
traditionally resides in Honiara (Solomon
Islands)
US diplomatic representation: embassy
closed July 1993; the ambassador to Papua
New Guinea is accredited to the Solomon
Islands
Flag: divided diagonally by a thin yellow
stripe from the lower hoist-side corner; the
upper triangle (hoist side) is blue with five
white five-pointed stars arranged in an X
pattern; the lower triangle is green

SOUTH KOREA

150 km

SEOUL
Inch'on
Wŏnju
Kangnŭng
Ullŭng-do
Yellow
Sea
Taejŏn
Sea of
Japan
Taegu
Kwangju
Ulsan
Pusan
Korea
Strait
Cheju-do

Boundary representation is
not necessarily authoritative.

Economy

Overview: The driving force behind the economy's dynamic growth has been the planned development of an export-oriented economy in a vigorously entrepreneurial society. Real GNP increased more than 10% annually between 1986 and 1991. This growth ultimately led to an overheated situation characterized by a tight labor market, strong inflationary pressures, and a rapidly rising current account deficit. As a result, in 1992, economic policy focused on slowing the growth rate of inflation and reducing the deficit. Annual growth slowed to 5%, still above the rate in most other countries of the world. Growth increased to 6.3% in 1993 as a result of fourth quarter manufacturing production growth of over 10% and is expected to be in the 8% range for 1994.
National product: GNP—purchasing power equivalent—$424 billion (1993 est.)
National product real growth rate: 6.3% (1993)
National product per capita: $9,500 (1993 est.)

Inflation rate (consumer prices): 4.8% (1993)
Unemployment rate: 2.6% (October 1993)
Budget:
revenues: $48.4 billion
expenditures: $48.4 billion, including capital expenditures of $NA (1993 est.)
Exports: $81 billion (f.o.b., 1993)
commodities: electronic and electrical equipment, machinery, steel, automobiles, ships, textiles, clothing, footwear, fish
partners: US 26%, Japan 17%, EC 14%
Imports: $78.9 billion (c.i.f., 1993)
commodities: machinery, electronics and electronic equipment, oil, steel, transport equipment, textiles, organic chemicals, grains
partners: Japan 26%, US 24%, EC 15%
External debt: $42 billion (1992)
Industrial production: growth rate 5.0% (1992 est.); accounts for about 45% of GNP
Electricity:
capacity: 27,016 kW (1993)
production: 105 billion kWh (1992)
consumption per capita: 2,380 kWh (1992)
Industries: electronics, automobile production, chemicals, shipbuilding, steel, textiles, clothing, footwear, food processing
Agriculture: accounts for 8% of GNP and employs 21% of work force (including fishing and forestry); principal crops—rice, root crops, barley, vegetables, fruit; livestock and livestock products—cattle, hogs, chickens, milk, eggs; self-sufficient in food, except for wheat; fish catch of 2.9 million metric tons, seventh-largest in world
Economic aid:
recipient: US commitments, including Ex-Im (FY70-89), $3.9 billion; non-US countries (1970-89), $3 billion
Currency: 1 South Korean won (W) = 100 chun (theoretical)
Exchange rates: South Korean won (W) per US$1—810.48 (January 1994), 802.68 (1993), 780.65 (1992), 733.35 (1991), 707.76 (1990), 671.46 (1989)

The Internationalist

Fiscal year: calendar year

Communications

Railroads: 3,091 km total (1991); 3,044 km 1.435 meter standard gauge, 47 km 0.610-meter narrow gauge, 847 km double track; 525 km electrified, government owned
Highways:
total: 63,201 km
paved: expressways 1,551 km
unpaved: NA
undifferentiated: national highway 12,190 km; provincial, local roads 49,460 km (1991)
Inland waterways: 1,609 km; use restricted to small native craft
Pipelines: petroleum products 455 km
Ports: Pusan, Inch'on, Kunsan, Mokp'o, Ulsan
Merchant marine: 417 ships (1,000 GRT or over) totaling 6,425,920 GRT/10,535,850 DWT, short-sea passenger 1, cargo 132, container 60, refrigerated cargo 11, vehicle carrier 9, oil tanker 47, chemical tanker 16, liquefied gas 13, combination ore/oil 2, bulk 123, combination bulk 2, multifunction large-load carrier 1
Airports:
total: 104
usable: 95
with permanent-surface runways: 61
with runways over 3,659 m: 0
with runways 2,440-3,659 m: 23
with runways 1,220-2,439 m: 18
Telecommunications: excellent domestic and international services; 13,276,449 telephone subscribers; broadcast stations—79 AM, 46 FM, 256 TV (57 of 1 kW or greater); satellite earth stations—2 Pacific Ocean INTELSAT and 1 Indian Ocean INTELSAT

Defense Forces

Branches: Army, Navy, Marine Corps, Air Force
Manpower availability: males age 15-49 13,435,598; fit for military service 8,623,325; reach military age (18) annually 417,055 (1994 est.)

Defense expenditures: exchange rate conversion—$12.2 billion, 3.6% of GNP (1993 est.)

Geography

Location: Eastern Asia, between North Korea and Japan
Map references: Asia, Standard Time Zones of the World
Area:
total area: 98,480 sq km
land area: 98,190 sq km
comparative area: slightly larger than Indiana
Land boundaries: total 238 km, North Korea 238 km
Coastline: 2,413 km
Maritime claims:
continental shelf: not specified
territorial sea: 12 nm; 3 nm in the Korea Strait
International disputes: Demarcation Line with North Korea; Liancourt Rocks claimed by Japan
Climate: temperate, with rainfall heavier in summer than winter
Terrain: mostly hills and mountains; wide coastal plains in west and south
Natural resources: coal, tungsten, graphite, molybdenum, lead, hydropower
Land use:
arable land: 21%
permanent crops: 1%
meadows and pastures: 1%
forest and woodland: 67%
other: 10%
Irrigated land: 13,530 sq km (1989)
Environment:
current issues: air pollution in large cities; water pollution from the discharge of sewage and industrial effluents
natural hazards: occasional typhoons bring high winds and floods; earthquakes in southwest
international agreements: party to—Antarctic Treaty, Climate Change, Environmental Modification, Hazardous Wastes, Nuclear Test Ban, Ozone Layer Protection, Ship Pollution, Tropical Timber, Whaling; signed, but not ratified—Antarctic-Environmental Protocol, Biodiversity, Law of the Sea

People

Population: 45,082,880 (July 1994 est.)
Population growth rate: 1.04% (1994 est.)
Birth rate: 15.7 births/1,000 population (1994 est.)
Death rate: 6.17 deaths/1,000 population (1994 est.)
Net migration rate: 0.91 migrant(s)/1,000 population (1994 est.)
Infant mortality rate: 21.7 deaths/1,000 live births (1994 est.)
Life expectancy at birth:
total population: 70.59 years
male: 67.39 years
female: 73.98 years (1994 est.)
Total fertility rate: 1.65 children born/woman (1994 est.)
Nationality:
noun: Korean(s)
adjective: Korean
Ethnic divisions: homogeneous (except for about 20,000 Chinese)
Religions: Christianity 48.6%, Buddhism 47.4%, Confucianism 3%, pervasive folk religion (shamanism), Chondogyo (Religion of the Heavenly Way) 0.2%
Languages: Korean, English widely taught in high school
Literacy: age 15 and over can read and write (1990 est.)
total population: 96%
male: 99%
female: 99%
Labor force: 20 million
by occupation: services and other 52%, mining and manufacturing 27%, agriculture, fishing, forestry 21% (1991)

Government

Names:
conventional long form: Republic of Korea
conventional short form: South Korea
local long form: Taehan-min'guk
local short form: none
Abbreviation: ROK
Digraph: KS
Type: republic

Capital: Seoul
Administrative divisions: 9 provinces (do, singular and plural) and 6 special cities* (jikhalsi, singular and plural); Cheju-do, Cholla-bukto, Cholla-namdo, Ch'ungch'ong-bukto, Ch'ungch'ong-namdo, Inch'on-jikhalsi*, Kangwon-do, Kwangju-jikhalsi*, Kyonggi-do, Kyongsang-bukto, Kyongsang-namdo, Pusan-jikhalsi*, Soul-t'ukpyolsi*, Taegu-jikhalsi*, Taejon-jikhalsi*
Independence: 15 August 1948
National holiday: Independence Day, 15 August (1948)
Constitution: 25 February 1988
Legal system: combines elements of continental European civil law systems, Anglo-American law, and Chinese classical thought
Suffrage: 20 years of age; universal
Executive branch:
chief of state: President KIM Yong-sam (since 25 February 1993); election last held on 18 December 1992 (next to be held NA December 1997); results—KIM Yong-sam (DLP) 41.9%, KIM Tae-chung (DP) 33.8%, CHONG Chu-yong (UPP) 16.3%, other 8%
head of government: Prime Minister YI Yong-tok (since 29 April 1994); Deputy Prime Minister CHONG Chae-sok (since 21 December 1993) and Deputy Prime Minister YI Hong-ku (since 30 April 1994)
cabinet: State Council; appointed by the president on the prime minister's recommendation
Legislative branch: unicameral
National Assembly (Kukhoe): elections last held on 24 March 1992; results—DLP 38.5%, DP 29.2%, Unification National Party (UNP) 17.3% (name later changed to UPP), other 15%; seats—(299 total) DLP 149, DP 97, UNP 31, other 22; the distribution of seats as of January 1994 was DLP 172, DP 96, UPP 11, other 20
note: the change in the distribution of seats reflects the fluidity of the current situation where party members are constantly switching from one party to another
Judicial branch: Supreme Court
Political parties and leaders:
majority party: Democratic Liberal Party

(DLP), KIM Yong-sam, president
opposition: Democratic Party (DP), YI
Ki-taek, executive chairman; United People's
Party (UPP), KIM Tong-kil, chairman; several
smaller parties
note: the DLP resulted from a merger of the
Democratic Justice Party (DJP), Reunification
Democratic Party (RDP), and New Democratic
Republican Party (NDRP) on 9 February 1990
Other political or pressure groups: Korean
National Council of Churches; National
Democratic Alliance of Korea; National
Federation of Student Associations; National
Federation of Farmers' Associations; National
Council of Labor Unions; Federation of
Korean Trade Unions; Korean Veterans'
Association; Federation of Korean Industries;
Korean Traders Association
Member of: AfDB, APEC, AsDB, CCC,
COCOM (cooperating), CP, EBRD, ESCAP,
FAO, G-77, GATT, IAEA, IBRD, ICAO, ICC,
ICFTU, IDA, IFAD, IFC, ILO, IMF, IMO,
INMARSAT, INTELSAT, INTERPOL, IOC,
IOM, ISO, ITU, LORCS, OAS (observer), UN,
UNCTAD, UNESCO, UNIDO, UNOSOM,
UPU, WHO, WIPO, WMO, WTO
Diplomatic representation in US:
chief of mission: Ambassador HAN Sung-su
chancery: 2450 Massachusetts Avenue NW,
Washington, DC 20008
telephone: (202) 939-5600
consulate(s) general: Agana (Guam),
Anchorage, Atlanta, Boston, Chicago,
Honolulu, Houston, Los Angeles, Miami, New
York, San Francisco, and Seattle
US diplomatic representation:
chief of mission: Ambassador James T.
LANEY
embassy: 82 Sejong-Ro, Chongro-ku, Seoul
mailing address: American Embassy, Unit
15550, Seoul; APO AP 96205-0001
telephone: [82] (2) 397-4000 through 4008 and
397-4114
FAX: [82] (2) 738-8845
consulate(s): Pusan
Flag: white with a red (top) and blue yin-yang
symbol in the center; there is a different black
trigram from the ancient I Ching (Book of
Changes) in each corner of the white field

U.S. Government Contacts:

U.S. Trade Desk: (202) 482-4390

American Embassy Commercial Section
82 Sejong-Ro, Chongro-ku
Seoul, Korea
APO AP 96205
Tel: 82-2-732-2601
Fax: 82-2-739-1628

Chambers of Commerce & Organizations:

American Chamber of Commerce in Korea
Room 307, Chosun Hotel
Seoul, Korea
Tel: (822) 753-6471/6516
Fax: (822) 755-6577

Legal Services

Myung Shin & Partners
12th Floor, Jindo Building
37, Dowha-Dong, Mapo-Gu
Seoul, Korea
Tel: 822 714-9922
Fax: 822 714-9933
*Industrial Property, Patent, Utility Model,
Design, Trademark, Unfair Competition and
Copyright Law.*

Travel:

International Airlines to Country:
Continental, Northwest, United

International Hotels in Country:
Seoul:
Seoul Hilton, Tel: 82 02 753 7788, Fax: 02
754 2510
Grand Hyatt Seoul, Tel: 82 2 797-1234, Fax:
82 2 798-6953

SRI LANKA

Economy

Overview: Industry—dominated by the fast-growing apparel industry—has surpassed agriculture as the main source of export earnings and accounts for over 16% of GDP. The economy has been plagued by high rates of unemployment since the late 1970s. Economic growth, which has been depressed by ethnic unrest, accelerated in 1991-93 as domestic conditions began to improve and conditions for foreign investment brightened.

National product: GDP—purchasing power equivalent—$53.5 billion (1993 est.)

National product real growth rate: 5% (1993 est.)

National product per capita: $3,000 (1993 est.)

Inflation rate (consumer prices): 11.6% (1992)

Unemployment rate: 15% (1991 est.)

Budget:
revenues: $2.3 billion
expenditures: $3.6 billion, including capital expenditures of $1.5 billion (1993)

Exports: $2.3 billion (f.o.b., 1992)
commodities: garments and textiles, teas, gems, petroleum products, coconuts, rubber, other agricultural products, marine products, graphite
partners: US 33.4%, Germany, UK, Netherlands, Japan, France, Singapore (1992)

Imports: $3 billion (c.i.f., 1992)
commodities: food and beverages, textiles and textile materials, petroleum and petroleum products, machinery and equipment
partners: Japan, India, US 4.3%, UK, Singapore, Germany, Hong King, Taiwan, South Korea (1991)

External debt: $5.2 billion (1991)

Industrial production: growth rate 7% (1991 est.); accounts for 16.5% of GDP

Electricity:
capacity: 1,300,000 kW
production: 3.6 billion kWh
consumption per capita: 200 kWh (1992)

Industries: processing of rubber, tea, coconuts, and other agricultural commodities; clothing, cement, petroleum refining, textiles, tobacco

Agriculture: accounts for one-fourth of GDP and nearly half of labor force; most important staple crop is paddy rice; other field crops—sugarcane, grains, pulses, oilseeds, roots, spices; cash crops—tea, rubber, coconuts; animal products—milk, eggs, hides, meat; not self-sufficient in rice production

Economic aid:
recipient: US commitments, including Ex-Im (FY70-89), $1 billion; Western (non-US) countries, ODA and OOF bilateral commitments (1980-89), $5.1 billion; OPEC bilateral aid (1979-89), $169 million; Communist countries (1970-89), $369 million

Currency: 1 Sri Lankan rupee (SLRe) = 100 cents

Exchange rates: Sri Lankan rupees (SLRes) per US$1—49.672 (January 1994), 48.322 (1993), 43.687 (1992), 41.372 (1991), 40.063 (1990), 36.047 (1989)

Fiscal year: calendar year

Communications

Railroads: 1,948 km total (1990); all 1.868-meter broad gauge; 102 km double track; no electrification; government owned

Highways:
total: 75,263 km
paved: mostly bituminous treated 27,637 km
unpaved: crushed stone, gravel 32,887 km; improved, unimproved earth 14,739 km

Inland waterways: 430 km; navigable by shallow-draft craft

Pipelines: crude oil and petroleum products 62 km (1987)

Ports: Colombo, Trincomalee

Merchant marine: 26 ships (1,000 GRT or over) totaling 289,115 GRT/453,609 DWT, cargo 12, refrigerated cargo 8, container 1, oil tanker 3, bulk 2

Airports:
total: 14
usable: 13
with permanent-surface runways: 12
with runways over 3,659 m: 0
with runways 2,440-3,659 m: 1
with runways 1,220-2,439 m: 8

Telecommunications: very inadequate domestic service, good international service; 114,000 telephones (1982); broadcast stations—12 AM, 5 FM, 5 TV; submarine cables extend to Indonesia and Djibouti; 2 Indian Ocean INTELSAT earth stations

Defense Forces

Branches: Army, Navy, Air Force, Police Force

Manpower availability: males age 15-49 4,906,666; fit for military service 3,825,774; reach military age (18) annually 178,213 (1994 est.)

Defense expenditures: exchange rate conversion—$365 million, 4.7% of GDP (1992)

Geography

Location: Southern Asia, 29 km southeast of India across the Palk Strait in the Indian Ocean

Map references: Asia, Standard Time Zones of the World

Area:
total area: 65,610 sq km
land area: 64,740 sq km
comparative area: slightly larger than West Virginia

Land boundaries: 0 km

Coastline: 1,340 km

Maritime claims:
contiguous zone: 24 nm
continental shelf: 200 nm or the edge of continental margin
exclusive economic zone: 200 nm
territorial sea: 12 nm

International disputes: none

Climate: tropical monsoon; northeast monsoon (December to March); southwest monsoon (June to October)

Terrain: mostly low, flat to rolling plain; mountains in south-central interior

Natural resources: limestone, graphite, mineral sands, gems, phosphates, clay

Land use:
arable land: 16%
permanent crops: 17%
meadows and pastures: 7%
forest and woodland: 37%
other: 23%

Irrigated land: 5,600 sq km (1989 est.)

Environment:
current issues: deforestation; soil erosion; wildlife populations threatened by poaching; coastal degradation from mining activities and increased pollution; freshwater resources being polluted by industrial wastes and sewage runoff
natural hazards: occasional cyclones and tornadoes
international agreements: party to—Biodiversity, Climate Change, Endangered Species, Environmental Modification, Hazardous Wastes, Nuclear Test Ban, Ozone Layer Protection, Wetlands; signed, but not ratified—Law of the Sea, Marine Life Conservation

Note: strategic location near major Indian Ocean sea lanes

People

Population: 18,129,850 (July 1994 est.)
note: since the outbreak of hostilities between the government and armed Tamil separatists in the mid-1980s, several hundred thousand Tamil civilians have fled the island; as of late 1992, nearly 115,000 were housed in refugee camps in south India, another 95,000 lived outside the Indian camps, and more than 200,000 Tamils have sought political asylum in the West
Population growth rate: 1.18% (1994 est.)
Birth rate: 18.51 births/1,000 population (1994 est.)
Death rate: 5.77 deaths/1,000 population (1994 est.)
Net migration rate: -0.91 migrant(s)/1,000 population (1994 est.)
Infant mortality rate: 21.9 deaths/1,000 live births (1994 est.)
Life expectancy at birth:
total population: 71.9 years
male: 69.37 years
female: 74.55 years (1994 est.)
Total fertility rate: 2.12 children born/woman (1994 est.)
Nationality:
noun: Sri Lankan(s)
adjective: Sri Lankan
Ethnic divisions: Sinhalese 74%, Tamil 18%, Moor 7%, Burgher, Malay, and Vedda 1%
Religions: Buddhist 69%, Hindu 15%, Christian 8%, Muslim 8%
Languages: Sinhala (official and national language) 74%, Tamil (national language) 18%
note: English is commonly used in government and is spoken by about 10% of the population
Literacy: age 15 and over can read and write (1990 est.)
total population: 88%
male: 93%
female: 84%
Labor force: 6.6 million
by occupation: agriculture 45.9%, mining and manufacturing 13.3%, trade and transport 12.4%, services and other 28.4% (1985 est.)

Government

Names:
conventional long form: Democratic Socialist Republic of Sri Lanka
conventional short form: Sri Lanka
former: Ceylon
Digraph: CE
Type: republic
Capital: Colombo
Administrative divisions: 8 provinces; Central, North Central, North Eastern, North Western, Sabaragamuwa, Southern, Uva, Western
Independence: 4 February 1948 (from UK)
National holiday: Independence and National Day, 4 February (1948)
Constitution: adopted 16 August 1978
Legal system: a highly complex mixture of English common law, Roman-Dutch, Muslim, Sinhalese, and customary law; has not accepted compulsory ICJ jurisdiction
Suffrage: 18 years of age; universal
Executive branch:
chief of state and head of government: President Dingiri Banda WIJETUNGA (since 7 May 1993); election last held 19 December 1988 (next to be held NA December 1994); results—Ranasinghe PREMADASA (UNP) 50%, Sirimavo BANDARANAIKE (SLFP) 45%, other 5%; note—following the assassination of President PREMADASA on 1 May 1993, Prime Minister WIJETUNGA became acting president; on 7 May 1993, he was confirmed by a vote of Parliament to finish out the term of the assassinated president
cabinet: Cabinet; appointed by the president in consultation with the prime minister
Legislative branch: unicameral
Parliament: elections last held 15 February 1989 (next to be held by NA February 1995); results—UNP 51%, SLFP 32%, SLMC 4%, TULF 3%, USA 3%, EROS 3%, MEP 1%, other 3%; seats—(225 total) UNP 125, SLFP 67, other 33
Judicial branch: Supreme Court
Political parties and leaders: United National Party (UNP), Dingiri Banda WIJETUNGA; Sri Lanka Freedom Party (SLFP), Sirimavo BANDARANAIKE; Sri

Lanka Muslim Congress (SLMC), M. H. M. ASHRAFF; All Ceylon Tamil Congress (ACTC), C. G. Kumar PONNAMBALAM; People's United Front (MEP, or Mahajana Eksath Peramuna), Dinesh GUNAWARDENE; Tamil United Liberation Front (TULF), M. SIVASITHAMBARAM; New Socialist Party (NSSP, or Nava Sama Samaja Party), Vasudeva NANAYAKKARA; Lanka Socialist Party/Trotskyite (LSSP, or Lanka Sama Samaja Party), Colin R. DE SILVA; Sri Lanka People's Party (SLMP, or Sri Lanka Mahajana Party), Ossie ABEYGUNASEKERA; Communist Party, K. P. SILVA; Communist Party/Beijing (CP/B), N. SHANMUGATHASAN; Democratic United National Front (DUNF), G. M. PREMACHANDRA; Eelam People's Democratic Party (EPDP), Douglas DEVANANDA; Tamil Eelam Liberation Organization (TELO), leader NA; Eelam People's Revolutionary Liberation Front (EPRL), Suresh PREMACHANDRAN; Eelam Revolutionary Organization of Students (EROS), Shankar RAJI; People's Liberation Organization of Tamil Eelam (PLOTE), Dharmalingam SIDARTHAN; Liberal Party (LP), Chanaka AMARATUNGA; Ceylon Workers Congress (CLDC), S. THONDAMAN; several ethnic Tamil and Muslim parties, represented in either parliament or provincial councils
note: the United Socialist Alliance (USA), which was formed in 1987 and included the NSSP, LSSP, SLMP, CP/M, and CP/B, was defunct as of 1993, following the formation of the People's Alliance Party (PEP)
Other political or pressure groups: Liberation Tigers of Tamil Eelam (LTTE) and other smaller Tamil separatist groups; other radical chauvinist Sinhalese groups; Buddhist clergy; Sinhalese Buddhist lay groups; labor unions
Member of: AsDB, C, CCC, CP, ESCAP, FAO, G-24, G-77, GATT, IAEA, IBRD, ICAO, ICC, ICFTU, IDA, IFAD, IFC, ILO, IMF, IMO, INMARSAT, INTELSAT, INTERPOL, IOC, IOM, ISO, ITU, LORCS, NAM, PCA, SAARC, UN, UNCTAD, UNESCO, UNIDO, UPU, WCL, WFTU, WHO, WIPO, WMO, WTO
Diplomatic representation in US:
chief of mission: Ambassador Ananda W.P. GURUGE
chancery: 2148 Wyoming Avenue NW, Washington, DC 20008
telephone: (202) 483-4025 through 4028
FAX: (202) 232-7181
consulate(s): New York
US diplomatic representation:
chief of mission: Ambassador Teresita C. SCHAFFER
embassy: 210 Galle Road, Colombo 3
mailing address: P. O. Box 106, Colombo
telephone: [94] (1) 44-80-07
FAX: [94] (1) 57-42-64
Flag: yellow with two panels; the smaller hoist-side panel has two equal vertical bands of green (hoist side) and orange; the other panel is a large dark red rectangle with a yellow lion holding a sword, and there is a yellow bo leaf in each corner; the yellow field appears as a border that goes around the entire flag and extends between the two panels

---

U.S. Government Contacts:

U.S. Trade Desk: (202) 482-2954

Chambers of Commerce & Organizations:

American Chamber of Commerce of Sri Lanka
PO Box 1000, Lotus Road
Colombo Hilton, Third Floor
Colombo 1, Sri Lanka
Tel: (94) 1-54-4644 Ext. 2318
Fax: (94) 1-437-165

Travel:

International Hotels in Country:
Colombo:
Colombo Hilton, Tel: 94 01 544644/437177, Fax: 01 544657/8

TAIWAN

100 km

Chi-lung
Taipei
Taiwan Strait
Su-ao
Chang-hua
Hua-lien
Pescadores
Taiwan
Philippine Sea
Ma-kung
Tai-nan
Kao-hsiung
T'ai-tung

Quemoy and Matsu islands are not shown

Economy

Overview: Taiwan has a dynamic capitalist economy with considerable government guidance of investment and foreign trade and partial government ownership of some large banks and industrial firms. Real growth in GNP has averaged about 9% a year during the past three decades. Export growth has been even faster and has provided the impetus for industrialization. Agriculture contributes about 4% to GDP, down from 35% in 1952. Taiwan currently ranks as number 13 among major trading countries. Traditional labor-intensive industries are steadily being replaced with more capital- and technology-intensive industries. Taiwan has become a major investor in China, Thailand, Indonesia, the Philippines, Malaysia, and Vietnam. The tightening of labor markets has led to an influx of foreign workers, both legal and illegal.
National product: GDP—purchasing power equivalent—$224 billion (1993 est.)
National product real growth rate: 6% (1993 est.)
National product per capita: $10,600 (1993 est.)

Inflation rate (consumer prices): 3.2% (1993 est.)
Unemployment rate: 1.5% (1992 est.)
Budget:
revenues: $30.3 billion
expenditures: $30.1 billion, including capital expenditures of $NA (1991 est.)
Exports: $85 billion (f.o.b., 1993 est.)
commodities: electrical machinery 19.7%, electronic products 19.6%, textiles 10.9%, footwear 3.3%, foodstuffs 1.0%, plywood and wood products 0.9% (1993 est.)
partners: US 27.6%, Hong Kong 21.7%, EC countries 15.2%, Japan 10.5% (1993 est.)
Imports: $77.1 billion (c.i.f., 1993 est.)
commodities: machinery and equipment 15.7%, electronic products 15.6%, chemicals 9.8%, iron and steel 8.5%, crude oil 3.9%, foodstuffs 2.1% (1993 est.)
partners: Japan 30.1%, US 21.7%, EC countries 17.6% (1993 est.)
External debt: $620 million (1992 est.)
Industrial production: growth rate 3.6% (1993 est.); accounts for more than 40% of GDP
Electricity:
capacity: 18,382,000 kW
production: 98.5 billion kWh
consumption per capita: 4,718 kWh (1992)
Industries: electronics, textiles, chemicals, clothing, food processing, plywood, sugar milling, cement, shipbuilding, petroleum refining
Agriculture: accounts for 4% of GNP and 16% of labor force (includes part-time farmers); heavily subsidized sector; major crops—vegetables, rice, fruit, tea; livestock—hogs, poultry, beef, milk; not self-sufficient in wheat, soybeans, corn; fish catch increasing, reached 1.4 million metric tons in 1988
Illicit drugs: an important heroin transit point; also a major drug money laundering center
Economic aid:
recipient: US, including Ex-Im (FY46-82),

$4.6 billion; Western (non-US) countries, ODA and OOF bilateral commitments (1970-89), $500 million
Currency: 1 New Taiwan dollar (NT$) = 100 cents
Exchange rates: New Taiwan dollars per US$1—26.6 (1993), 25.4 (1992), 25.748 (1991), 27.108 (1990), 26.407 (1989)
Fiscal year: 1 July—30 June

Communications

Railroads: about 4,600 km total track with 1,075 km common carrier lines and 3,525 km industrial lines; common carrier lines consist of the 1.067-meter gauge 708 km West Line and the 367 km East Line; a 98.25 km South Link Line connection was completed in late 1991; common carrier lines owned by the government and operated by the Railway Administration under Ministry of Communications; industrial lines owned and operated by government enterprises
Highways:
total: 20,041 km
paved: bituminous, concrete pavement 17,095 km
unpaved: crushed stone, gravel 2,371 km; graded earth 575 km
Pipelines: petroleum products 615 km, natural gas 97 km
Ports: Kao-hsiung, Chi-lung (Keelung), Hua-lien, Su-ao, T'ai-tung
Merchant marine: 212 ships (1,000 GRT or over) totaling 5,910,453 GRT/9,098,315 DWT, passenger-cargo 1, cargo 38, refrigerated cargo 11, container 85, oil tanker 17, combination ore/oil 2, bulk 54, roll-on/roll-off cargo 1, combination bulk 2, chemical tanker 1
Airports:
total: 40
usable: 38
with permanent-surface runways: 36
with runways over 3,659 m: 3
with runways 2,440-3,659 m: 16
with runways 1,220-2,439 m: 7
Telecommunications: best developed system in Asia outside of Japan; 7,800,000 telephones; extensive microwave radio relay links on east and west coasts; broadcast stations—91 AM, 23 FM, 15 TV (13 repeaters); 8,620,000 radios; 6,386,000 TVs (5,680,000 color, 706,000 monochrome); satellite earth stations—1 Pacific Ocean INTELSAT and 1 Indian Ocean INTELSAT; submarine cable links to Japan (Okinawa), Philippines, Guam, Singapore, Hong Kong, Indonesia, Australia, Middle East, and Western Europe

Defense Forces

Branches: General Staff, Ministry of National Defense, Army, Navy (including Marines), Air Force, Coastal Patrol and Defense Command, Armed Forces Reserve Command, Military Police Command
Manpower availability: males age 15-49 6,205,707; fit for military service 4,806,456; reach military age (19) annually 192,083 (1994 est.)
Defense expenditures: exchange rate conversion—$10.9 billion, 5.4% of GNP (FY93/94 est.)

Geography

Location: Eastern Asia, off the southeastern coast of China, between Japan and the Philippines
Map references: Asia, Oceania, Southeast Asia
Area:
total area: 35,980 sq km
land area: 32,260 sq km
comparative area: slightly larger than Maryland and Delaware combined
note: includes the Pescadores, Matsu, and Quemoy
Land boundaries: 0 km
Coastline: 1,448 km
Maritime claims:
exclusive economic zone: 200 nm
territorial sea: 12 nm
International disputes: involved in complex dispute over the Spratly Islands with China, Malaysia, Philippines, Vietnam, and possibly Brunei; Paracel Islands occupied by China, but

claimed by Vietnam and Taiwan; Japanese-administered Senkaku-shoto (Senkaku Islands/ Diaoyu Tai) claimed by China and Taiwan

Climate: tropical; marine; rainy season during southwest monsoon (June to August); cloudiness is persistent and extensive all year

Terrain: eastern two-thirds mostly rugged mountains; flat to gently rolling plains in west

Natural resources: small deposits of coal, natural gas, limestone, marble, and asbestos

Land use:
arable land: 24%
permanent crops: 1%
meadows and pastures: 5%
forest and woodland: 55%
other: 15%

Irrigated land: NA sq km

Environment:
current issues: water pollution from industrial emissions, untreated sewage; air pollution; contamination of drinking water supplies
natural hazards: subject to earthquakes and typhoons
international agreements: signed, but not ratified—Marine Life Conservation

People

Population: 21,298,930 (July 1994 est.)
Population growth rate: 0.96% (1994 est.)
Birth rate: 15.6 births/1,000 population (1994 est.)
Death rate: 5.63 deaths/1,000 population (1994 est.)
Net migration rate: -0.38 migrant(s)/1,000 population (1994 est.)
Infant mortality rate: 5.7 deaths/1,000 live births (1994 est.)
Life expectancy at birth:
total population: 75.25 years
male: 72.01 years
female: 78.66 years (1994 est.)
Total fertility rate: 1.81 children born/ woman (1994 est.)
Nationality:
noun: Chinese (singular and plural)
adjective: Chinese
Ethnic divisions: Taiwanese 84%, mainland Chinese 14%, aborigine 2%

Religions: mixture of Buddhist, Confucian, and Taoist 93%, Christian 4.5%, other 2.5%
Languages: Mandarin Chinese (official), Taiwanese (Min), Hakka dialects
Literacy: age 15 and over can read and write (1980)
total population: 86%
male: 93%
female: 79%
Labor force: 7.9 million
by occupation: industry and commerce 53%, services 22%, agriculture 15.6%, civil administration 7% (1989)

Administration

Names:
conventional long form: none
conventional short form: Taiwan
local long form: none
local short form: T'ai-wan
Digraph: TW
Type: multiparty democratic regime; opposition political parties legalized in March, 1989
Capital: Taipei
Administrative divisions: some of the ruling party in Taipei claim to be the government of all China; in keeping with that claim, the central administrative divisions include 2 provinces (sheng, singular and plural) and 2 municipalities* (shih, singular and plural)— Fu-chien (some 20 offshore islands of Fujian Province including Quemoy and Matsu), Kao-hsiung*, T'ai-pei*, and Taiwan (the island of Taiwan and the Pescadores islands); the more commonly referenced administrative divisions are those of Taiwan Province—16 counties (hsien, singular and plural), 5 municipalities* (shih, singular and plural), and 2 special municipalities** (chuan-shih, singular and plural); Chang-hua, Chia-i, Chia-i*, Chi-lung*, Hsin-chu, Hsin-chu*, Hua-lien, I-lan, Kao-hsiung, Kao-hsiung**, Miao-li, Nan-t'ou, P'eng-hu, P'ing-tung, T'ai-chung, T'ai-chung*, T'ai-nan, T'ai-nan*, T'ai-pei, T'ai-pei**, T'ai-tung, T'ao-yuan, and Yun-lin; the provincial capital is at Chung-hsing-hsin-ts'un
note: Taiwan uses the Wade-Giles system for romanization

National holiday: National Day, 10 October (1911) (Anniversary of the Revolution)
Constitution: 1 January 1947, amended in 1992, presently undergoing revision
Legal system: based on civil law system; accepts compulsory ICJ jurisdiction, with reservations
Suffrage: 20 years of age; universal
Executive branch:
chief of state: President LI Teng-hui (since 13 January 1988); Vice President LI Yuan-zu (since 20 May 1990)
head of government: Premier (President of the Executive Yuan) LIEN Chan (since 23 February 1993); Vice Premier (Vice President of the Executive Yuan) HSU Li-teh (since 23 February 1993) presidential election last held 21 March 1990 (next to be held NA March 1996); results—President LI Teng-hui was reelected by the National Assembly; vice presidential election last held 21 March 1990 (next election will probably be a direct popular election and will be held NA March 1996); results—LI Yuan-zu was elected by the National Assembly
cabinet: Executive Yuan; appointed by the president
Legislative branch: unicameral Legislative Yuan and unicameral National Assembly
Legislative Yuan: elections last held 19 December 1992 (next to be held near the end of 1995); results—KMT 60%, DPP 31%, independents 9%; seats—(304 total, 161 elected) KMT 96, DPP 50, independents 15
National Assembly: elections—first National Assembly elected in November 1946 with a supplementary election in December 1986; second and present National Assembly elected in December 1991; seats—(403 total) KMT 318, DPP 75, other 10; (next election to be held in 1997)
Judicial branch: Judicial Yuan
Political parties and leaders: Kuomintang (KMT, Nationalist Party), LI Teng-hui, chairman; Democratic Progressive Party (DPP); Chinese New Party (CNP); Labor Party (LP)
Other political or pressure groups: Taiwan independence movement, various environmental groups

note: debate on Taiwan independence has become acceptable within the mainstream of domestic politics on Taiwan; political liberalization and the increased representation of the opposition Democratic Progressive Party in Taiwan's legislature have opened public debate on the island's national identity; advocates of Taiwan independence, both within the DPP and the ruling Kuomintang, oppose the ruling party's traditional stand that the island will eventually unify with mainland China; the aims of the Taiwan independence movement include establishing a sovereign nation on Taiwan and entering the UN; other organizations supporting Taiwan independence include the World United Formosans for Independence and the Organization for Taiwan Nation Building
Member of: expelled from UN General Assembly and Security Council on 25 October 1971 and withdrew on same date from other charter-designated subsidiary organs; expelled from IMF/World Bank group April/May 1980; seeking to join GATT; attempting to retain membership in INTELSAT; suspended from IAEA in 1972, but still allows IAEA controls over extensive atomic development, APEC, AsDB, BCIE, ICC, IOC, COCOM (cooperating), WCL
Diplomatic representation in US: none; unofficial commercial and cultural relations with the people of the US are maintained through a private instrumentality, the Coordination Council for North American Affairs (CCNAA) with headquarters in Taipei and field offices in Washington and 10 other US cities
US diplomatic representation: unofficial commercial and cultural relations with the people of Taiwan are maintained through a private institution, the American Institute in Taiwan (AIT), which has offices in Taipei at #7, Lane 134, Hsin Yi Road, Section 3, telephone [886] (2) 709-2000, and in Kaohsiung at #2 Chung Cheng 3d Road, telephone [886] (7) 224-0154 through 0157, and the American Trade Center at Room 3207 International Trade Building, Taipei World Trade Center, 333 Keelung Road Section 1, Taipei 10548, telephone [886] (2) 720-1550

Flag: red with a dark blue rectangle in the upper hoist-side corner bearing a white sun with 12 triangular rays

U.S. Government Contacts:

U.S. Trade Desk: (202) 482-4390

Chambers of Commerce & Organizations:

American Chamber of Commerce in Taiwan
Rm 1012, Chia Hsin Building Annex
96 Chung Shan Road, Section 2
P.O. Box 17-277
Taipei, Taiwan
Tel: 866-2-551-2515
Fax: 886-2-542-3376

American Institue in Taiwan (AIT - WashDC)
1700 North Moore Street
17th Floor
Arlington, VA 22209
Tel: (703) 525-8474

American Institute in Taiwan (AIT - Taipei)
American Trade Center
Room 3207, International Trade Building
Taipei World Trade Center
333 Keelung Road Section 1
Taipei 10548, Taiwan
Tel: 886-2-720-1550
Fax: 886-2-757-7162

Coordination Council for North American Affairs Economic Division
4301 Connecticut Avenue, N.W.
Suite 420
Washington, DC 20008
Tel: (202) 686-6400

Legal Services:

Bennett Jones Verchere/Weston
Suite 1466, Asia Enterprise Centre
144 Min Chaun East Road, Section 3
Taipei, Taiwan
Tel: 8862 719-5008

Fax: 8862 717-6088
Energy and Natural Resources, Banking, Reulatory and Intellectual Properties, Corporate and Commercial.

Travel:

International Airlines to Country:
Continental, Northwest, United

International Hotels in Country:
Taipei:
Taipei Hilton, Tel: 886 02 311 5151, Fax: 02 331 9944
Grand Hyatt Taipei, Tel: 886 2 720-1234, Fax: 886 2 720-1111

THAILAND

Economy

Overview: Thailand's economy recovered rapidly from the political unrest in May 1992 to post an impressive 7.5% growth rate for the year and 7.8% in 1993. One of the more advanced developing countries in Asia, Thailand depends on exports of manufactures and the development of the service sector to fuel the country's rapid growth. The trade and current account deficits fell in 1992; much of Thailand's recent imports have been for capital equipment suggesting that the export sector is poised for further growth. With foreign investment slowing, Bangkok is working to increase the generation of domestic capital. Prime Minister CHUAN's government—Thailand's fifth government in less than two years—is pledged to continue Bangkok's probusiness policies, and the return of a democratically elected government has improved business confidence. Nevertheless, CHUAN must overcome divisions within his ruling coalition to complete much needed infrastructure development programs if Thailand is to remain an attractive place for business investment. Over the longer-term, Bangkok must produce more college graduates with technical training and upgrade workers' skills to continue its rapid economic development.

National product: GDP—purchasing power equivalent—$323 billion (1993 est.)

National product real growth rate: 7.8% (1993 est.)

National product per capita: $5,500 (1993 est.)

Inflation rate (consumer prices): 4.1% (1992 est.)

Unemployment rate: 3.1% (1992 est.)

Budget:

revenues: $21.36 billion

expenditures: $22.4 billion, including capital expenditures of $6.24 billion (1993 est.)

Exports: $28.4 billion (f.o.b., 1992)

commodities: machinery and manufactures 76.9%, agricultural products 14.9%, fisheries products 5.9% (1992)

partners: US 22%, Japan 18%, Singapore 8%, Hong Kong 5%, Germany 4%, Netherlands 4%, UK 4%, Malaysia, France, China (1992)

Imports: $37.6 billion (c.i.f., 1992)

commodities: capital goods 41.4%, intermediate goods and raw materials 32.8%, consumer goods 10.4%, oil 8.2%

partners: Japan 29.3%, US 11.4%, Singapore 7.6%, Taiwan 5.5%, Germany 5.4%, South Korea 4.6%, Malaysia 4.2%, China 3.3%, Hong Kong 3.3%, UK (1992)

External debt: $33.4 billion (1991)

Industrial production: growth rate 9% (1992); accounts for about 26% of GDP

Electricity:

capacity: 10,000,000 kW

production: 43.75 billion kWh

consumption per capita: 760 kWh (1992)

Industries: tourism is the largest source of foreign exchange; textiles and garments, agricultural processing, beverages, tobacco, cement, light manufacturing, such as jewelry; electric appliances and components, integrated circuits, furniture, plastics; world's second-largest tungsten producer and third-largest tin producer

Agriculture: accounts for 12% of GDP and 60% of labor force; leading producer and exporter of rice and cassava (tapioca); other crops—rubber, corn, sugarcane, coconuts, soybeans; except for wheat, self-sufficient in food

Illicit drugs: a minor producer of opium and marijuana; major illicit trafficker of heroin, particularly from Burma and Laos, for the international drug market; eradication efforts have reduced the area of cannabis cultivation and shifted some production to neighboring countries; opium poppy cultivation has been affected by eradication efforts; also a major drug money laundering center

Economic aid:
recipient: US commitments, including Ex-Im (FY70-89), $870 million; Western (non-US) countries, ODA and OOF bilateral commitments (1970-89), $8.6 billion; OPEC bilateral aid (1979-89), $19 million

Currency: 1 baht (B) = 100 satang

Exchange rates: baht (B) per US$1—25.446 (December 1993), 25.400 (1992), 25.517 (1991), 25.585 (1990), 25.702 (1989)

Fiscal year: 1 October-30 September

Communications

Railroads: 3,940 km 1.000-meter gauge, 99 km double track

Highways:
total: 77,697 km
paved: 35,855 km (including 88 km of expressways)
unpaved: gravel, other stabilization 14,092 km; earth 27,750 km (1988)

Inland waterways: 3,999 km principal waterways; 3,701 km with navigable depths of 0.9 m or more throughout the year; numerous minor waterways navigable by shallow-draft native craft

Pipelines: natural gas 350 km, petroleum products 67 km

Ports: Bangkok, Pattani, Phuket, Sattahip, Si Racha

Merchant marine: 198 ships (1,000 GRT or over) totaling 998,372 GRT/1,561,824 DWT, short-sea passenger 1, cargo 105, container 13, oil tanker 43, liquefied gas 9, chemical tanker 2, bulk 14, refrigerated cargo 6, combination bulk 2, passenger 1, roll-on/roll-off cargo 1, specialized tanker 1

Airports:
total: 105
usable: 96
with permanent-surface runways: 51
with runways over 3,659 m: 1
with runways 2,440-3,659 m: 14
with runways 1,220-2,439 m: 28

Telecommunications: service to general public inadequate; bulk of service to government activities provided by multichannel cable and microwave radio relay network; 739,500 telephones (1987); broadcast stations—over 200 AM, 100 FM, and 11 TV in government-controlled networks; satellite earth stations—1 Indian Ocean INTELSAT and 1 Pacific Ocean INTELSAT; domestic satellite system being developed

Defense Forces

Branches: Royal Thai Army, Royal Thai Navy (including Royal Thai Marine Corps), Royal Thai Air Force, Paramilitary Forces

Manpower availability: males age 15-49 16,982,226; fit for military service 10,312,744; reach military age (18) annually 599,240 (1994 est.)

Defense expenditures: exchange rate conversion—$2.6 billion, about 2% of GNP (FY92/93 est.)

Geography

Location: Southeastern Asia, bordering the Gulf of Thailand, between Burma and Cambodia

Map references: Asia, Southeast Asia, Standard Time Zones of the World

Area:
total area: 514,000 sq km
land area: 511,770 sq km
comparative area: slightly more than twice the size of Wyoming

Land boundaries: total 4,863 km, Burma 1,800 km, Cambodia 803 km, Laos 1,754 km, Malaysia 506 km

Coastline: 3,219 km
Maritime claims:
exclusive economic zone: 200 nm
territorial sea: 12 nm
International disputes: boundary dispute with Laos; unresolved maritime boundary with Vietnam; parts of border with Thailand in dispute; maritime boundary with Thailand not clearly defined
Climate: tropical; rainy, warm, cloudy southwest monsoon (mid-May to September); dry, cool northeast monsoon (November to mid-March); southern isthmus always hot and humid
Terrain: central plain; Khorat plateau in the east; mountains elsewhere
Natural resources: tin, rubber, natural gas, tungsten, tantalum, timber, lead, fish, gypsum, lignite, fluorite
Land use:
arable land: 34%
permanent crops: 4%
meadows and pastures: 1%
forest and woodland: 30%
other: 31%
Irrigated land: 42,300 sq km (1989 est.)
Environment:
current issues: air pollution increasing from vehicle emissions; water pollution from organic and factory wastes; deforestation; wildlife populations threatened by illegal hunting
natural hazards: land subsidence in Bangkok area resulting from the depletion of the water table
international agreements: party to—Endangered Species, Marine Life Conservaiton, Nuclear Test Ban, Ozone Layer Protection, Tropical Timber; signed, but not ratified—Biodiversity, Climate Change, Hazardous Wastes, Law of the Sea
Note: controls only land route from Asia to Malaysia and Singapore

People

Population: 59,510,471 (July 1994 est.)
Population growth rate: 1.3% (1994 est.)
Birth rate: 19.43 births/1,000 population (1994 est.)

Death rate: 6.41 deaths/1,000 population (1994 est.)
Net migration rate: 0 migrant(s)/1,000 population (1994 est.)
Infant mortality rate: 37.1 deaths/1,000 live births (1994 est.)
Life expectancy at birth:
total population: 68.35 years
male: 64.99 years
female: 71.87 years (1994 est.)
Total fertility rate: 2.1 children born/woman (1994 est.)
Nationality:
noun: Thai (singular and plural)
adjective: Thai
Ethnic divisions: Thai 75%, Chinese 14%, other 11%
Religions: Buddhism 95%, Muslim 3.8%, Christianity 0.5%, Hinduism 0.1%, other 0.6% (1991)
Languages: Thai, English the secondary language of the elite, ethnic and regional dialects
Literacy: age 15 and over can read and write (1990 est.)
total population: 93%
male: 96%
female: 90%
Labor force: 30.87 million
by occupation: agriculture 62%, industry 13%, commerce 11%, services (including government) 14% (1989 est.)

Government

Names:
conventional long form: Kingdom of Thailand
conventional short form: Thailand
Digraph: TH
Type: constitutional monarchy
Capital: Bangkok
Administrative divisions: 73 provinces (changwat, singular and plural); Ang Thong, Buriram, Chachoengsao, Chai Nat, Chaiyaphum, Chanthaburi, Chiang Mai, Chiang Rai, Chon Buri, Chumphon, Kalasin, Kamphaeng Phet, Kanchanaburi, Khon Kaen,

Krabi, Krung Thep Mahanakhon, Lampang, Lamphun, Loei, Lop Buri, Mae Hong Son, Maha Sarakham, Mukdahan, Nakhon Nayok, Nakhon Pathom, Nakhon Phanom, Nakhon Ratchasima, Nakhon Sawan, Nakhon Si Thammarat, Nan, Narathiwat, Nong Khai, Nonthaburi, Pathum Thani, Pattani, Phangnga, Phatthalung, Phayao, Phetchabun, Phetchaburi, Phichit, Phitsanulok, Phra Nakhon Si Ayutthaya, Phrae, Phuket, Prachin Buri, Prachuap Khiri Khan, Ranong, Ratchaburi, Rayong, Roi Et, Sakon Nakhon, Samut Prakan, Samut Sakhon, Samut Songkhram, Sara Buri, Satun, Sing Buri, Sisaket, Songkhla, Sukhothai, Suphan Buri, Surat Thani, Surin, Tak, Trang, Trat, Ubon Ratchathani, Udon Thani, Uthai Thani, Uttaradit, Yala, Yasothon

Independence: 1238 (traditional founding date; never colonized)

National holiday: Birthday of His Majesty the King, 5 December (1927)

Constitution: new constitution approved 7 December 1991; amended 10 June 1992

Legal system: based on civil law system, with influences of common law; has not accepted compulsory ICJ jurisdiction; martial law in effect since 23 February 1991 military coup

Suffrage: 21 years of age; universal

Executive branch:

chief of state: King PHUMIPHON Adunyadet (since 9 June 1946); Heir Apparent Crown Prince WACHIRALONGKON (born 28 July 1952)

head of government: Prime Minister CHUAN Likphai (since 23 September 1992)

cabinet: Council of Ministers

Privy Council: NA

Legislative branch: bicameral National Assembly (Rathasatha)

Senate (Vuthisatha): consists of a 270-member appointed body

House of Representatives(Saphaphoothan-Rajsadhorn): elections last held 13 September 1992 (next to be held by NA); results—percent of vote by party NA; seats—(360 total) DP 79, TNP 77, NDP 60, NAP 51, Phalang Tham 47, SAP 22, LDP 8, SP 8, Mass Party 4, Thai Citizen's Party 3, People's Party 1, People's Force Party 0

Judicial branch: Supreme Court (Sarndika)

Political parties and leaders: Democrat Party (DP), Chuan LIKPHAI; Thai Nation Pary (TNP or Chat Thai Party), Banhan SINLAPA-ACHA; National Development Party (NDP or Chat Phattana), Chatchai CHUNHAWAN; New Aspiration Party (NAP), Gen. Chawalit YONGCHAIYUT; Phalang Tham (Palang Dharma), Bunchu ROTCHANASATIEN; Social Action Party (SAP), Montri PHONGPHANIT; Liberal Democratic Party (LDP or Seri Tham), Athit URAIRAT; Solidarity Party (SP), Uthai PHIMCHAICHON; Mass Party (Muanchon), Pol. Cpt. Choem YUBAMRUNG; Thai Citizen's Party (Prachakon Thai), Samak SUNTHONWET; People's Party (Ratsadon), Chaiphak SIRIWAT; People's Force Party (Phalang Prachachon), Col. Sophon HANCHAREON

Member of: APEC, AsDB, ASEAN, CCC, CP, ESCAP, FAO, G-77, GATT, IAEA, IBRD, ICAO, ICFTU, IDA, IFAD, IFC, ILO, IMF, IMO, INTELSAT, INTERPOL, IOC, IOM, ISO, ITU, LORCS, NAM (observer), PCA, UN, UNCTAD, UNESCO, UNHCR, UNIDO, UNIKOM, UNTAC, UPU, WCL, WFTU, WHO, WIPO, WMO

Diplomatic representation in US:

chief of mission: Ambassador PHIRAPHONG Kasemsi

chancery: 2300 Kalorama Road NW, Washington, DC 20008

telephone: (202) 483-7200

FAX: (202) 234-4498

consulate(s) general: Chicago, Los Angeles, and New York

US diplomatic representation:

chief of mission: Ambassador David F. LAMBERTSON

embassy: 95 Wireless Road, Bangkok

mailing address: APO AP 96546

telephone: [66] (2) 252-5040

FAX: [66] (2) 254-2990

consulate(s) general: Chiang Mai

consulate(s): Udorn (Udon Thani)

Flag: five horizontal bands of red (top), white, blue (double width), white, and red

U.S. Trade Desk: (202) 482-3877

American Embassy Commercial Section
95 Wireless Road
Bangkok, Thailand
APO AP 96546
Tel: 66-2-253-4920
Fax: 66-2-255-9215

Thailand Government Contacts:

Embassy of Thailand Commercial Section
2300 Kalorama Road, N.W.
Washington, DC 20008
Tel: (202) 467-6790

Chambers of Commerce & Organizations:

American Chamber of Commerce in Thailand
7th Floor, Kian Gwan Building
140 Wireless Road
PO Box 11-1095
Bangkok, Thailand
Tel: 66-2-251-9266
Fax: 66-2-255-2454

Legal Services:

Boonsom & Manoch Interlaw Limited
Panawongse Building, 9th Floor
104 Surawongse Road
Bangkok 10500, Thailand
Tel: 662 2354625
Fax: 662 2369268
Mineral, Petroleum, Trials and Appeals, General Practice, Investment and International Business Law.

Ukrit Mongkolnavin Law Office
10 Sukhumvit 5
Bangkok 10110, Thailand
Tel: 662 255-4015
662 253 5529
Maritime and International Law, Trials and Appeals, Business Law, Patent and Trademarks, Securities and Investment Law, Commercial Arbitration.

Travel:

International Airlines to Country:
Northwest, United

International Hotels in Country:
Bangkok:
Dusit Thani, Tel: 66-2-233-1130, Fax: 66-2-800-223-5652
Oriental Hotel, Tel: 66-2-236-0400, Fax: 66-2-236-1939
Shangi-La Hotel, Tel: 66-2-236-7777, Fax: 66-2-236-8579/

VIETNAM

400 km

HANOI

Vinh — Gulf of Tonkin

Hue

Boundary representation is not necessarily authoritative.

South China Sea

Cam Ranh

Ho Chi Minh City

Gulf of Thailand — Can Tho

Con Dao

Economy

Overview: Vietnam has made significant progress in recent years moving away from the planned economic model toward a more effective market-based economic system. Most prices are now fully decontrolled, and the Vietnamese currency has been effectively devalued and floated at world market rates. In addition, the scope for private sector activity has been expanded, primarily through decollectivization of the agricultural sector and introduction of laws giving legal recognition to private business. Nearly three-quarters of export earnings are generated by only two commodities, rice and crude oil. Led by industry and construction, the economy did well in 1993 with output rising perhaps 7%. However, the industrial sector remains burdened by uncompetitive state-owned enterprises the government is unwilling or unable to privatize. Unemployment looms as a serious problem with roughly 25% of the workforce without jobs and with population growth swelling the ranks of the unemployed yearly.

National product: GNP—purchasing power equivalent—$72 billion (1993 est.)
National product real growth rate: 7% (1993 est.)
National product per capita: $1,000 (1993 est.)
Inflation rate (consumer prices): 5.2% (1993 est.)
Unemployment rate: 25% (1993 est.)
Budget:
revenues: $1.9 billion
expenditures: $2 billion, including capital expenditures of $NA (1992)
Exports: $2.6 billion (f.o.b., 1993 est.)
commodities: petroleum, rice, agricultural products, marine products, coffee
partners: Japan, Hong Kong, Thailand, Germany, Indonesia
Imports: $3.1 billion (f.o.b., 1993 est.)
commodities: petroleum products, steel products, railroad equipment, chemicals, medicines, raw cotton, fertilizer, grain
partners: Hong Kong, Japan, Indonesia, South Korea, Taiwan
External debt: $3.4 billion Western countries; $4.5 billion CEMA debts primarily to Russia; $700 million commercial debts (1993 est.)
Industrial production: growth rate 15% (1992); accounts for 20% of GDP
Electricity:
capacity: 3,300,000 kW
production: 9 billion kWh
consumption per capita: 130 kWh (1992)
Industries: food processing, textiles, machine building, mining, cement, chemical fertilizer, glass, tires, oil
Agriculture: accounts for almost 40% of GDP; paddy rice, corn, potatoes make up 50% of farm output; commercial crops (rubber, soybeans, coffee, tea, bananas) and animal products 50%; since 1989 self-sufficient in food staple rice; fish catch of 943,100 metric tons (1989 est.)
Illicit drugs: minor opium producer and secondary transit point for Southeast Asian

heroin destined for the US and Europe
Economic aid:
recipient: $1.9 billion in credits and grants pledged by international donors for 1994, Japan largest contributor with $550 million
Currency: 1 new dong (D) = 100 xu
Exchange rates: new dong (D) per US$1— 10,800 (November 1993), 8,100 (July 1991), 7,280 (December 1990), 3,996 (March 1990); note—1985-89 figures are end of year
Fiscal year: calendar year

Communications

Railroads: 3,059 km total; 2,454 1.000-meter gauge, 151 km 1.435-meter (standard) gauge, 230 km dual gauge (three rails), and 224 km not restored to service after war damage
Highways:
total: 85,000 km
paved: 9,400 km
unpaved: gravel, improved earth 48,700 km; unimproved earth 26,900 km
Inland waterways: 17,702 km navigable; more than 5,149 km navigable at all times by vessels up to 1.8 meter draft
Pipelines: petroleum products 150 km
Ports: Da Nang, Haiphong, Ho Chi Minh City
Merchant marine: 101 ships (1,000 GRT or over) totaling 460,225 GRT/741,231 DWT, cargo 86, refrigerated cargo 3, roll-on/roll-off cargo 1, oil tanker 8, bulk 3
Airports:
total: 100
usable: 100
with permanent-surface runways: 50
with runways over 3,659 m: 0
with runways 2,440-3,659 m: 10
with runways 1,220-2,439 m: 20
Telecommunications: the inadequacies of the obsolete switching equipment and cable system is a serious constraint on the business sector and on economic growth, and restricts access to the international links that Vietnam has established with most major countries; the telephone system is not generally available for private use (25 telephones for each 10,000 persons); 3 satellite earth stations; broadcast stations—NA AM, 288 FM; 36 (77 repeaters)

TV; about 2,500,000 TV receivers and 7,000,000 radio receivers in use (1991)

Defense Forces

Branches:
People's Army of Vietnam (PAVN) including: Ground, Navy (including Naval Infantry), Air Force
Manpower availability: males age 15-49 18,281,483; fit for military service 11,602,318; reach military age (17) annually 762,943 (1994 est.)
Defense expenditures: exchange rate conversion—$NA, NA% of GNP

Geography

Location: Southeastern Asia, bordering the South China Sea, between Laos and the Philippines
Map references: Asia, Southeast Asia, Standard Time Zones of the World
Area:
total area: 329,560 sq km
land area: 325,360 sq km
comparative area: slightly larger than New Mexico
Land boundaries: total 3,818 km, Cambodia 982 km, China 1,281 km, Laos 1,555 km
Coastline: 3,444 km (excludes islands)
Maritime claims:
contiguous zone: 24 nm
continental shelf: 200 nm or the edge of continental margin
exclusive economic zone: 200 nm
territorial sea: 12 nm
International disputes: maritime boundary with Cambodia not defined; involved in a complex dispute over the Spratly Islands with China, Malaysia, Philippines, Taiwan, and possibly Brunei; unresolved maritime boundary with Thailand; maritime boundary dispute with China in the Gulf of Tonkin; Paracel Islands occupied by China but claimed by Vietnam and Taiwan
Climate: tropical in south; monsoonal in north with hot, rainy season (mid-May to mid-September) and warm, dry season (mid-October to mid-March)

Terrain: low, flat delta in south and north; central highlands; hilly, mountainous in far north and northwest

Natural resources: phosphates, coal, manganese, bauxite, chromate, offshore oil deposits, forests

Land use:
arable land: 22%
permanent crops: 2%
meadows and pastures: 1%
forest and woodland: 40%
other: 35%

Irrigated land: 18,300 sq km (1989 est.)

Environment:
current issues: deforestation; soil degradation; water pollution and overfishing threatening marine life populations
natural hazards: occasional typhoons (May to January) with extensive flooding
international agreements: party to— Environmental Modification, Ozone Layer Protection, Ship Pollution, Wetlands; signed, but not ratified—Biodiversity, Climate Change, Endangered Species, Law of the Sea, Nuclear Test Ban

---

People

Population: 73,103,898 (July 1994 est.)
Population growth rate: 1.78% (1994 est.)
Birth rate: 27.13 births/1,000 population (1994 est.)
Death rate: 7.76 deaths/1,000 population (1994 est.)
Net migration rate: -1.53 migrant(s)/1,000 population (1994 est.)
Infant mortality rate: 45.5 deaths/1,000 live births (1994 est.)
Life expectancy at birth:
total population: 65.41 years
male: 63.37 years
female: 67.58 years (1994 est.)
Total fertility rate: 3.33 children born/ woman (1994 est.)
Nationality:
noun: Vietnamese (singular and plural)
adjective: Vietnamese
Ethnic divisions: Vietnamese 85-90%, Chinese 3%, Muong, Thai, Meo, Khmer, Man, Cham

Religions: Buddhist, Taoist, Roman Catholic, indigenous beliefs, Islamic, Protestant
Languages: Vietnamese (official), French, Chinese, English, Khmer, tribal languages (Mon-Khmer and Malayo-Polynesian)
Literacy: age 15 and over can read and write (1990)
total population: 88%
male: 93%
female: 83%
Labor force: 32.7 million
by occupation: agricultural 65%, industrial and service 35% (1990 est.)

Government

Names:
conventional long form: Socialist Republic of Vietnam
conventional short form: Vietnam
local long form: Cong Hoa Chu Nghia Viet Nam
local short form: Viet Nam
Abbreviation: SRV
Digraph: VM
Type: Communist state
Capital: Hanoi
Administrative divisions: 50 provinces (tinh, singular and plural), 3 municipalities* (thanh pho, singular and plural); An Giang, Ba Ria-Vung Tau, Bac Thai, Ben Tre, Binh Dinh, Binh Thuan, Can Tho, Cao Bang, Dac Lac, Dong Nai, Dong Thap, Gia Lai, Ha Bac, Ha Giang, Ha Noi*, Ha Tay, Ha Tinh, Hai Hung, Hai Phong*, Ho Chi Minh*, Hoa Binh, Khanh Hoa, Kien Giang, Kon Tum, Lai Chau, Lam Dong, Lang Son, Lao Cai, Long An, Minh Hai, Nam Ha, Nghe An, Ninh Binh, Ninh Thuan, Phu Yen, Quang Binh, Quang Nam-Da Nang, Quang Ngai, Quang Ninh, Quang Tri, Soc Trang, Son La, Song Be, Tay Ninh, Thai Binh, Thanh Hoa, Thua Thien, Tien Giang, Tra Vinh, Tuyen Quang, Vinh Long, Vinh Phu, Yen Bai
Independence: 2 September 1945 (from France)
National holiday: Independence Day, 2 September (1945)
Constitution: 15 April 1992
Legal system: based on Communist legal theory and French civil law system

Suffrage: 18 years of age; universal

Executive branch:

chief of state: President Le Duc ANH (since 23 September 1992)

head of government: Prime Minister Vo Van KIET (since 9 August 1991); First Deputy Prime Minister Phan Van KHAI (since 10 August 1991); Deputy Prime Minister Nguyen KHANH (since NA February 1987); Deputy Prime Minister Tran Duc LUONG (since NA February 1987)

cabinet: Cabinet; appointed by the president on proposal of the prime minister and ratification of the Assembly

Legislative branch: unicameral

National Assembly (Quoc-Hoi): elections last held 19 July 1992 (next to be held NA July 1997); results—VCP is the only party; seats— (395 total) VCP or VCP-approved 395

Judicial branch: Supreme People's Court

Political parties and leaders: only party— Vietnam Communist Party (VCP), DO MUOI, general secretary

Member of: ACCT, AsDB, ASEAN (observer), ESCAP, FAO, G-77, IAEA, IBRD, ICAO, IDA, IFAD, IFC, ILO, IMF, IMO, INTELSAT, INTERPOL, IOC, IOM (observer), ISO, ITU, LORCS, NAM, UN, UNCTAD, UNESCO, UNIDO, UPU, WCL, WFTU, WHO, WIPO, WMO, WTO

Diplomatic representation in US: none; Ambassador Le Van BANG is the Permanent Representative to the UN

US diplomatic representation: none

Flag: red with a large yellow five-pointed star in the center

---

U.S. Government Contacts:

U.S. Trade Desk: (202) 482-3877

Travel:

International Hotels in Country:
Saigon:
Continental, Tel: 84-8-994456
Rex (Ben Thanh) Hotel, Tel: 84-8-292185
Saigon Floating Hotel, Tel: 84-8-290783.

ADDENDA

Abbreviations & Definitions

avdp.	avoirdupois
c.i.f.	cost, insurance, and freight
CY	calendar year
DWT	deadweight ton
est.	estimate
Ex-Im	Export-Import Bank of the United States
f.o.b.	free on board
FRG	Federal Republic of Germany (West Germany); used for information dated before 3 October 1990 or CY91
FSU	former Soviet Union
FY	fiscal year
FYROM	The Former Yugoslav Republic of Macedonia
GDP	gross domestic product
GDR	German Democratic Republic (East Germany); used for information dated before 3 October 1990 or CY91
GNP	gross national product
GRT	gross register ton
GWP	gross world product
km	kilometer
kW	kilowatt
kWh	kilowatt hour
m	meter
NA	not available
NEGL	negligible
nm	nautical mile
NZ	New Zealand
ODA	official development assistance
OOF	other official flows
PDRY	People's Democratic Republic of Yemen [Yemen (Aden) or South Yemen]; used for information dated before 22 May 1990 or CY91
sq km	square kilometer
sq mi	square mile
UAE	United Arab Emirates
UK	United Kingdom
US	United States
USSR	Union of Soviet Socialist Republics (Soviet Union); used for information dated before 25 December 1991
YAR	Yemen Arab Republic [Yemen (Sanaa) or North Yemen]; used for information dated before 22 May 1990 or CY91

Administrative divisions: The numbers, designatory terms, and first-order administrative divisions are generally those approved by the US Board on Geographic Names (BGN). Changes that have been reported but not yet acted on by BGN are noted.

Area: Total area is the sum of all land and water areas delimited by international boundaries and/or coastlines. Land area is the aggregate of all surfaces delimited by international boundaries and/or coastlines, excluding inland water bodies (lakes, reservoirs, rivers). Comparative areas are based on total area equivalents. Most entities are compared with the entire US or one of the 50 states. The smaller entities are compared with Washington, DC (178 sq km, 69 sq mi) or The Mall in Washington, DC (0.59 sq km, 0.23 sq mi, 146 acres).

Birth rate: The average annual number of births during a year per 1,000 population at midyear; also known as crude birth rate.

Dates of information: In general, information available as of 1 January 1994 was used in the preparation of this edition. Population figures are estimates for 1 July 1994, with population growth rates estimated for calendar year 1994. Major political events have been updated through May 1994.

Death rate: The average annual number of deaths during a year per 1,000 population at midyear; also known as crude death rate.

Digraphs: The digraph is a two-letter "country code" that precisely identifies every entity without overlap, duplication, or omission. AF, for example, is the digraph for Afghanistan. It is a standardized geopolitical data element promulgated in the *Federal Information Processing Standards Publication* (FIPS) 10-3 by the National Institute of Standards and Technology (US Department of Commerce) and maintained by the Office of the Geographer (US Department of State). The digraph is used to eliminate confusion and incompatibility in the collection, processing, and dissemination of area-specific data and is particularly useful for interchanging data between databases.

Diplomatic representation: The US Government has diplomatic relations with 183 nations, including 177 of the 184 UN members (excluded UN members are Bhutan, Cuba, Iran, Iraq, North Korea, Vietnam, and former Yugoslavia). In addition, the US has diplomatic relations with 6 nations that are not in the UN—Holy See, Kiribati, Nauru, Switzerland, Tonga, and Tuvalu.

Economic aid: This entry refers to bilateral commitments of official development assistance (ODA) and other official flows (OOF). ODA is defined as financial assistance which is concessional in character, has the main objective to promote economic development and welfare of LDCs. and contains a grant element of at least 25%. OOF transactions are also official government assistance, but with a main objective other than development and with a grant element less than 25%. OOF transactions include official export credits (such as Ex-Im Bank credits), official equity and portfolio investment, and debt reorganization by the official sector that does not meet concessional terms. Aid is considered to have been committed when agreements are initialed by the parties involved and constitute a formal declaration of intent.

Entities: Some of the nations, dependent areas, areas of special sovereignty, and governments included in this publication are not independent, and others are not officially recognized by the US Government. "Nation" refers to a people politically organized into a sovereign state with a definite territory. "Dependent area" refers to a broad category of political entities that are associated in some way with a nation. Names used for page headings are usually the short-form names as approved by the US Board on Geographic Names. There are 266 entities in *The World Factbook* that may be categorized as follows:

NATIONS

183 UN members (excluding both the Socialist Federal Republic of Yugoslavia and the Federal Republic of Yugoslavia; membership status in the UN is still to be determined)

7 nations that are not members of the UN—Holy See, Kiribati, Nauru, Serbia and Montenegro, Switzerland, Tonga, Tuvalu

OTHER

1 Taiwan

DEPENDENT AREAS

6 Australia—Ashmore and Cartier Islands, Christmas Island, Cocos (Keeling) Islands, Coral Sea Islands, Heard Island and McDonald Islands, Norfolk Island

2 Denmark—Faroe Islands, Greenland

16 France—Bassas da India, Clipperton Island, Europa Island, French Guiana, French Polynesia, French Southern and Antarctic Lands, Glorioso Islands, Guadeloupe, Juan de Nova Island, Martinique, Mayotte, New Caledonia, Reunion, Saint Pierre and Miquelon, Tromelin Island, Wallis and Futuna

2 Netherlands—Aruba, Netherlands Antilles

3 New Zealand—Cook Islands, Niue, Tokelau

3 Norway—Bouvet Island, Jan Mayen, Svalbard

1 Portugal—Macau

16 United Kingdom—Anguilla, Bermuda, British Indian Ocean Territory, British Virgin Islands, Cayman Islands, Falkland Islands, Gibraltar, Guernsey, Hong Kong, Jersey, Isle of Man, Montserrat, Pitcairn Islands, Saint Helena, South Georgia and the South Sandwich Islands, Turks and Caicos Islands

15 United States—American Samoa, Baker Island, Guam, Howland Island, Jarvis Island, Johnston Atoll, Kingman Reef, Midway

Islands, Navassa Island, Northern Mariana Islands, Trust Territory of
the Pacific Islands (Palau), Palmyra Atoll, Puerto Rico, Virgin
Islands, Wake Island

MISCELLANEOUS

6   Antarctica, Gaza Strip, Paracel Islands, Spratly Islands, West Bank,
     Western Sahara

OTHER ENTITIES

4   oceans—Arctic Ocean, Atlantic Ocean, Indian Ocean, Pacific Ocean

1   World

266 total

Exchange rate: The value of a nation's monetary unit at a given date or
over a given period of time, as expressed in units of local currency per US
dollar and as determined by international market forces or official fiat.

Gross domestic product (GDP): The value of all final goods and
services produced within a nation in a given year.

Gross national product (GNP): The value of all final goods and services
produced within a nation in a given year, plus income earned abroad,
minus income earned by foreigners from domestic production.

Gross world product (GWP): The aggregate value of all goods and
services produced worldwide in a given year.

GNP/GDP methodology: In the "Economy" section, GNP/GDP dollar
estimates for the great majority of countries are derived from *purchasing
power parity* (PPP) calculations rather than from conversions at official
currency exchange rates. The PPP method normally involves the use of
international dollar price weights, which are applied to the quantities of
goods and services produced in a given economy. In addition to the lack
of reliable data from the majority of countries, the statistician faces a
major difficulty in specifying, identifying, and allowing for the quality of
goods and services. The division of a GNP/GDP estimate in local currency
by the corresponding PPP estimate in dollars gives *the PPP conversion
rate*. On average, one thousand dollars will buy the same market basket of
goods in the US as one thousand dollars—converted to the local currency
at the PPP conversion rate—will buy in the other country. Whereas PPP
estimates for OECD countries are quite reliable, PPP estimates for
developing countries are often rough approximations. The latter estimates
are based on extrapolation of numbers published by the UN International
Comparison Program and by Professors Robert Summers and Alan
Heston of the University of Pennsylvania and their colleagues. Because
currency exchange rates depend on a variety of international and domestic
financial forces that often have little relation to domestic output, use of
these rates is less satisfactory for calculating GNP/GDP than the PPP
method. In developing countries with weak currencies the exchange rate
estimate of GNP/GDP in dollars is typically one-fourth to one-half the

PPP estimate. Furthermore, exchange rates may suddenly go up or down by 10% or more because of market forces or official fiat whereas real output has remained unchanged. On 12 January 1994, for example, the 14 countries of the African Financial Community (whose currencies are tied to the French franc) devalued their currencies by 50%. This move, of course, did not cut the real output of these countries by half. One additional caution: the proportion of, say, defense expenditures as a percent of GNP/GDP in local currency accounts may differ substantially from the proportion when GNP/GDP accounts are expressed in PPP terms, as, for example, when an observer estimates the dollar level of Russian or Japanese military expenditures.

Growth rate (population): The annual percent change in the population, resulting from a surplus (or deficit) of births over deaths and the balance of migrants entering and leaving a country. The rate may be positive or negative.

Illicit drugs: There are five categories of illicit drugs—narcotics, stimulants, depressants (sedatives), hallucinogens, and cannabis. These categories include many drugs legally produced and prescribed by doctors as well as those illegally produced and sold outside medical channels.

Cannabis (Cannabis sativa) is the common hemp plant, which provides hallucinogens with some sedative properties, and includes marijuana (pot, Acapulco gold, grass, reefer), tetrahydrocannabinol (THC, Marinol), hashish (hash), and hashish oil (hash oil).

Coca (Erythroxylon coca) is a bush, and the leaves contain the stimulant cocaine. Coca is not to be confused with cocoa, which comes from cacao seeds and is used in making chocolate, cocoa, and cocoa butter.

Cocaine is a stimulant derived from the leaves of the coca bush.

Depressants (sedatives) are drugs that reduce tension and anxiety and include chloral hydrate, barbiturates (Amytal, Nembutal, Seconal, phenobarbital), benzodiazepines (Librium, Valium), methaqualone (Quaalude), glutethimide (Doriden), and others (Equanil, Placidyl, Valmid).

Drugs are any chemical substances that effect a physical, mental, emotional, or behavioral change in an individual.

Drug abuse is the use of any licit or illicit chemical substance that results in physical, mental, emotional, or behavioral impairment in an individual.

Hallucinogens are drugs that affect sensation, thinking, self-awareness, and emotion. Hallucinogens include LSD (acid, microdot), mescaline and peyote (mexc, buttons, cactus), amphetamine variants (PMA, STP, DOB), phencyclidine (PCP, angel dust, hog), phencyclidine analogues (PCE, PCPy, TCP), and others (psilocybin, psilocyn).

Hashish is the resinous exudate of the cannabis or hemp plant (Cannabis sativa).

Heroin is a semisynthetic derivative of morphine.

Mandrax is a synthetic chemical depressant, the same as, or similar to, Quaalude.

Marijuana is the dried leaves of the cannabis or hemp plant (Cannabis sativa).

Narcotics are drugs that relieve pain, often induce sleep, and refer to opium, opium derivatives, and synthetic substitutes. Natural narcotics include opium (paregoric, parepectolin), morphine (MS-Contin, Roxanol), codeine (Tylenol with codeine, Empirin with codeine, Robitussan AC), and thebaine. Semisynthetic narcotics include heroin (horse, smack), and hydromorphone (Dilaudid). Synthetic narcotics include meperidine or Pethidine (Demerol, Mepergan), methadone (Dolophine, Methadose), and others (Darvon, Lomotil).

Opium is the milky exudate of the incised, unripe seedpod of the opium poppy.

Opium poppy (Papaver somniferum) is the source for many natural and semisynthetic narcotics.

Poppy straw concentrate is the alkaloid derived from the mature dried opium poppy.

Qat (kat, khat) is a stimulant from the buds or leaves of catha edulis that is chewed or drunk as tea.

Stimulants are drugs that relieve mild depression, increase energy and activity, and include cocaine (coke, snow, crack), amphetamines (Desoxyn, Dexedrine), phenmetrazine (Preludin), methylphenidate (Ritalin), and others (Cylert, Sanorex, Tenuate).

Infant mortality rate: The number of deaths to infants under one year old in a given year per 1,000 live births occurring in the same year.

International disputes: This category includes a wide variety of situations that range from traditional bilateral boundary disputes to unilateral claims of one sort or another. Information regarding disputes over international boundaries and maritime boundaries has been reviewed by the Department of State. References to other situations involving borders or frontiers may also be included, such as resource disputes, geopolitical questions, or irredentist issues. However, inclusion does not necessarily constitute official acceptance or recognition by the US Government.

Irrigated land: The figure refers to the land area that is artificially supplied with water.

Land use: Human use of the land surface is categorized as *arable land*—land cultivated for crops that are replanted after each harvest (wheat, maize, rice); *permanent crops*—land cultivated for crops that are not replanted after each harvest (citrus, coffee, rubber); *meadows and pastures*—land permanently used for herbaceous forage crops; *forest and woodland*—under dense or open stands of trees; and *other*—any land type not specifically mentioned above (urban areas, roads, desert).

Leaders: The chief of state is the titular leader of the country who represents the state at official and ceremonial functions but is not involved with the day-to-day activities of the government. The head of government is the administrative leader who manages the day-to-day activities of the government. In the UK, the monarch is the chief of state, and the Prime Minister is the head of government. In the US, the President is both the chief of state and the head of government.

Life expectancy at birth: The average number of years to be lived by a group of people all born in the same year, if mortality at each age remains constant in the future.

Literacy: There are no universal definitions and standards of literacy. Unless otherwise noted, all rates are based on the most common definition—the ability to read and write at a specified age. Detailing the standards that individual countries use to assess the ability to read and write is beyond the scope of this publication.

Maritime claims: The proximity of neighboring states may prevent some national claims from being extended the full distance.

Merchant marine: All ships engaged in the carriage of goods. All commercial vessels (as opposed to all nonmilitary ships), which excludes tugs, fishing vessels, offshore oil rigs, etc.; also, a grouping of merchant ships by nationality or register.

Captive register—A register of ships maintained by a territory, possession, or colony primarily or exclusively for the use of ships owned in the parent country; also referred to as an offshore register, the offshore equivalent of an internal register. Ships on a captive register will fly the same flag as the parent country, or a local variant of it, but will be subject to the maritime laws and taxation rules of the offshore territory. Although the nature of a captive register makes it especially desirable for ships owned in the parent country, just as in the internal register, the ships may also be owned abroad. The captive register then acts as a flag of convenience register, except that it is not the register of an independent state.

Flag of convenience register—A national register offering registration to a merchant ship not owned in the flag state. The major flags of convenience (FOC) attract ships to their register by virtue of low fees, low or nonexistent taxation of profits, and liberal manning requirements. True FOC registers are characterized by having relatively few of the ships registered actually owned in the flag state. Thus, while virtually any flag can be used for ships under a given set of circumstances, an FOC register is one where the majority of the merchant fleet is owned abroad. It is also referred to as an open register.

Flag state—The nation in which a ship is registered and which holds legal jurisdiction over operation of the ship, whether at home or abroad. Differences in flag state maritime legislation determine how a ship is manned and taxed and whether a foreign-owned ship may be placed on the register.

Internal register—A register of ships maintained as a subset of a national register. Ships on the internal register fly the national flag and have that nationality but are subject to a separate set of maritime rules from those on the main national register. These differences usually include lower taxation of profits, manning by foreign nationals, and, usually, ownership outside the flag state (when it functions as an FOC register). The Norwegian International Ship Register and Danish International Ship

Register are the most notable examples of an internal register. Both have been instrumental in stemming flight from the national flag to flags of convenience and in attracting foreign owned ships to the Norwegian and Danish flags.

Merchant ship—A vessel that carries goods against payment of freight; commonly used to denote any nonmilitary ship but accurately restricted to commercial vessels only.

Register—The record of a ship's ownership and nationality as listed with the maritime authorities of a country; also, the compendium of such individual ships' registrations. Registration of a ship provides it with a nationality and makes it subject to the laws of the country in which registered (the flag state) regardless of the nationality of the ship's ultimate owner.

Money figures: All money figures are expressed in contemporaneous US dollars unless otherwise indicated.

National product: The total output of goods and services in a country in a given year. See Gross domestic product (GDP), Gross national product (GNP), and GNP/GDP methodology.

Net migration rate: The balance between the number of persons entering and leaving a country during the year per 1,000 persons (based on midyear population). An excess of persons entering the country is referred to as net immigration (3.56 migrants/1,000 population); an excess of persons leaving the country as net emigration (-9.26 migrants/1,000 population).

Population: Figures are estimates from the Bureau of the Census based on statistics from population censuses, vital statistics registration systems, or sample surveys pertaining to the recent past, and on assumptions about future trends. Starting with the 1993 Factbook, demographic estimates for some countries (mostly African) have taken into account the effects of the growing incidence of AIDS infections; in 1993 these countries were Burkina, Burundi, Central African Republic, Congo, Cote d'Ivoire, Haiti, Kenya, Malawi, Rwanda, Tanzania, Uganda, Zaire, Zambia, Zimbabwe, Thailand, and Brazil.

Total fertility rate: The average number of children that would be born per woman if all women lived to the end of their childbearing years and bore children according to a given fertility rate at each age.

Years: All year references are for the calendar year (CY) unless indicated as fiscal year (FY).

International Organizations Abbreviations

ABEDA	Arab Bank for Economic Development in Africa
ACC	Arab Cooperation Council
ACCT	Agence de Cooperation Culturelle et Technique; see Agency for Cultural and Technical Cooperation
ACP	African, Caribbean, and Pacific Countries
AfDB	African Development Bank
AFESD	Arab Fund for Economic and Social Development
AG	Andean Group
AL	Arab League
ALADI	Asociacion Latinoamericana de Integracion; see Latin American Integration Association (LAIA)
AMF	Arab Monetary Fund
AMU	Arab Maghreb Union
ANZUS	Australia-New Zealand-United States Security Treaty
APEC	Asia Pacific Economic Cooperation
AsDB	Asian Development Bank
ASEAN	Association of Southeast Asian Nations
BAD	Banque Africaine de Developpement; see African Development Bank (AfDB)
BADEA	Banque Arabe de Developpement Economique en Afrique; see Arab Bank for Economic Development in Africa (ABEDA)
BCIE	Banco Centroamericano de Integracion Economico; see Central American Bank for Economic Integration (BCIE)
BDEAC	Banque de Developpment des Etats de l'Afrique Centrale; see Central African States Development Bank (BDEAC)
Benelux	Benelux Economic Union
BID	Banco Interamericano de Desarrollo; see Inter-American Development Bank (IADB)
BIS	Bank for International Settlements
BOAD	Banque Ouest-Africaine de Developpement; see West African Development Bank (WADB)
BSEC	Black Sea Economic Cooperation Zone
C	Commonwealth
CACM	Central American Common Market
CAEU	Council of Arab Economic Unity

CARICOM	Caribbean Community and Common Market
CBSS	Council of the Baltic Sea States
CCC	Customs Cooperation Council
CDB	Caribbean Development Bank
CE	Council of Europe
CEAO	Communaute Economique de l'Afrique de l'Ouest; see West African Economic Community (CEAO)
CEEAC	Communaute Economique des Etats de l'Afrique Centrale; see Economic Community of Central African States (CEEAC)
CEI	Central European Initiative
CEMA	Council for Mutual Economic Assistance; also known as CMEA or Comecon; abolished 1 January 1991
CEPGL	Communaute Economique des Pays des Grands Lacs; see Economic Community of the Great Lakes Countries (CEPGL)
CERN	Conseil Europeen pour la Recherche Nucleaire; see European Organization for Nuclear Research (CERN)
CG	Contadora Group
CIS	Commonwealth of Independent States
CMEA	Council for Mutual Economic Assistance (CEMA); also known as Comecon; abolished 1 January 1991
COCOM	Coordinating Committee on Export Controls
Comecon	Council for Mutual Economic Assistance (CEMA); also known as CMEA; abolished 1 January 1991
CP	Colombo Plan
CSCE	Conference on Security and Cooperation in Europe
DC	developed country
EADB	East African Development Bank
EBRD	European Bank for Reconstruction and Development
EC	European Community; see European Union (EU)
ECA	Economic Commission for Africa
ECAFE	Economic Commission for Asia and the Far East; see Economic and Social Commission for Asia and the Pacific (ESCAP)
ECE	Economic Commission for Europe
ECLA	Economic Commission for Latin America; see Economic Commission for Latin America and the Caribbean (ECLAC)
ECLAC	Economic Commission for Latin America and the Caribbean
ECO	Economic Cooperation Organization
ECOSOC	Economic and Social Council
ECOWAS	Economic Community of West African States

ECSC	European Coal and Steel Community
ECWA	Economic Commission for Western Asia; see Economic and Social Commission for Western Asia (ESCWA)
EEC	European Economic Community
EFTA	European Free Trade Association
EIB	European Investment Bank
Entente	Council of the Entente
ESA	European Space Agency
ESCAP	Economic and Social Commission for Asia and the Pacific
ESCWA	Economic and Social Commission for Western Asia
EU	European Union
Euratom	European Atomic Energy Community
FAO	Food and Agriculture Organization
FLS	Front Line States
FZ	Franc Zone
G-2	Group of 2
G-3	Group of 3
G-5	Group of 5
G-6	Group of 6 (not to be confused with the Big Six)
G-7	Group of 7
G-8	Group of 8
G-9	Group of 9
G-10	Group of 10
G-11	Group of 11
G-15	Group of 15
G-19	Group of 19
G-24	Group of 24
G-30	Group of 30
G-33	Group of 33
G-77	Group of 77
GATT	General Agreement on Tariffs and Trade
GCC	Gulf Cooperation Council
Habitat	Commission on Human Settlements
IADB	Inter-American Development Bank
IAEA	International Atomic Energy Agency
IBEC	International Bank for Economic Cooperation

IBRD	International Bank for Reconstruction and Development
ICAO	International Civil Aviation Organization
ICC	International Chamber of Commerce
ICEM	Intergovernmental Committee for European Migration; see International Organization for Migration (IOM)
ICFTU	International Confederation of Free Trade Unions
ICJ	International Court of Justice
ICM	Intergovernmental Committee for Migration; see International Organization for Migration (IOM)
ICRC	International Committee of the Red Cross
IDA	International Development Association
IDB	Islamic Development Bank
IEA	International Energy Agency
IFAD	International Fund for Agricultural Development
IFC	International Finance Corporation
IFCTU	International Federation of Christian Trade Unions
IGADD	Inter-Governmental Authority on Drought and Development
IIB	International Investment Bank
ILO	International Labor Organization
IMCO	Intergovernmental Maritime Consultative Organization; see International Maritime Organization (IMO)
IMF	International Monetary Fund
IMO	International Maritime Organization
INMARSAT	International Maritime Satellite Organization
INTELSAT	International Telecommunications Satellite Organization
INTERPOL	International Criminal Police Organization
IOC	International Olympic Committee
IOM	International Organization for Migration
ISO	International Organization for Standardization
ITU	International Telecommunication Union
LAES	Latin American Economic System
LAIA	Latin American Integration Association
LAS	League of Arab States; see Arab League (AL)
LDC	less developed country
LLDC	least developed country
LORCS	League of Red Cross and Red Crescent Societies

MERCOSUR	Mercado Comun del Cono Sur; see Southern Cone Common Market
MINURSO	United Nations Mission for the Referendum in Western Sahara
MTCR	Missile Technology Control Regime
NACC	North Atlantic Cooperation Council
NAM	Nonaligned Movement
NATO	North Atlantic Treaty Organization
NC	Nordic Council
NEA	Nuclear Energy Agency
NIB	Nordic Investment Bank
NIC	newly industrializing country; see newly industrializing economy (NIE)
NIE	newly industrializing economy
NSG	Nuclear Suppliers Group
OAPEC	Organization of Arab Petroleum Exporting Countries
OAS	Organization of American States
OAU	Organization of African Unity
OECD	Organization for Economic Cooperation and Development
OECS	Organization of Eastern Caribbean States
OIC	Organization of the Islamic Conference
ONUSAL	United Nations Observer Mission in El Salvador
OPANAL	Organismo para la Proscripcion de las Armas Nucleares en la America Latina y el Caribe; see Agency for the Prohibition of Nuclear Weapons in Latin America and the Caribbean
OPEC	Organization of Petroleum Exporting Countries
PCA	Permanent Court of Arbitration
RG	Rio Group
SAARC	South Asian Association for Regional Cooperation
SACU	Southern African Customs Union
SADC	Southern African Development Community
SADCC	Southern African Development Coordination Conference
SELA	Sistema Economico Latinoamericana; see Latin American Economic System (LAES)
SPARTECA	South Pacific Regional Trade and Economic Cooperation Agreement
SPC	South Pacific Commission
SPF	South Pacific Forum
UDEAC	Union Douaniere et Economique de l'Afrique Centrale; see Central African Customs and Economic Union (UDEAC)

UN	United Nations
UNAVEM II	United Nations Angola Verification Mission
UNCTAD	United Nations Conference on Trade and Development
UNDOF	United Nations Disengagement Observer Force
UNDP	United Nations Development Program
UNEP	United Nations Environment Program
UNESCO	United Nations Educational, Scientific, and Cultural Organization
UNFICYP	United Nations Force in Cyprus
UNFPA	United Nations Fund for Population Activities; see UN Population Fund (UNFPA)
UNHCR	United Nations Office of the High Commissioner for Refugees
UNICEF	United Nations Children's Fund
UNIDO	United Nations Industrial Development Organization
UNIFIL	United Nations Interim Force in Lebanon
UNIKOM	United Nations Iraq-Kuwait Observation Mission
UNMOGIP	United Nations Military Observer Group in India and Pakistan
UNOMIG	United Nations Observer Mission in Georgia
UNOMOZ	United Nations Operation in Mozambique
UNOMUR	United Nations Observer Mission Uganda-Rwanda
UNOSOM	United Nations Operation in Somalia
UNPROFOR	United Nations Protection Force
UNRWA	United Nations Relief and Works Agency for Palestine Refugees
UNTAC	United Nations Transitional Authority in Cambodia
UNTSO	United Nations Truce Supervision Organization
UPU	Universal Postal Union
WADB	West African Development Bank
WCL	World Confederation of Labor
WEU	Western European Union
WFC	World Food Council
WFP	World Food Program
WFTU	World Federation of Trade Unions
WHO	World Health Organization
WIPO	World Intellectual Property Organization
WMO	World Meteorological Organization
WP	Warsaw Pact (members met 1 July 1991 to dissolve the alliance)
WTO	World Tourism Organization
ZC	Zangger Committee

International Economic Statistics

Selected World Statistics [a]

	1990	1991	1992	1993
Gross domestic product *(billion 1993 US $)* [b]	28,028.0	28,044.0	28,528.0	29,132.0
Population *(million persons, midyear)*	5,295.0	5,381.0	5,469.0	5,556.0
Exports *(billion US $)*	3,424.6	3,533.2	3,759.6	3,730.7
Crude oil, excluding natural gas liquids *(million b/d)*	60.6	60.1	60.0	59.6
Natural gas *(trillion cubic meters)*	2.1	2.1	2.1	2.1
Hard coal *(million metric tons)* [c]	3,515.0	3,450.0	3,530.0	3,640.0
Brown coal and lignite *(million metric tons)*	1,210.0	1,180.0	970.0	945.0
Electricity *(billion kilowatt-hours)*	11,800.0	12,035.0	11,460.0	11,985.0
Iron ore *(million metric tons)*	893.0	956.0	930.0	940.0
Bauxite *(million metric tons)*	109.0	107.9	101.6	105.6
Pig iron *(million metric tons)*	555.0	526.0	517.0	528.0
Crude steel *(million metric tons)*	771.0	736.0	722.0	725.0
Refined copper *(thousand metric tons)*	10,696.0	10,637.0	10,917.0	NA
Primary aluminum *(million metric tons)*	19.3	19.6	19.5	19.8
Smelter lead *(thousand metric tons)*	3,098.0	3,008.0	3,042.0	NA
Refined zinc *(thousand metric tons)*	7,109.0	7,101.0	6,210.0	NA
Primary tin *(thousand metric tons)*	227.0	183.0	190.0	NA
Mineral fertilizer [d] *(million metric tons)*	152.6	147.9	144.2	138.3
Nitrogen fertilizer [d] *(million metric tons of N)*	84.6	81.9	80.6	79.9
Phosphate fertilizer [d] *(million metric tons of P_2O_5)*	39.7	39.0	38.6	34.8
Potassium fertilizer [d] *(million metric tons of K_2O)*	28.3	26.7	25.0	23.5
Synthetic fibers *(thousand metric tons)*	13,265.0	11,598.0	11,200.0	11,300.0
Automobiles *(thousand units)*	35,700.0	34,400.0	34,000.0	NA
Grain *(million metric tons)*	1,930.0	1,860.0	1,936.0	1,853.0
Wheat *(million metric tons)*	589.0	543.0	560.0	562.0
Coarse grain *(million metric tons)*	821.0	803.0	856.0	777.0
Rice *(million metric tons)*	518.0	515.0	520.0	514.0
Sugar *(million metric tons)*	113.6	115.9	111.3	112.7
Coffee *(thousand metric tons)*	6,028.0	6,259.0	5,575.0	5,650.0

[a] For more detailed descriptions and definitions, refer to the respective table.

[b] Data were converted to US dollars by the use of purchasing power parities used by international organizations and academia.

[c] Including brown coal at its hard coal equivalent.

[d] Fertilizer year ending 30 June of the stated year.

Percent

Share of Global Exports of High-Technology Products

Microelectronics		Computers	
1980	1990	1980	1990
United States (18.3)	United States (27.5)	United States (38.6)	United States (24.2)
Japan (13.2)	Japan (21.7)	Germany[a] (11.5)	Japan (17.3)
Singapore (10.1)	Malaysia (7.2)	United Kingdom (10.4)	United Kingdom (8.7)
Malaysia (8.9)	South Korea (6.7)	France (8.6)	Germany[a] (6.6)
Germany[a] (8.4)	Germany[a] (4.0)	Italy (6.6)	Taiwan (6.3)
France (4.9)	Taiwan (3.8)	Japan (4.3)	Singapore (6.1)
Hong Kong (4.8)	Singapore (3.6)	Canada (3.4)	Netherlands (4.2)
United Kingdom (4.5)	United Kingdom (3.5)	Sweden (2.9)	France (4.0)
South Korea (4.2)	France (2.7)	Hong Kong (1.9)	Italy (3.3)
Philippines (3.8)	Canada (2.3)	Netherlands (1.6)	South Korea (2.5)

Machine Tools and Robotics		Scientific/Precision Equipment	
1980	1990	1980	1990
Germany[a] (25.8)	Japan (21.8)	United States (28.3)	United States (27.4)
United States (14.1)	Germany[a] (20.2)	Germany[a] (18.1)	Germany[a] (16.9)
Japan (11.3)	United States (13.1)	United Kingdom (9.4)	Japan (12.9)
Switzerland (9.1)	Italy (9.7)	France (8.0)	United Kingdom (7.0)
Italy (8.7)	Switzerland (7.3)	Japan (7.1)	France (5.6)
United Kingdom (6.9)	United Kingdom (4.5)	Switzerland (5.5)	Switzerland (4.1)
France (6.3)	France (3.6)	Netherlands (4.2)	Netherlands (3.8)
Sweden (2.4)	Netherlands (2.5)	Italy (3.0)	Italy (2.9)
Canada (1.8)	Sweden (2.5)	Belgium (2.7)	Sweden (2.4)
Netherlands (1.8)	Taiwnan (2.1)	Sweden (2.7)	Belgium (2.3)

Telecommunications Equipment		Aerospace	
1980	1990	1980	1990
Germany[a] (16.7)	Japan (28.4)	United States (47.6)	United States (50.3)
Sweden (15.3)	United States (15.9)	United Kingdom (19.7)	France (17.5)
United States (10.9)	Sweden (6.9)	Germany[a] (9.1)	United Kingdom (7.7)
Japan (10.3)	Germany[a] (6.5)	France (6.0)	Germany[a] (4.1)
Netherlands (9.3)	Canada (4.7)	Canada (4.4)	Canada (4.0)
Belgium (7.4)	Taiwan (3.9)	Netherlands (2.5)	Netherlands (2.5)
France (6.5)	South Korea (3.4)	Italy (2.1)	Italy (0.9)
Canada (5.1)	Netherlands (3.3)	Belgium (1.2)	Japan (0.9)
United Kingdom (4.1)	France (3.1)	Switzerland (0.8)	Sweden (0.9)
Italy (2.7)	United Kingdom (3.1)	Japan (0.6)	Switzerland (0.5)

Medicine and Biologicals		Organic Chemicals	
1980	1990	1980	1990
Germany[a] (16.7)	Germany[a] (15.4)	Germany[a] (19.1)	Germany[a] (16.0)
Switzerland (12.5)	United States (13.5)	United States (13.9)	United States (14.9)
United Kingdom (12.0)	Switzerland (12.3)	Netherlands (10.9)	Netherlands (11.8)
France (11.9)	United Kingdom (12.2)	France (10.7)	France (9.2)
United States (11.4)	France (8.6)	United Kingdom (8.4)	United Kingdom (7.2)
Italy (5.4)	Italy (5.1)	Japan (6.3)	Japan (7.1)
Belgium (5.2)	Belgium (4.9)	Belgium (6.1)	Belgium, (6.7)
Netherlands (4.7)	Netherlands (4.7)	Italy (4.6)	Italy (4.8)
Sweden (2.5)	Sweden (4.6)	Switzerland (3.3)	Switzerland (3.3)
Japan (2.2)	Japan (2.8)	Canada (2.5)	Canada (2.1)

Primary Energy Production[a]

Thousand barrels per day of oil equivalent

	1990	1991	1992	1993
OECD				
United States	33,015	33,285	33,175	32,525
Canada	5,510	5,730	5,900	6,275
Japan	1,380	1,455	1,480	1,485
Norway	2,400	2,615	2,910	3,050
European Union				
Germany	3,700	3,325	3,220	3,010
France	2,085	2,185	2,230	2,215
Netherlands	1,195	1,335	1,335	1,360
United Kingdom	4,150	4,275	4,270	4,325
Selected East European				
Russia	25,260	23,890	22,270	20,900
Ukraine	NA	2,040	1,978	1,770
Bulgaria	195	179	176	173
Hungary	297	294	276	256
Poland	1,955	1,900	1,790	1,792
Romania	818	729	693	692
Other				
China	14,470	NA	NA	NA

[a]Data are for coal, crude oil, natural gas, natural gas liquids, and hydroelectric
and nuclear electric power expressed in terms of oil equivalent.

Primary Energy Production, by Type[a]

Thousand barrels per day of oil equivalent

	1993 Coal	Crude Oil	Natural Gas	Hydro/ Nuclear
OECD				
United States	11,725	8,000	8,650	4,150
Canada	925	2,075	2,300	975
Japan	80	15	40	1,350
European Union				
Germany	1,825	60	275	850
France	200	65	50	1,900
Netherlands	5	60	1,275	20
United Kingdom	850	2,000	1,050	425
Selected East European				
Russia	2,560	7,040	9,965	1,335
Ukraine	980	85	310	395
Bulgaria	97	1	NEGL	75
Hungary	60	32	90	74
Poland	1,702	4	70	16
Romania	156	139	334	63
Other				
China	10,700 [b]	2,770 [b]	290 [b]	710 [b]

[a] Data are for coal, crude oil, natural gas, natural gas liquids, and hydroelectric and nuclear electric power expressed in terms of oil equivalent.
[b] Data are for 1990.

Thousand barrels per day

Crude Oil Production[a]

	1990	1991	1992	1993
OECD[b]				
United States	7,355	7,417	7,171	6,838
Canada	1,518	1,548	1,604	1,684
Norway	1,620	1,876	2,144	2,247
European Union				
United Kingdom	1,850	1,823	1,864	1,866
Selected East European				
Russia[c]	10,320	9,220	7,880	7,040
Kazakhstan[c]	510	530	514	460
Azerbaijan[c]	248	234	226	201
Hungary	40	39	33	32
Romania	160	140	136	139
OPEC				
Algeria	794	803	772	750
Indonesia	1,289	1,411	1,346	1,323
Iran	3,252	3,358	3,455	3,640
Iraq	2,080	283	425	436
Kuwait[d]	1,235	200	1,050	1,873
Libya	1,374	1,509	1,493	1,367
Nigeria	1,811	1,867	1,902	1,896
Saudi Arabia[d]	6,414	8,223	8,308	8,162
United Arab Emirates	2,117	2,416	2,322	2,225
Venezuela	2,085	2,350	2,314	2,332
Other				
China	2,769	2,785	2,835	2,900
Mexico	2,648	2,774	2,668	2,664

[a] Unless otherwise indicated, data are for crude oil and exclude natural gas liquids, shale oil, natural gasoline, and synthetic crude oil.
[b] Including shale oil.
[c] Including natural gas liquids.
[d] Including about one-half of Neutral Zone production.

World Crude Oil Prices

	1990	1991	1992	1993
OPEC official average sales price[a]				
US $ per barrel	21.76	18.58	18.33	16.08
1993 US $ per barrel[c]	23.86	19.60	18.80	16.08
World average price				
US $ per barrel	22.12	18.72	18.24	16.13
1993 US $ per barrel[c]	24.25	19.75	18.71	16.13

[a]F.o.b. prices set by the OPEC governments for direct sales
[b]Posted prices.
[c]Nominal price deflated by the US GDP deflator.

Proved Reserves of Crude Oil, and Natural Gas, Yearend 1993

	Crude Oil (Billion barrels)	Natural Gas (Trillion cubic feet)
OECD		
United States	24	165
Canada	5	95
Norway	9	70
European Union		
Germany	NEGL	12
Italy	1	11
Netherlands	NEGL	68
United Kingdom	5	22
Selected East European		
Russia	35	1,748
Poland	NEGL	5
Romania	2	8
Other		
OPEC		
Algeria	9	128
Indonesia	6	64
Iran	93	730
Iraq	100	110
Kuwait	94	52
Libya	23	46
Nigeria	18	120
Qatar	4	250
Saudi Arabia	259	185
United Arab Emirates	98	205
Venezuela	63	129
Other		
Brazil	4	5
Egypt	6	15
India	6	25
Malaysia	4	77
Mexico	51	71
Oman	5	20
Syria	2	7

Table 76   *Thousand troy ounces*
Selected Countries: Platinum-Group Metals Production

	1990	1991	1992	1993
South Africa[a]	4,563	4,593	4,916	4,800
Russia	4,019	3,906	3,346	2,400
Canada	376	376	329	444
United States[b]	249	250	267	268
Colombia	42	52	63	64
Japan	79	66	52	60
Australia	16	16	16	16
Finland	5	5	5	5
Serbia[c]	5	4	2	2
Zimbabwe	2	2	1	1

[a]Platinum-group metals from platinum ores and osmium and iridium from gold ores.
[b]Crude placer platinum and byproduct metals recovered largely from domestic copper refining.
[c]Including Montenegro.

Table 77   *Million troy ounces*
Selected Countries: Gold Production

	1990	1991	1992	1993
South Africa	19.45	19.33	19.74	19.92
United States	9.33	8.96	9.52	NA
Australia	7.85	7.53	7.83	7.72
China	3.22	3.86	4.50	5.14
Canada	5.45	5.68	5.17	4.92
Russia	NA	NA	4.69	4.18
Papua New Guinea	1.03	1.95	2.29	2.85
Uzbekistan	NA	NA	2.60	2.60
Brazil	3.28	2.87	2.86	1.89
Colombia	.94	1.12	1.03	1.06

Million persons, annual average

Industrial Employment [a]

	1990	1991	1992	1993
OECD				
United States	29.61	28.25	27.65	27.45
Canada	2.96	2.73	2.63	2.61
Japan	20.89	21.52	21.85	21.69
European Union				
France	6.42	6.33	6.12	5.87
Germany[b]	10.88	10.93	10.85	10.43
Italy	6.84	6.91	6.85	NA
United Kingdom	7.47	6.90	6.50	6.17
Selected East European				
Russia	25.09	25.28	25.55	25.66
Ukraine	6.87	6.91	NA	NA
Bulgaria[c]	1.77	1.55	1.35	1.14 [d]
Czech Republic	NA	NA	NA	2.04
Hungary[ce]	1.69	1.52	1.32	1.20 [d]
Poland[c]	5.76	5.18	4.81	4.45 [d]
Romania[ce]	4.58	4.15	3.30	NA
Slovakia	NA	NA	NA	.83
Other				
China[e]	121.58	124.71	NA	NA

[a] Includes employment in manufacturing, mining, and construction.
[b] Western area only.
[c] Official statistics. Beginning in 1990, figures are distorted because government statistical officials are not able to track all of private sector employment.
[d] Midyear data.
[e] Yearend data.

Million persons

Nonagricultural Labor Force [a]

	1990	1991	1992	1993
OECD				
United States	121.43	121.91	123.60	124.78
Canada	13.15	13.20	13.27	13.40
Japan	58.78	60.29	61.13	61.82
European Union				
France	23.05	23.28	23.39	23.52
Germany [b]	28.44	28.85	29.17	29.12
Italy	20.79	21.13	21.18	NA
United Kingdom	27.97	27.84	27.68	27.62
Selected East European				
Russia	71.88	71.93	73.26	73.58
Ukraine	22.81	22.95	23.40	23.44
Bulgaria [c]	3.40	3.16	3.05	NA
Czech Republic	NA	NA	NA	NA
Hungary [c]	4.79	4.81	4.74	4.67 [d]
Poland [c]	12.54	12.90	13.19	13.44 [d]
Romania [c]	7.69	7.91	7.94	NA
Slovakia	NA	NA	NA	2.14
Other				
China [e]	225.63	233.48	NA	NA

[a] Excludes the armed forces but includes the unemployed. Annual averages of monthly data, unless otherwise indicated.
[b] Western area only.
[c] Official statistics. Beginning in 1990, figures are distorted because government statistical officials are not able to track all of private sector employment.
[d] Midyear data.
[e] Yearend data, series revised in 1985.

Gross Domestic Product Per Capita, 1993[a]
(in 1993 US $)

More than $15,000

Aruba	Denmark	Liechtenstein	Singapore
Australia	Finland	Luxembourg	Sweden
Austria	France	Monaco	Switzerland
Bahamas, The	Germany	Netherlands	United Arab Emirates
Belgium	Hong Kong	New Zealand	United Kingdom
Bermuda	Iceland	Norway	United States
Canada	Italy	Qatar	
Cayman Islands	Japan	San Marino	

$10,001 to $15,000

Andorra	Faroe Islands	Korea, South	Spain
Bahrain	Guam	Kuwait	Taiwan
Brunei	Ireland	Northern Mariana Islands	Virgin Islands, British
Cyprus	Israel	Saudi Arabia	Virgin Islands, US

$3,001 to $10,000

Algeria	Falkland Islands	Malaysia	Reunion
American Samoa	Fiji	Malta	Russia
Anguilla	French Guiana	Man, Isle of	St. Kitts and Nevis
Antigua and Barbuda	French Polynesia	Martinique	St. Pierre and Miquelon
Argentina	Gabon	Mauritius	Seychelles
Barbados	Gibraltar	Mexico	Slovakia
Belarus	Greece	Moldova	Slovenia
Bosnia and Herzegovina	Greenland	Montserrat	South Africa
Botswana	Grenada	Nauru	Syria
Brazil	Guadeloupe	Netherlands Antilles	Thailand
Bulgaria	Hungary	New Caledonia	Trinidad and Tobago
Chile	Iran	Oman	Tunisia
Colombia	Jamaica	Pacific Islands, Trust	Turkey
Costa Rica	Kazakhstan	Territory of the	Turkmenistan
Croatia	Latvia	Panama	Turks and Caicos Islands
Czech Republic	Libya	Poland	Ukraine
Ecuador	Lithuania	Portugal	Uruguay
Estonia	Macau	Puerto Rico	Venezuela

$1,000 to $3,000

Albania	Gaza Strip	Mongolia	Sierra Leone
Armenia	Georgia	Morocco	Solomon Islands
Azerbaijan	Ghana	Namibia	Sri Lanka
Bangladesh	Guatemala	Nepal	Suriname
Belize	Guyana	Nicaragua	Swaziland
Benin	Honduras	Nigeria	Tajikistan
Bolivia	India	Niue	The Former Yugoslav
Cameroon	Indonesia	Pakistan	Republic of Macedonia
Cape Verde	Iraq	Papua New Guinea	Tokelau
China	Jordan	Paraguay	Tonga
Congo	Kenya	Peru	Uganda
Cook Islands	Korea, North	Philippines	Uzbekistan
Cote d'Ivoire	Kyrgyzstan	Romania	Vanuatu
Cuba	Lebanon	Saint Lucia	Vietnam
Djibouti	Lesotho	Saint Vincent and	Wallis and Futuna
Dominica	Marshall Islands	the Grenadines	West Bank
Dominican Republic	Mauritania	Senegal	Western Samoa
Egypt	Micronesia, Federated	Serbia and Montenegro	Zimbabwe
El Salvador	States of		

[a] GDP per capita data are calculated using GDP converted at purchasing power exchange rates.

Geographic Name Reference Guide

Name	Geographic Area
Abidjan [US Embassy]	Cote d'Ivoire
Abu Dhabi [US Embassy]	United Arab Emirates
Abuja [US Embassy Branch Office]	Nigeria
Acapulco [US Consular Agency]	Mexico
Accra [US Embassy]	Ghana
Adamstown	Pitcairn Islands
Adana [US Consulate]	Turkey
Addis Ababa [US Embassy]	Ethiopia
Adelaide [US Consular Agency]	Australia
Adelie Land (Terre Adelie) [claimed by France]	Antarctica
Aden	Yemen
Aden, Gulf of	Indian Ocean
Admiralty Islands	Papua New Guinea
Adriatic Sea	Atlantic Ocean
Aegean Islands	Greece
Aegean Sea	Atlantic Ocean
Afars and Issas, French Territory of the (F.T.A.I.)	Djibouti
Agalega Islands	Mauritius
Agana	Guam
Aland Íslands	Finland
Alaska	United States
Alaska, Gulf of	Pacific Ocean
Aldabra Islands	Seychelles
Alderney	Guernsey
Aleutian Islands	United States
Alexander Island	Antarctica
Alexandria [US Consulate General]	Egypt
Algiers [US Embassy]	Algeria
Alhucemas, Penon de	Spain
Alma-Ata (Almaty)	Kazakhstan
Almaty (Alma-Ata) [US Embassy]	Kazakhstan
Alofi	Niue
Alphonse Island	Seychelles
Amami Strait	Pacific Ocean
Amindivi Islands	India
Amirante Isles	Seychelles
Amman [US Embassy]	Jordan
Amsterdam [US Consulate General]	Netherlands
Amsterdam Island (Ile Amsterdam)	French Southern and Antarctic
Amundsen Sea	Pacific Ocean

Name	Geographic Area
Amur	China; Russia
Andaman Islands	India
Andaman Sea	Indian Ocean
Andorra la Vella	Andorra
Anegada Passage	Atlantic Ocean
Anglo-Egyptian Sudan	Sudan
Anjouan	Comoros
Ankara [US Embassy]	Turkey
Annobon	Equatorial Guinea
Antananarivo [US Embassy]	Madagascar
Antipodes Islands	New Zealand
Antwerp [US Consulate General]	Belgium
Aozou Strip	Chad
Apia [US Embassy]	Western Samoa
Aqaba, Gulf of	Indian Ocean
Arabian Sea	Indian Ocean
Arafura Sea	Pacific Ocean
Argun	China; Russia
Ascension Island	Saint Helena
Ashgabat (Ashkhabad)	Turkmenistan
Ashkhabad [US Embassy]	Turkmenistan
Asmara [US Embassy]	Eritrea
Asmera (see Asmara)	Eritrea
Assumption Island	Seychelles
Asuncion [US Embassy]	Paraguay
Asuncion Island	Northern Mariana Islands
Atacama	Chile
Athens [US Embassy]	Greece
Attu	United States
Auckland [US Consulate General]	New Zealand
Auckland Islands	New Zealand
Australes Iles (Iles Tubuai)	French Polynesia
Avarua	Cook Islands
Axel Heiberg Island	Canada
Azores	Portugal
Azov, Sea of	Atlantic Ocean
Bab el Mandeb	Indian Ocean
Babuyan Channel	Pacific Ocean
Babuyan Islands	Philippines
Baffin Bay	Arctic Ocean
Baffin Island	Canada
Baghdad [US Embassy temporarily suspended; US Interests Section located in Poland's embassy in Baghdad]	Iraq
Baku [US Embassy]	Azerbaijan

The Internationalist

Name

Baky (Baku)
Balabac Strait
Balearic Islands
Balearic Sea (Iberian Sea)
Bali [US Consular Agency]
Bali Sea
Balintang Channel
Balintang Islands
Balleny Islands
Balochistan
Baltic Sea
Bamako [US Embassy]
Banaba (Ocean Island)
Bandar Seri Begawan [US Embassy]
Banda Sea
Bangkok [US Embassy]
Bangui [US Embassy]
Banjul [US Embassy]
Banks Island
Banks Islands (Iles Banks)
Barcelona [US Consulate General]
Barents Sea
Barranquilla [US Consulate]
Bashi Channel
Basilan Strait
Bass Strait
Basse-Terre
Basseterre
Batan Islands
Basutoland
Bavaria (Bayern)
Beagle Channel
Bear Island (Bjornoya)
Beaufort Sea
Bechuanaland
Beijing [US Embassy]
Beirut [US Embassy]
Belau
Belem [US Consular Agency]
Belep Islands (Iles Belep)
Belfast [US Consulate General]
Belgian Congo
Belgrade [US Embassy; US does not maintain full diplomatic relations with Serbia and Montenegro]

Geographic Area

Azerbaijan
Pacific Ocean
Spain
Atlantic Ocean
Indonesia
Indian Ocean
Pacific Ocean
Philippines
Antarctica
Pakistan
Atlantic Ocean
Mali
Kiribati
Brunei
Pacific Ocean
Thailand
Central African Republic
Gambia, The
Canada
Vanuatu
Spain
Arctic Ocean
Colombia
Pacific Ocean
Pacific Ocean
Indian Ocean
Gaudeloupe
Saint Kitts and Nevis
Philippines
Lesotho
Germany
Atlantic Ocean
Svalbard
Arctic Ocean
Botswana
China
Lebanon
Pacific Islands, Trust Territory
Brazil
New Caledonia
United Kingdom
Zaire
Serbia and Montenegro

169

Name	Geographic Area
Belize City [US Embassy]	Belize
Belle Isle, Strait of	Atlantic Ocean
Bellingshausen Sea	Pacific Ocean
Belmopan	Belize
Belorussia	Belarus
Bengal, Bay of	Indian Ocean
Bering Sea	Pacific Ocean
Bering Strait	Pacific Ocean
Berkner Island	Antarctica
Berlin [US Branch Office]	Germany
Berlin, East	Germany
Berlin, West	Germany
Bern [US Embassy]	Switzerland
Bessarabia	Romania; Moldova
Bijagos, Arquipelago dos	Guinea-Bissau
Bikini Atoll	Marshall Islands
Bilbao [US Consulate]	Spain
Bioko	Equatorial Guinea
Biscay, Bay of	Atlantic Ocean
Bishkek [Interim Chancery]	Kyrgyzstan
Bishop Rock	United Kingdom
Bismarck Archipelago	Papua New Guinea
Bismarck Sea	Pacific Ocean
Bissau [US Embassy]	Guinea-Bissau
Bjornoya (Bear Island)	Svalbard
Black Rock	Falkland Islands (Islas Malvinas)
Black Sea	Atlantic Ocean
Bloemfontein	South Africa
Boa Vista	Cape Verde
Bogota [US Embassy]	Colombia
Bombay [US Consulate General]	India
Bonaire	Netherlands Antilles
Bonifacio, Strait of	Atlantic Ocean
Bonin Islands	Japan
Bonn [US Embassy]	Germany
Bophuthatswana	South Africa
Bora-Bora	French Polynesia
Bordeaux [US Consulate General]	France
Borneo	Brunei; Indonesia; Malaysia
Bornholm	Denmark
Bosporus	Atlantic Ocean
Bothnia, Gulf of	Atlantic Ocean
Bougainville Island	Papua New Guinea

Name	Geographic Area
Bougainville Strait	Pacific Ocean
Bounty Islands	New Zealand
Brasilia [US Embassy]	Brazil
Bratislava [US Embassy]	Slovakia
Brazzaville [US Embassy]	Congo
Bridgetown [US Embassy]	Barbados
Brisbane [US Consulate]	Australia
British East Africa	Kenya
British Guiana	Guyana
British Honduras	Belize
British Solomon Islands	Solomon Islands
British Somaliland	Somalia
Brussels [US Embassy, US Mission to European Communities, US Mission to the North Atlantic Treaty Organization (USNATO)]	Belgium
Bucharest [US Embassy]	Romania
Budapest [US Embassy]	Hungary
Buenos Aires [US Embassy]	Argentina
Bujumbura [US Embassy]	Burundi
Burnt Pine	Norfolk Island
Byelorussia	Belarus
Cabinda	Angola
Cabot Strait	Atlantic Ocean
Caicos Islands	Turks and Caicos Islands
Cairo [US Embassy]	Egypt
Calcutta [US Consulate General]	India
Calgary [US Consulate General]	Canada
California, Gulf of	Pacific Ocean
Campbell Island	New Zealand
Canal Zone	Panama
Canary Islands	Spain
Canberra [US Embassy]	Australia
Cancun [US Consular Agency]	Mexico
Canton (Guangzhou)	China
Canton Island	Kiribati
Cape Town [US Consulate General]	South Africa
Caracas [US Embassy]	Venezuela
Cargados Carajos Shoals	Mauritius
Caroline Islands	Micronesia, Federated States of Territory of the
Caribbean Sea	Atlantic Ocean
Carpentaria, Gulf of	Pacific Ocean
Casablanca [US Consulate General]	Morocco
Castries	Saint Lucia

Name	Geographic Area
Cato Island	Australia
Cayenne	French Guiana
Cebu [US Consulate General]	Philippines
Celebes	Indonesia
Celebes Sea	Pacific Ocean
Celtic Sea	Atlantic Ocean
Central African Empire	Central African Republic
Ceuta	Spain
Ceylon	Sri Lanka
Chafarinas, Islas	Spain
Chagos Archipelago (Oil Islands)	British Indian Ocean Territory
Channel Islands	Guernsey; Jersey
Charlotte Amalie	Virgin Islands
Chatham Islands	New Zealand
Cheju-do	Korea, South
Cheju Strait	Pacific Ocean
Chengdu [US Consulate General]	China
Chesterfield Islands (Iles Chesterfield)	New Caledonia
Chiang Mai [US Consulate General]	Thailand
Chihli, Gulf of (Bo Hai)	Pacific Ocean
China, People's Republic of	China
China, Republic of	Taiwan
Chisinau [US Embassy]	Moldova
Choiseul	Solomon Islands
Christchurch [US Consular Agency]	New Zealand
Christmas Island [Indian Ocean]	Australia
Christmas Island [Pacific Ocean] (Kiritimati)	Kiribati
Chukchi Sea	Arctic Ocean
Ciskei	South Africa
Ciudad Juarez [US Consulate General]	Mexico
Cochabamba [US Consular Agency]	Bolivia
Coco, Isla del	Costa Rica
Cocos Islands	Cocos (Keeling) Islands
Colombo [US Embassy]	Sri Lanka
Colon [US Consular Agency]	Panama
Colon, Archipielago de (Galapagos Islands)	Ecuador
Commander Islands (Komandorskiye Ostrova)	Russia
Conakry [US Embassy]	Guinea
Congo (Brazzaville)	Congo
Congo (Kinshasa)	Zaire
Congo (Leopoldville)	Zaire
Con Son Islands	Vietnam
Cook Strait	Pacific Ocean
Copenhagen [US Embassy]	Denmark

Name	Geographic Area
Coral Sea	Pacific Ocean
Corn Islands (Islas del Maiz)	Nicaragua
Corsica	France
Cosmoledo Group	Seychelles
Cotonou [US Embassy]	Benin
Crete	Greece
Crooked Island Passage	Atlantic Ocean
Crozet Islands (Iles Crozet)	French Southern and Antarctic
Curacao [US Consulate General]	Netherlands Antilles
Cusco [US Consular Agency]	Peru
Czechoslovakia	Czech Republic; Slovakia
Dahomey	Benin
Daito Islands	Japan
Dakar [US Embassy]	Senegal
Daman (Damao)	India
Damascus [US Embassy]	Syria
Danger Atoll	Cook Islands
Danish Straits	Atlantic Ocean
Danzig (Gdansk)	Poland
Dao Bach Long Vi	Vietnam
Dardanelles	Atlantic Ocean
Dar es Salaam [US Embassy]	Tanzania
Davis Strait	Atlantic Ocean
Deception Island	Antarctica
Denmark Strait	Atlantic Ocean
D'Entrecasteaux Islands	Papua New Guinea
Devon Island	Canada
Dhahran [US Consulate General]	Saudi Arabia
Dhaka [US Embassy]	Bangladesh
Diego Garcia	British Indian Ocean Territory
Diego Ramirez	Chile
Diomede Islands	Russia [Big Diomede]
Diu	India
Djibouti [US Embassy]	Djibouti
Dodecanese	Greece
Dodoma	Tanzania
Doha [US Embassy]	Qatar
Douala [US Consulate]	Cameroon
Douglas	Man, Isle of
Dover, Strait of	Atlantic Ocean
Drake Passage	Atlantic Ocean
Dubai (Dubayy) [US Consulate General]	United Arab Emirates
Dublin [US Embassy]	Ireland
Durango [US Consular Agency]	Mexico

Name	Geographic Area
Durban [US Consulate General]	South Africa
Dushanbe [Interim Chancery]	Tajikistan
Dusseldorf [US Consulate General]	Germany
Dutch East Indies	Indonesia
Dutch Guiana	Suriname
East China Sea	Pacific Ocean
Easter Island (Isla de Pascua)	Chile
Eastern Channel (East Korea Strait or Tsushima Strait)	Pacific Ocean
East Germany (German Democratic Republic)	Germany
East Korea Strait (Eastern Channel or Tsushima Strait)	Pacific Ocean
East Pakistan	Bangladesh
East Siberian Sea	Arctic Ocean
East Timor (Portuguese Timor)	Indonesia
Edinburgh [US Consulate General]	United Kingdom
Elba	Italy
Ellef Ringnes Island	Canada
Ellesmere Island	Canada
Ellice Islands	Tuvalu
Elobey, Islas de	Equatorial Guinea
Enderbury Island	Kiribati
Enewetak Atoll (Eniwetok Atoll)	Marshall Islands
England	United Kingdom
English Channel	Atlantic Ocean
Eniwetok Atoll	Marshall Islands
Epirus, Northern	Albania; Greece
Essequibo [claimed by Venezuela]	Guyana
Etorofu	Russia [de facto]
Farquhar Group	Seychelles
Fernando de Noronha	Brazil
Fernando Po (Bioko)	Equatorial Guinea
Finland, Gulf of	Atlantic Ocean
Florence [US Consulate General]	Italy
Florida, Straits of	Atlantic Ocean
Formosa	Taiwan
Formosa Strait (Taiwan Strait)	Pacific Ocean
Fort-de-France [US Consulate General]	Martinique
Frankfurt am Main [US Consulate General]	Germany
Franz Josef Land	Russia
Freetown [US Embassy]	Sierra Leone
French Cameroon	Cameroon
French Indochina	Cambodia; Laos; Vietnam
French Guinea	Guinea
French Sudan	Mali

Name	Geographic Area
French Territory of the Afars and Issas (F.T.A.I.)	Djibouti
French Togo	Togo
Friendly Islands	Tonga
Frunze (Bishkek)	Kyrgyzstan
Fukuoka [US Consulate]	Japan
Funafuti	Tuvalu
Funchal [US Consular Agency]	Portugal
Fundy, Bay of	Atlantic Ocean
Futuna Islands (Hoorn Islands)	Wallis and Futuna
Gaborone [US Embassy]	Botswana
Galapagos Islands (Archipielago de Colon)	Ecuador
Galleons Passage	Atlantic Ocean
Gambier Islands (Iles Gambier)	French Polynesia
Gaspar Strait	Indian Ocean
Geneva [Branch Office of the US Embassy, US Mission to European Office of the UN and Other International Organizations]	Switzerland
Genoa [US Consulate General]	Italy
George Town [US Consular Agency]	Cayman Islands
Georgetown [US Embassy]	Guyana
German Democratic Republic (East Germany)	Germany
German Federal Republic of (West Germany)	Germany
Gibraltar	Gibraltar
Gibraltar, Strait of	Atlantic Ocean
Gilbert Islands	Kiribati
Goa	India
Gold Coast	Ghana
Golan Heights	Syria
Good Hope, Cape of	South Africa
Goteborg	Sweden
Gotland	Sweden
Gough Island	Saint Helena
Grand Banks	Atlantic Ocean
Grand Cayman	Cayman Islands
Grand Turk [US Consular Agency]	Turks and Caicos Islands
Great Australian Bight	Indian Ocean
Great Belt (Store Baelt)	Atlantic Ocean
Great Britain	United Kingdom
Great Channel	Indian Ocean
Greater Sunda Islands	Brunei; Indonesia; Malaysia
Green Islands	Papua New Guinea
Greenland Sea	Arctic Ocean
Grenadines, Northern	Saint Vincent and the Grenadines
Grenadines, Southern	Grenada

Name	Geographic Area
Guadalajara [US Consulate General]	Mexico
Guadalcanal	Solomon Islands
Guadalupe, Isla de	Mexico
Guangzhou [US Consulate General]	China
Guantanamo [US Naval Base]	Cuba
Guatemala [US Embassy]	Guatemala
Gubal, Strait of	Indian Ocean
Guinea, Gulf of	Atlantic Ocean
Guayaquil [US Consulate General]	Ecuador
Ha'apai Group	Tonga
Habomai Islands	Russia [de facto]
Hague, The [US Embassy]	Netherlands
Haifa [US Consular Agency]	Israel
Hainan Dao	China
Halifax [US Consulate General]	Canada
Halmahera	Indonesia
Hamburg [US Consulate General]	Germany
Hamilton [US Consulate General]	Bermuda
Hanoi	Vietnam
Harare [US Embassy]	Zimbabwe
Hatay	Turkey
Havana [US post not maintained; representation by US Interests Section (USINT) of the Swiss Embassy]	Cuba
Hawaii	United States
Heard Island	Heard Island
Helsinki [US Embassy]	Finland
Hermosillo [US Consulate]	Mexico
Hispaniola	Dominican Republic; Haiti
Hokkaido	Japan
Hong Kong [US Consulate General]	Hong Kong
Honiara [US Consulate]	Solomon Islands
Honshu	Japan
Hormuz, Strait of	Indian Ocean
Horn, Cape (Cabo de Hornos)	Chile
Horne, Iles de	Wallis and Futuna
Horn of Africa	Ethiopia; Somalia
Hudson Bay	Arctic Ocean
Hudson Strait	Arctic Ocean
Inaccessible Island	Saint Helena
Indochina	Cambodia; Laos; Vietnam
Inner Mongolia (Nei Mongol)	China
Ionian Islands	Greece
Ionian Sea	Atlantic Ocean
Irian Jaya	Indonesia

Name	Geographic Area
Irish Sea	Atlantic Ocean
Islamabad [US Embassy]	Pakistan
Islas Malvinas	Falkland Islands
Istanbul [US Consulate General]	Turkey
Italian Somaliland	Somalia
Ivory Coast	Cote d'Ivoire
Iwo Jima	Japan
Izmir [US Consulate General]	Turkey
Jakarta [US Embassy]	Indonesia
Jamestown	Saint Helena
Japan, Sea of	Pacific Ocean
Java	Indonesia
Java Sea	Indian Ocean
Jeddah [US Consulate General]	Saudi Arabia
Jerusalem [US Consulate General]	Israel; West Bank
Johannesburg [US Consulate General]	South Africa
Juan de Fuca, Strait of	Pacific Ocean
Juan Fernandez, Isla de	Chile
Juventud, Isla de la (Isle of Youth)	Cuba
Kabul [US Embassy now closed]	Afghanistan
Kaduna [US Consulate General]	Nigeria
Kalimantan	Indonesia
Kamchatka Peninsula (Poluostrov Kamchatka)	Russia
Kampala [US Embassy]	Uganda
Kampuchea	Cambodia
Karachi [US Consulate General]	Pakistan
Kara Sea	Arctic Ocean
Karimata Strait	Indian Ocean
Kathmandu [US Embassy]	Nepal
Kattegat	Atlantic Ocean
Kauai Channel	Pacific Ocean
Keeling Islands	Cocos (Keeling) Islands
Kerguelen, Iles	French Southern and Antarctic
Kermadec Islands	New Zealand
Khabarovsk	Russia
Khartoum [US Embassy]	Sudan
Khmer Republic	Cambodia
Khuriya Muriya Islands (Kuria Muria Islands)	Oman
Khyber Pass	Pakistan
Kiel Canal (Nord-Ostsee Kanal)	Atlantic Ocean
Kiev [US Embassy]	Ukraine
Kigali [US Embassy]	Rwanda
Kingston [US Embassy]	Jamaica

Name	Geographic Area
Kingston	Norfolk Island
Kingston	Saint Vincent and the Grenadines
Kinshasa [US Embassy]	Zaire
Kirghiziya	Kyrgyzstan
Kiritimati (Christmas Island)	Kiribati
Kishinev (Chisinau)	Moldova
Kithira Strait	Atlantic Ocean
Kodiak Island	United States
Kola Peninsula (Kol'skiy Poluostrov)	Russia
Kolonia [US Embassy]	Micronesia, Federated States
Korea Bay	Pacific Ocean
Korea, Democratic People's Republic of	Korea, North
Korea, Republic of	Korea, South
Korea Strait	Pacific Ocean
Koror [US Liaison Office]	Pacific Islands, Trust Territory
Kosovo	Serbia and Montenegro
Kowloon	Hong Kong
Krakow [US Consulate General]	Poland
Kuala Lumpur [US Embassy]	Malaysia
Kunashiri (Kunashir)	Russia [de facto]
Kuril Islands	Russia [de facto]
Kuwait [US Embassy]	Kuwait
Kwajalein Atoll	Marshall Islands
Kyushu	Japan
Kyyiv (Kiev)	Ukraine
Labrador	Canada
Laccadive Islands	India
Laccadive Sea	Indian Ocean
La Coruna [US Consular Agency]	Spain
Lagos [US Embassy]	Nigeria
Lahore [US Consulate General]	Pakistan
Lakshadweep	India
La Paz [US Embassy]	Bolivia
La Perouse Strait	Pacific Ocean
Laptev Sea	Arctic Ocean
Las Palmas [US Consular Agency]	Spain
Lau Group	Fiji
Leipzig [US Consulate General]	Germany
Leningrad (see Saint Petersburg)	Russia
Lesser Sunda Islands	Indonesia
Leyte	Philippines
Liancourt Rocks [claimed by Japan]	Korea, South
Libreville [US Embassy]	Gabon
Ligurian Sea	Atlantic Ocean

Name	Geographic Area
Lilongwe [US Embassy]	Malawi
Lima [US Embassy]	Peru
Lincoln Sea	Arctic Ocean
Line Islands	Kiribati; Palmyra Atoll
Lisbon [US Embassy]	Portugal
Ljubljana [US Embassy]	Slovenia
Lobamba	Swaziland
Lombok Strait	Indian Ocean
Lome [US Embassy]	Togo
London [US Embassy]	United Kingdom
Longyearbyen	Svalbard
Lord Howe Island	Australia
Louisiade Archipelago	Papua New Guinea
Loyalty Islands (Iles Loyaute)	New Caledonia
Luanda [US Liaison Office]	Angola
Lubumbashi [US Consulate General closed since October 1991]	Zaire
Lusaka [US Embassy]	Zambia
Luxembourg [US Embassy]	Luxembourg
Luzon	Philippines
Luzon Strait	Pacific Ocean
Lyon [US Consulate General]	France
Macao	Macau
Macedonia	The Former Yugoslav Republic
Macquarie Island	Australia
Madeira Islands	Portugal
Madras [US Consulate General]	India
Madrid [US Embassy]	Spain
Magellan, Strait of	Atlantic Ocean
Maghreb	Algeria, Libya, Mauritania
Mahe Island	Seychelles
Maiz, Islas del (Corn Islands)	Nicaragua
Majorca (Mallorca)	Spain
Majuro [US Embassy]	Marshall Islands
Makassar Strait	Pacific Ocean
Malabo [US Embassy]	Equatorial Guinea
Malacca, Strait of	Indian Ocean
Malaga [US Consular Agency]	Spain
Malagasy Republic	Madagascar
Male [US post not maintained; representation from Colombo, Sri Lanka]	Maldives
Mallorca (Majorca)	Spain
Malpelo, Isla de	Colombia
Malta Channel	Atlantic Ocean

Name

Name	Geographic Area
Malvinas, Islas	Falkland Islands
Mamoutzou	Mayotte
Managua [US Embassy]	Nicaragua
Manama [US Embassy]	Bahrain
Manaus [US Consular Agency]	Brazil
Manchukuo	China
Manchuria	China
Manila [US Embassy]	Philippines
Manipa Strait	Pacific Ocean
Mannar, Gulf of	Indian Ocean
Manua Islands	American Samoa
Maputo [US Embassy]	Mozambique
Maracaibo [US Consulate]	Venezuela
Marcus Island (Minami-tori-shima)	Japan
Mariana Islands	Guam; Northern Mariana Islands
Marion Island	South Africa
Marmara, Sea of	Atlantic Ocean
Marquesas Islands (Iles Marquises)	French Polynesia
Marseille [US Consulate General]	France
Martin Vaz, Ilhas	Brazil
Mas a Tierra (Robinson Crusoe Island)	Chile
Mascarene Islands	Mauritius; Reunion
Maseru [US Embassy]	Lesotho
Matamoros [US Consulate]	Mexico
Mata Utu	Wallis and Futuna
Mazatlan [US Consulate]	Mexico
Mbabane [US Embassy]	Swaziland
McDonald Islands	Heard Island and McDonald
Medan [US Consulate]	Indonesia
Mediterranean Sea	Atlantic Ocean
Melbourne [US Consulate General]	Australia
Melilla	Spain
Mensk (Minsk)	Belarus
Merida [US Consulate]	Mexico
Messina, Strait of	Atlantic Ocean
Mexico [US Embassy]	Mexico
Mexico, Gulf of	Atlantic Ocean
Milan [US Consulate General]	Italy
Minami-tori-shima	Japan
Mindanao	Philippines
Mindoro Strait	Pacific Ocean
Minicoy Island	India
Minsk [US Embassy]	Belarus
Mogadishu [US Liaison Office]	Somalia

Name	Geographic Area
Moldovia	Moldova
Mombasa [US Consulate]	Kenya
Monaco	Monaco
Mona Passage	Atlantic Ocean
Monrovia [US Embassy]	Liberia
Montego Bay [US Consular Agency]	Jamaica
Montenegro	Serbia and Montenegro
Monterrey [US Consulate General]	Mexico
Montevideo [US Embassy]	Uruguay
Montreal [US Consulate General, US Mission to the International Civil Aviation Organization (ICAO)]	Canada
Moravian Gate	Czech Republic
Moroni [US Embassy]	Comoros
Mortlock Islands	Micronesia, Federated States of
Moscow [US Embassy]	Russia
Mozambique Channel	Indian Ocean
Mulege [US Consular Agency]	Mexico
Munich [US Consulate General]	Germany
Musandam Peninsula	Oman; United Arab Emirates
Muscat [US Embassy]	Oman
Muscat and Oman	Oman
Myanma, Myanmar	Burma
Naha [US Consulate General]	Japan
Nairobi [US Embassy]	Kenya
Nampo-shoto	Japan
Naples [US Consulate General]	Italy
Nassau [US Embassy]	Bahamas, The
Natuna Besar Islands	Indonesia
N'Djamena [US Embassy]	Chad
Netherlands East Indies	Indonesia
Netherlands Guiana	Suriname
Nevis	Saint Kitts and Nevis
New Delhi [US Embassy]	India
Newfoundland	Canada
New Guinea	Indonesia; Papua New Guinea
New Hebrides	Vanuatu
New Siberian Islands	Russia
New Territories	Hong Kong
New York, New York [US Mission to the United Nations (USUN)]	United States
Niamey [US Embassy]	Niger
Nice [US Consular Agency]	France
Nicobar Islands	India
Nicosia [US Embassy]	Cyprus
Nightingale Island	Saint Helena

Name	Geographic Area
North Atlantic Ocean	Atlantic Ocean
North Channel	Atlantic Ocean
Northeast Providence Channel	Atlantic Ocean
Northern Epirus	Albania; Greece
Northern Grenadines	Saint Vincent and the Grenadines
Northern Ireland	United Kingdom
Northern Rhodesia	Zambia
North Island	New Zealand
North Korea	Korea, North
North Pacific Ocean	Pacific Ocean
North Sea	Atlantic Ocean
North Vietnam	Vietnam
Northwest Passages	Arctic Ocean
North Yemen (Yemen Arab Republic)	Yemen
Norwegian Sea	Atlantic Ocean
Nouakchott [US Embassy]	Mauritania
Noumea	New Caledonia
Nuku'alofa	Tonga
Novaya Zemlya	Russia
Nuevo Laredo [US Consulate]	Mexico
Nuuk (Godthab)	Greenland
Nyasaland	Malawi
Oahu	United States
Oaxaca [US Consular Agency]	Mexico
Ocean Island (Banaba)	Kiribati
Ocean Island (Kure Island)	United States
Ogaden	Ethiopia; Somalia
Oil Islands (Chagos Archipelago)	British Indian Ocean Territory
Okhotsk, Sea of	Pacific Ocean
Okinawa	Japan
Oman, Gulf of	Indian Ocean
Ombai Strait	Pacific Ocean
Oporto [US Consulate]	Portugal
Oran [US Consulate]	Algeria
Oranjestad	Aruba
Oresund (The Sound)	Atlantic Ocean
Orkney Islands	United Kingdom
Osaka-Kobe [US Consulate General]	Japan
Oslo [US Embassy]	Norway
Otranto, Strait of	Atlantic Ocean
Ottawa [US Embassy]	Canada
Ouagadougou [US Embassy]	Burkina
Outer Mongolia	Mongolia

Name	Geographic Area
Pagan	Northern Mariana Islands
Pago Pago	American Samoa
Palau	Pacific Islands, Trust Territory
Palawan	Philippines
Palermo [US Consulate General]	Italy
Palk Strait	Indian Ocean
Palma de Mallorca [US Consular Agency]	Spain
Pamirs	China; Tajikistan
Panama [US Embassy]	Panama
Panama Canal	Panama
Panama, Gulf of	Pacific Ocean
Papeete	French Polynesia
Paramaribo [US Embassy]	Suriname
Parece Vela	Japan
Paris [US Embassy	France
Pascua, Isla de (Easter Island)	Chile
Passion, Ile de la	Clipperton Island
Pashtunistan	Afghanistan; Pakistan
Peking (Beijing)	China
Pemba Island	Tanzania
Pentland Firth	Atlantic Ocean
Perim	Yemen
Perouse Strait, La	Pacific Ocean
Persian Gulf	Indian Ocean
Perth [US Consulate General]	Australia
Pescadores	Taiwan
Peshawar [US Consulate]	Pakistan
Peter I Island	Antarctica
Philip Island	Norfolk Island
Philippine Sea	Pacific Ocean
Phnom Penh [US Embassy]	Cambodia
Phoenix Islands	Kiribati
Pines, Isle of (Isla de la Juventud)	Cuba
Piura [US Consular Agency]	Peru
Pleasant Island	Nauru
Plymouth	Montserrat
Ponape (Pohnpei)	Micronesia
Ponta Delgada [US Consulate]	Portugal
Port-au-Prince [US Embassy]	Haiti
Port Louis [US Embassy]	Mauritius
Port Moresby [US Embassy]	Papua New Guinea
Porto Alegre [US Consulate]	Brazil
Port-of-Spain [US Embassy]	Trinidad and Tobago
Porto-Novo	Benin

Name	Geographic Area
Port Said [US Consular Agency]	Egypt
Portuguese Guinea	Guinea-Bissau
Portuguese Timor (East Timor)	Indonesia
Port-Vila	Vanuatu
Poznan [US Consulate General]	Poland
Prague [US Embassy]	Czech Republic
Praia [US Embassy]	Cape Verde
Pretoria [US Embassy]	South Africa
Pribilof Islands	United States
Prince Edward Island	Canada
Prince Edward Islands	South Africa
Prince Patrick Island	Canada
Principe	Sao Tome and Principe
Puerto Plata [US Consular Agency]	Dominican Republic
Puerto Vallarta [US Consular Agency]	Mexico
Pusan [US Consulate]	Korea, South
P'yongyang	Korea, North
Quebec [US Consulate General]	Canada
Queen Charlotte Islands	Canada
Queen Elizabeth Islands	Canada
Queen Maud Land [claimed by Norway]	Antarctica
Quito [US Embassy]	Ecuador
Rabat [US Embassy]	Morocco
Ralik Chain	Marshall Islands
Rangoon [US Embassy]	Burma
Ratak Chain	Marshall Islands
Recife [US Consulate]	Brazil
Redonda	Antigua and Barbuda
Red Sea	Indian Ocean
Revillagigedo Island	United States
Revillagigedo Islands	Mexico
Reykjavik [US Embassy]	Iceland
Rhodes	Greece
Rhodesia	Zimbabwe
Rhodesia, Northern	Zambia
Rhodesia, Southern	Zimbabwe
Riga [US Embassy]	Latvia
Rio de Janeiro [US Consulate General]	Brazil
Rio de Oro	Western Sahara
Rio Muni	Equatorial Guinea
Riyadh [US Embassy]	Saudi Arabia
Road Town	British Virgin Islands
Robinson Crusoe Island (Mas a Tierra)	Chile

Name	Geographic Area
Rocas, Atol das	Brazil
Rockall [disputed]	United Kingdom
Rodrigues	Mauritius
Rome [US Embassy, US Mission to the UN Agencies for Food and Agriculture (FODAG)]	Italy
Roncador Cay	Colombia
Roosevelt Island	Antarctica
Roseau	Dominica
Ross Dependency [claimed by New Zealand]	Antarctica
Ross Island	Antarctica
Ross Sea	Antarctica
Rota	Northern Mariana Islands
Rotuma	Fiji
Ryukyu Islands	Japan
Saba	Netherlands Antilles
Sabah	Malaysia
Sable Island	Canada
Sahel	Burkina, Cape Verde, Chad Mali, Mauritania, Niger
Saigon (Ho Chi Minh City)	Vietnam
Saint Brandon	Mauritius
Saint Christopher and Nevis	Saint Kitts and Nevis
Saint-Denis	Reunion
Saint George's [US Embassy]	Grenada
Saint George's Channel	Atlantic Ocean
Saint Heliar	Jersey
Saint John's [US Embassy]	Antigua and Barbuda
Saint Lawrence, Gulf of	Atlantic Ocean
Saint Lawrence Island	United States
Saint Lawrence Seaway	Atlantic Ocean
Saint Martin	Guadeloupe
Saint Martin (Sint Maarten)	Netherlands Antilles
Saint Paul Island	Canada
Saint Paul Island	United States
Saint Paul Island (Ile Saint-Paul)	French Southern and Antarctic
Saint Peter and Saint Paul Rocks (Penedos de Sao Pedro e Sao Paulo)	Brazil
Saint Peter Port	Guernsey
Saint Petersburg [US Consulate]	Russia
Saint-Pierre	Saint Pierre and Miquelon
Saint Vincent Passage	Atlantic Ocean
Saipan	Northern Mariana Islands
Sakhalin Island (Ostrov Sakhalin)	Russia
Sala y Gomez, Isla	Chile

Name

Name	Geographic Area
Salisbury (Harare)	Zimbabwe
Salvador de Bahia [US Consular Agency]	Brazil
Salzburg [US Consulate General]	Austria
Sanaa [US Embassy]	Yemen
San Ambrosio	Chile
San Andres y Providencia, Archipielago	Colombia
San Bernardino Strait	Pacific Ocean
San Felix, Isla	Chile
San Jose [US Embassy]	Costa Rica
San Juan	Puerto Rico
San Luis Potosi [US Consular Agency]	Mexico
San Marino	San Marino
San Miguel Allende [US Consular Agency]	Mexico
San Salvador [US Embassy]	El Salvador
Santa Cruz [US Consular Agency]	Bolivia
Santa Cruz Islands	Solomon Islands
Santiago [US Embassy]	Chile
Santo Domingo [US Embassy]	Dominican Republic
Sao Luis [US Consular Agency]	Brazil
Sao Paulo [US Consulate General]	Brazil
Sao Pedro e Sao Paulo, Penedos de	Brazil
Sao Tome	Sao Tome and Principe
Sapporo [US Consulate General]	Japan
Sapudi Strait	Indian Ocean
Sarajevo	Bosnia and Herzegovina
Sarawak	Malaysia
Sardinia	Italy
Sargasso Sea	Atlantic Ocean
Sark	Guernsey
Scotia Sea	Atlantic Ocean
Scotland	United Kingdom
Scott Island	Antarctica
Senyavin Islands	Micronesia, Federated States of
Seoul [US Embassy]	Korea, South
Serbia	Serbia and Montenegro
Serrana Bank	Colombia
Serranilla Bank	Colombia
Settlement, The	Christmas Island
Severnaya Zemlya (Northland)	Russia
Seville [US Consular Agency]	Spain
Shag Island	Heard Island and McDonald Islan
Shag Rocks	Falkland Islands (Islas Malvinas)
Shanghai [US Consulate General]	China
Shenyang [US Consulate General]	China

Name	Geographic Area
Shetland Islands	United Kingdom
Shikoku	Japan
Shikotan (Shikotan-to)	Japan
Siam	Thailand
Sibutu Passage	Pacific Ocean
Sicily	Italy
Sicily, Strait of	Atlantic Ocean
Sikkim	India
Sinai	Egypt
Singapore [US Embassy]	Singapore
Singapore Strait	Pacific Ocean
Sinkiang (Xinjiang)	China
Sint Eustatius	Netherlands Antilles
Sint Maarten (Saint Martin)	Netherlands Antilles
Skagerrak	Atlantic Ocean
Skopje	The Former Yugoslav Republic
Society Islands (Iles de la Societe)	French Polynesia
Socotra	Yemen
Sofia [US Embassy]	Bulgaria
Solomon Islands, northern	Papua New Guinea
Solomon Islands, southern	Solomon Islands
Soloman Sea	Pacific Ocean
Songkhla [US Consulate]	Thailand
Sound, The (Oresund)	Atlantic Ocean
South Atlantic Ocean	Atlantic Ocean
South China Sea	Pacific Ocean
Southern Grenadines	Grenada
Southern Rhodesia	Zimbabwe
South Georgia	South Georgia
South Island	New Zealand
South Korea	Korea, South
South Orkney Islands	Antarctica
South Pacific Ocean	Pacific Ocean
South Sandwich Islands	South Georgia
South Shetland Islands	Antarctica
South Tyrol	Italy
South Vietnam	Vietnam
South-West Africa	Namibia
South Yemen (People's Democratic Republic of Yemen)	Yemen
Spanish Guinea	Equatorial Guinea
Spanish Sahara	Western Sahara

Name

Name	Geographic Area
Spitsbergen	
Stanley	Falkland Islands
Stockholm [US Embassy]	Sweden
Strasbourg [US Consulate General]	France
Stuttgart [US Consulate General]	Germany
Suez, Gulf of	Indian Ocean
Sulu Archipelago	Philippines
Sulu Sea	Pacific Ocean
Sumatra	Indonesia
Sumba	Indonesia
Sunda Islands (Soenda Isles)	Indonesia; Malaysia
Sunda Strait	Indian Ocean
Surabaya [US Consulate]	Indonesia
Surigao Strait	Pacific Ocean
Surinam	Suriname
Suva [US Embassy]	Fiji
Swains Island	American Samoa
Swan Islands	Honduras
Sydney [US Consulate General]	Australia
Tahiti	French Polynesia
Taipei	Taiwan
Taiwan Strait	Pacific Ocean
Tallin [US Embassy]	Estonia
Tampico [US Consular Agency]	Mexico
Tanganyika	Tanzania
Tangier	Morocco
Tarawa	Kiribati
Tartar Strait	Pacific Ocean
Tashkent [US Embassy]	Uzbekistan
Tasmania	Australia
Tasman Sea	Pacific Ocean
Taymyr Peninsula (Poluostrov Taymyra)	Russia
Tegucigalpa [US Embassy]	Honduras
Tehran [US post not maintained; representation by Swiss Embassy]	Iran
Tel Aviv [US Embassy]	Israel
Terre Adelie (Adelie Land) [claimed by France]	Antarctica
Thailand, Gulf of	Pacific Ocean
Thessaloniki [US Consulate General]	Greece
Thimphu	Bhutan
Thurston Island	Antarctica
Tibet (Xizang)	China
Tibilisi (Tbilisi) [US Embassy]	Georgia
Tierra del Fuego	Argentina; Chile

Name	Geographic Area
Tijuana [US Consulate General]	Mexico
Timor	Indonesia
Timor Sea	Indian Ocean
Tinian	Northern Mariana Islands
Tiran, Strait of	Indian Ocean
Tirane [US Embassy]	Albania
Tobago	Trinidad and Tobago
Tokyo [US Embassy]	Japan
Tonkin, Gulf of	Pacific Ocean
Toronto [US Consulate General]	Canada
Torres Strait	Pacific Ocean
Torshavn	Faroe Islands
Toshkent (Tashkent)	Uzbekistan
Transjordan	Jordan
Transkei	South Africa
Transylvania	Romania
Trieste [US Consular Agency]	Italy
Trindade, Ilha de	Brazil
Tripoli [US post not maintained; representation by Belgian Embassy]	Libya
Tristan da Cunha Group	Saint Helena
Trobriand Islands	Papua New Guinea
Trucial States	United Arab Emirates
Truk Islands	Micronesia
Tsugaru Strait	Pacific Ocean
Tuamotu Islands (Iles Tuamotu)	French Polynesia
Tubuai Islands (Iles Tubuai)	French Polynesia
Tunis [US Embassy]	Tunisia
Turin	Italy
Turkish Straits	Atlantic Ocean
Turkmeniya	Turkmenistan
Turks Island Passage	Atlantic Ocean
Tyrol, South	Italy
Tyrrhenian Sea	Atlantic Ocean
Udorn [US Consulate]	Thailand
Ulaanbaatar [US Embassy]	Mongolia
Ullung-do	Korea, South
Unimak Pass [strait]	Pacific Ocean
United Arab Republic	Egypt; Syria
Upper Volta	Burkina
Vaduz [US post not maintained; representation from Zurich, Switzerland]	Liechtenstein
Vakhan Corridor (Wakhan)	Afghanistan

Name	Geographic Area
Valencia [US Consular Agency]	Spain
Valletta [US Embassy]	Malta
Valley, The	Anguilla
Vancouver [US Consulate General]	Canada
Vancouver Island	Canada
Van Diemen Strait	Pacific Ocean
Vatican City [US Embassy]	Holy See
Velez de la Gomera, Penon de	Spain
Venda	South Africa
Veracruz [US Consular Agency]	Mexico
Verde Island Passage	Pacific Ocean
Victoria [US Embassy]	Seychelles
Vienna [US Embassy, US Mission to International Organizations in Vienna (UNVIE)]	Austria
Vientiane [US Embassy]	Laos
Vilnius [US Embassy]	Lithuania
Vladivostok [US Consulate]	Russia
Volcano Islands	Japan
Vostok Island	Kiribati
Vrangelya, Ostrov (Wrangel Island)	Russia
Wakhan Corridor (now Vakhan Corridor)	Afghanistan
Wales	United Kingdom
Walvis Bay	South Africa
Warsaw [US Embassy]	Poland
Washington, DC [The Permanent Mission of the USA to the Organization of American States (OAS)]	United States
Weddell Sea	Atlantic Ocean
Wellington [US Embassy]	New Zealand
Western Channel (West Korea Strait)	Pacific Ocean
West Germany (Federal Republic of Germany)	Germany
West Island	Cocos (Keeling) Islands
West Korea Strait (Western Channel)	Pacific Ocean
West Pakistan	Pakistan
Wetar Strait	Pacific Ocean
White Sea	Arctic Ocean
Willemstad	Netherlands Antilles
Windhoek [US Embassy]	Namibia
Windward Passage	Atlantic Ocean
Winnipeg [US Consular Agency]	Canada
Wrangel Island (Ostrov Vrangelya)	Russia [de facto]
Yamoussoukro	Cote d'Ivoire
Yaounde [US Embassy]	Cameroon
Yap Islands	Micronesia

Name

Geographic Area

Name	Geographic Area
Yellow Sea	Pacific Ocean
Yemen (Aden) [People's Democratic Republic of Yemen]	Yemen
Yemen Arab Republic	Yemen
Yemen, North [Yemen Arab Republic]	Yemen
Yemen (Sanaa) [Yemen Arab Republic]	Yemen
Yemen, People's Democratic Republic of	Yemen
Yemen, South [People's Democratic Republic of Yemen]	Yemen
Yerevan [US Embassy]	Armenia
Youth, Isle of (Isla de la Juventud)	Cuba
Yucatan Channel	Atlantic Ocean
Zagreb [US Embassy]	Croatia
Zanzibar	Tanzania
Zurich [US Consulate General]	Switzerland

Export Resources

Department of Commerce

The scope of services provided by the Department of Commerce to exporters is vast, but it is often overlooked by many companies. Most of the information and programs of interest to U.S. exporters are concentrated in the department's International Trade Administration (ITA), of which the subdivision called the U.S. and Foreign Commercial Service (US&FCS) maintains a network of international trade specialists in the United States and commercial officers in foreign cities to help American companies do business abroad. By contacting the nearest Department of Commerce district office, the U.S. exporter can tap into all assistance programs available from ITA and all trade information gathered by U.S. embassies and consulates worldwide. Addresses and phone numbers for all district offices, listed by state, are given in appendix III. The following sections detail the kinds of assistance offered.

Export assistance available in the United States

Department of Commerce District Offices

Sixty-eight Department of Commerce district and branch offices in cities throughout the United States and Puerto Rico provide information and professional export counseling to business people. Each district office is headed by a director and supported by trade specialists and other staff. Branch offices usually consist of one trade specialist. These professionals can counsel companies on the steps involved in exporting, help them assess the export potential of their products, target markets, and locate and check out potential overseas partners. In fact, because Commerce has a worldwide network of international business experts, district offices can answer almost any question exporters are likely to ask – or put them in touch with someone who can.

Each district office can offer information about

- international trade opportunities abroad,
- foreign markets for U.S. products and services,
- services to locate and evaluate overseas buyers and representatives,
- financial aid to exporters,
- international trade exhibitions,
- export documentation requirements,
- foreign economic statistics,
- U.S. export licensing and foreign nation import requirements, and
- export seminars and conferences.

Most district offices also maintain business libraries containing Commerce's latest reports as well as other publications of interest to U.S. exporters. Important data bases, such as the NTDB, are also available through many district offices that provide trade leads, foreign business contacts, in-depth country market research, export-import trade statistics, and other valuable information.

District Export Councils

Besides the immediate services of its district offices, the Department of Commerce gives the exporter direct contact with seasoned exporters experienced in all phases of export trade. The district offices work closely with 51 district export councils (DECs) comprising nearly 1,800 business and trade experts who volunteer to help U.S. firms develop solid export strategies.

These DECs assist in many of the workshops and seminars on exporting arranged by the district offices (see below) or sponsor their own. DEC members may also provide direct, personal counseling to less experienced exporters, suggesting marketing strategies, trade contacts, and ways to maximize success in overseas markets.

Assistance from DECs may be obtained through the Department of Commerce district offices with which they are affiliated.

Export Seminars and Educational Programming

In addition to individual counseling sessions, an effective method of informing local business communities of the various aspects of international trade is through the conference and seminar program. Each year, Commerce district offices conduct approximately 5,000 conferences, seminars, and workshops on topics such as export documentation and licensing procedures, country-specific market opportunities, export trading companies, and U.S. trade promotion and trade policy initiatives. The seminars are usually held in conjunction with DECs, local chambers of commerce, state agencies, and world trade clubs. For information on scheduled seminars across the country, or for educational programming assistance, contact the nearest district office.

Assistance Available From Department of Commerce Specialists in Washington, D.C.

Among the most valuable resources available to U.S. exporters are the hundreds of trade specialists, expert in various areas of international business, that the Department of Commerce has assembled in its Washington headquarters.

Country counseling. Every country in the world is assigned a *country desk officer.* These desk officers (see appendix II for a list), in Commerce's International Economic Policy (IEP) area, look at the needs of an individual U.S. firm wishing to sell in a particular country, taking into account that country's overall economy, trade policies, political situation, and other relevant factors. Each desk officer collects up-to-date information on the country's trade regulations, tariffs and value-added taxes, business practices, economic and political developments, trade data and trends, market size and growth, and so on. Desk officers also participate in preparing Commerce's country-specific market research reports, such as *Foreign Economic Trends* and *Overseas Business Reports* (see appendix V), available from the U.S. Government Printing Office and through the NTDB. The value of IEP's market data may be gauged from the fact that this agency develops much of the country-specific background for negotiating positions of the U.S. trade representative.

Product and service sector counseling. Complementing IEP's country desks are the *industry desk officers* of Commerce's Trade Development area. They are grouped in units (with telephone numbers):

- Aerospace, 202-377-2835.

- Automotive Affairs and Consumer Goods, 202-377-0823.

- Basic Industries, 202-377-0614.

- Capital Goods and International Construction, 202-377-5023.

- Science and Electronics, 202-377-3548.

- Services, 202-377-5261.

- Textiles and Apparel, 202-377-3737.

The industry desk officers (see appendix II for a list) participate in preparing reports on the competitive strength of selected U.S. industries in domestic and international markets for the publication *U.S. Industrial Outlook* (available from the U.S. Government Printing Office). They also promote exports for their industry sectors through marketing seminars, trade missions and trade fairs, foreign buyer groups, business counseling, and information on market opportunities.

Export counseling and international market analysis. The Market Analysis Division provides U.S. firms with assistance in market research efforts and export counseling on market research. Many of the research reports described in this chapter are planned and prepared by the Office of Product Development and Distribution, Market Analysis Division (202-377-5037).

Major projects. For major projects abroad, the International Construction unit works with American planning, engineering, and construction firms to win bid contracts. The Major Projects Reference Room in Commerce's Washington headquarters keeps detailed project documents on multilateral development bank and U.S. foreign assistance projects. Companies able to bid on major overseas projects can reach the Major Projects Reference Room on 202-377-4876.

The Office of Telecommunications (202-377-4466) has major projects information exclusively for that sector.

Other assistance. Rounding out the Trade Development area is a unit that cuts across industry sector issues. Trade Information and Analysis gathers, analyzes, and disseminates trade and investment data for use in trade promotion and policy formulation. It also includes specialists in technical areas of international trade finance, such as countertrade and barter, foreign sales corporations, export financing, and the activities of multilateral development banks. For more information, contact the nearest Department of Commerce district office.

Export marketing information and assistance available overseas

US&FCS Overseas Posts

Much of the information about trends and actual trade leads in foreign countries is gathered on site by the commercial officers of the US&FCS. About half of the approximately 186 US&FCS American officers working in 67 countries (with 127 offices) have been hired from the private sector, many with international trade experience. All understand firsthand the problems encountered by U.S. companies in their efforts to trade abroad. U.S.-based regional directors for the US&FCS can be contacted at the following telephone numbers:

- Africa, Near East and South Asia, 202-377-4836.

- East Asia and Pacific, 202-377-8422.

- Europe, 202-377-1599.

- Western Hemisphere, 202-377-2736.

- Fax (Europe and Western Hemisphere), 202-377-3159.

- Fax (all others), 202-377-5179.

In addition, a valued asset of the US&FCS is a group of about 525 foreign nationals, usually natives of the foreign country, who are employed in the U.S. embassy or consulate and bring with them a wealth of personal understanding of local market conditions and business practices. The US&FCS staff overseas provides a range of services to help companies sell abroad: background information on foreign companies, agency-finding services, market research, business counseling, assistance in making appointments with key buyers and government officials, and representations on behalf of companies adversely affected by trade barriers. (Some of the more important services are described fully in chapter 7.)

U.S. exporters usually tap into these services by contacting the Department of Commerce district office in their state. While exporters are strongly urged to contact their district office *before* going overseas, U.S. business travelers abroad can also contact U.S. embassies and consulates directly for help during their trips. District offices can provide business travel facilitation assistance before departure by arranging advance appointments with embassy personnel, market briefings, and other assistance in cities to be visited.

US&FCS posts also cooperate with overseas representatives of individual states. Almost all 50 states have such representation in overseas markets, and their efforts are closely coordinated with the resources of the US&FCS.

Other Commerce export services

Besides ITA, a number of other Department of Commerce agencies offer export services.

The Internationalist

Export Administration

The under secretary for export administration is responsible for U.S. export controls (see chapter 11). Assistance in complying with export controls can be obtained directly from local district offices or from the Exporter Counseling Division within the Bureau of Export Administration (BXA) Office of Export Licensing in Washington, DC (202-377-4811). BXA also has four field offices that specialize in counseling on export controls and regulations: the Western Regional Office (714-660-0144), the Northern California Branch Office (408-748-7450), the Portland Branch Office (503-326-5159), and the Eastern Regional Office (603-834-6300).

Trade Adjustment Assistance

Trade Adjustment Assistance, part of Commerce's Economic Development Administration, helps firms that have been adversely affected by imported products to adjust to international competition. Companies eligible for trade adjustment assistance may receive technical consulting to upgrade operations such as product engineering, marketing, information systems, export promotion, and energy management. The federal government may assume up to 75 percent of the cost of these services. For more information call 202-377-3373.

Travel and Tourism

The U.S. Travel and Tourism Administration (USTTA) promotes U.S. export earnings through trade in tourism. USTTA stimulates foreign demand, helps to remove barriers, increases the number of small and medium-sized travel businesses participating in the export market, provides timely data, and forms marketing partnerships with private industry and with state and local governments.

To maintain its programs in international markets, USTTA has offices in Toronto, Montreal, Vancouver, Mexico City, Tokyo, London, Paris, Amsterdam, Milan, Frankfurt, Sydney, and (serving South America) Miami.

Travel development activities in countries without direct USTTA representation are carried out under the direction of USTTA regional directors, who cooperate with Visit USA committees composed of representatives from the U.S. and foreign travel industry in those countries, and also with the US&FCS. For more information, U.S. destinations and suppliers of tourism services interested in the overseas promotion of travel to the United States should call 202-377-4003.

Foreign Requirements for U.S. Products and Services

For information about foreign standards and certification systems, write National Center for Standards and Certificates Information, National Institute for Standards and Technology (NIST), Administration Building, A629, Gaithersburg, MD 20899; telephone 301-975-4040, 4038, or 4036. NIST maintains a General Agreement on Tariffs and Trade (GATT) hotline (301-975-4041) with a recording that reports on the latest notifications of proposed foreign regulations that may affect trade. Exporters can also get information from the nongovernmental American National Standards Institute (212-354-3300).

Minority Business Development Agency (MBDA)

The MBDA identifies minority business enterprises (MBEs) in selected industries to increase their awareness of their relative size and product advantages and to aggressively take them through the advanced stages of market development.

Through an interagency agreement with the ITA, MBDA provides information on market and product needs worldwide. MBDA and ITA coordinate MBE participation in Matchmaker and other trade delegations.

MBDA provides counseling through the Minority Business Development Center network to help MBEs prepare international marketing plans and promotional materials and to identify financial resources.

For general export information, the field organizations of both MBDA and ITA provide information kits and information on local seminars. Contact Minority Business Development Agency, Office of Program Development, U.S. Department of Commerce, Washington, DC 20230; telephone 202-377-3237.

Foreign Metric Regulations

The Office of Metric Programs (202-377-0944) provides exporters with guidance and assistance on matters relating to U.S. transition to the metric system. It can also give referrals to metric contacts in state governments.

Fishery Products Exports

The National Oceanic and Atmospheric Administration (NOAA) assists seafood exporters by facilitating access to foreign markets. NOAA's National Marine Fisheries Service provides inspection services for fishery exports and issues official U.S. government certification attesting to the findings. Contact Office of Trade and Industry Services, National Marine Fisheries Service, Room 6490, 1335 East-West Highway, Silver Spring, MD 20910. Telephone numbers are as follows: Trade Matters, 301-427-2379 or 2383; Export Inspection, 301-427-2355; and Fisheries Promotion, 301-427-2379.

Bureau of the Census

The Bureau of the Census is the primary source of trade statistics that break down the quantity and dollar value of U.S. exports and imports by commodity (product) and country. Commerce district offices can help retrieve Census export statistics for exporters who want to identify potential export markets for their products. Firms interested in more extensive statistical data can contact the Bureau of the Census at 301-763-5140.

Census can also provide authoritative guidance on questions concerning shippers' export declarations (see chapter 12). Call 301-763-5310.

Department of State

The Department of State has a diverse staff capable of providing U.S. exporters with trade contacts. These staff members include bureau commercial coordinators, country desk officers, policy officers in the functional bureaus (such as the Bureau of Economic and Business

Affairs), and all U.S. embassies and consular posts abroad. While the Department of Commerce's US&FCS is present in 67 countries, the Department of State provides commercial services in 84 embassies and numerous consular posts. Their addresses and telephone numbers are published in the directory titled *Key Officers of Foreign Service Posts,* available from the U.S. Government Printing Office (202-783-3238).

The ambassador takes the lead in promoting U.S. trade and investment interests in every U.S. embassy. All members of U.S. diplomatic missions abroad have the following continuing obligations:

* To ascertain the views of the American business sector on foreign policy issues that affect its interests, in order to ensure that those views are fully considered in the development of policy.

* To seek to ensure that the ground rules for conducting international trade are fair and nondiscriminatory.

* To be responsive when U.S. firms seek assistance, providing them with professional advice and analysis as well as assistance in making and developing contacts abroad.

* To vigorously encourage and promote the export of U.S. goods, services, and agricultural commodities and represent the interests of U.S. business to foreign governments where appropriate.

* To assist U.S. business in settling investment disputes with foreign governments amicably and, in cases of expropriation or similar action, to obtain prompt, adequate, and effective compensation.

Bureau of Economic and Business Affairs

The Bureau of Economic and Business Affairs has primary responsibility within the Department of State for (1) formulating and implementing policies regarding foreign economic matters, trade promotion, and business services of an international nature and (2) coordinating regional economic policy with other bureaus. The bureau is divided functionally as follows: Planning and Economic Analysis Staff; Office of Commercial, Legislative, and Public Affairs; Trade and Commercial Affairs (including textiles and food policy); International Finance and Development (including investment and business practices); Transportation (including aviation and maritime affairs); International Energy and Resources Policy; and International Trade Controls. For more information, contact Commercial Coordinator, Bureau of Economic and Business Affairs; telephone 202-647-1942.

Regional bureaus

Regional bureaus, each under the direction of an assistant secretary of state, are responsible for U.S. foreign affairs activities in specific major regions of the world. Bureau commercial coordinators can be reached on the following telephone numbers:

* Bureau of African Affairs, 202-647-3503.

* Bureau of East Asian and Pacific Affairs, 202-647-2006.

* Bureau of Near Eastern and South Asian Affairs, 202-647-4835.

* Bureau of European and Canadian Affairs, 202-647-2395.

* Bureau of International Communications and Information Policy, 202-647-5832.

Country desk officers maintain day-to-day contact with overseas diplomatic posts and provide country-specific economic and political analysis and commercial counseling to U.S. business.

Cooperation between state and commerce

The Departments of State and Commerce provide many services to U.S. business jointly. Firms interested in establishing a market for their products or expanding sales abroad should first seek assistance from their nearest Department of Commerce district office, which can tap into the worldwide network of State and Commerce officials serving in U.S. missions abroad and in Washington.

Small Business Administration

Through its 107 field offices in cities throughout the United States (see appendix III for addresses and telephone numbers), the U.S. Small Business Administration (SBA) provides counseling to potential and current small business exporters. These no-cost services include the following:

* **Legal advice.** Through an arrangement with the Federal Bar Association (FBA), exporters may receive initial export legal assistance. Under this program, qualified attorneys from the International Law Council of the FBA, working through SBA field offices, provide free initial consultations to small companies on the legal aspects of exporting.

* **Export training.** SBA field offices cosponsor export training programs with the Department of Commerce, other federal agencies, and various private sector international trade organizations. These programs are conducted by experienced international traders.

* **Small Business Institute and small business development centers.** Through the Small Business Institute, advanced business students from more than 500 colleges and universities provide in-depth, long-term counseling under faculty supervision to small businesses. Additional export counseling and assistance are offered through small business development centers, which are located in some colleges and universities. Students in these two programs provide technical help by developing an export marketing feasibility study and analysis for their client firms.

* **Export counseling.** Export counseling services are also furnished to potential and current small business exporters by executives and professional consultants. Members of the Service Corps of Retired Executives, with practical experience in international trade, help small firms evaluate their export potential and strengthen their domestic operations by identifying financial, managerial, or technical problems. These advisers also can help small firms develop and implement basic export marketing plans, which show where and how to sell goods abroad.

For information on any of the programs funded by SBA, contact the nearest SBA field office (see appendix III).

Department of Agriculture

The U.S. Department of Agriculture (USDA) export promotion efforts are centered in the Foreign Agricultural Service (FAS), whose marketing programs are discussed in chapter 7. However, other USDA agencies also offer services to U.S. exporters of agricultural products: the Economic Research Service, the Office of Transportation, the Animal and Plant Health Inspection Service, the Food Safety and Inspection Service, and the Federal Grain Inspection Service. A wide variety of other valuable programs is offered, such as promotion of U.S. farm products in foreign markets; services of commodity and marketing specialists in Washington, D.C.; trade fair exhibits; publications and information services; and financing programs. For more information on programs contact the director of the High-Value Product Services Division, Foreign Agricultural Service, U.S. Department of Agriculture, Washington, DC 20250; telephone 202-447-6343.

State governments

State economic development agencies, departments of commerce, and other departments of state governments often provide valuable assistance to exporters. State export development programs are growing rapidly. In many areas, county and city economic development agencies also have export assistance programs. The aid offered by these groups typically includes the following:

- **Export education** – helping exporters analyze export potential and orienting them to export techniques and strategies. This help may take the form of group seminars or individual counseling sessions.

- **Trade missions** – organizing trips abroad enabling exporters to call on potential foreign customers. (For more information on trade missions, see chapter 7.)

- **Trade shows** – organizing and sponsoring exhibitions of state-produced goods and services in overseas markets.

Appendix III lists the agencies in each state responsible for export assistance to local firms. Also included are the names of other government and private organizations, with their telephone numbers and addresses. Readers interested in the role played by state development agencies in promoting and supporting exports may also wish to contact the National Association of State Development Agencies, 444 North Capitol Street, Suite 611, Washington, DC 20001; telephone 202-624-5411.

To determine if a particular county or city has local export assistance programs, contact the appropriate economic development agency. Appendix III includes contact information for several major cities.

Commercial banks

More than 300 U.S. banks have international banking departments with specialists familiar with specific foreign countries and various types of commodities and transactions. These large banks, located in major U.S. cities, maintain correspondent relationships with smaller banks throughout the country. Larger banks also maintain correspondent relationships with banks in most foreign countries or operate their own overseas branches, providing a direct channel to foreign customers.

International banking specialists are generally well informed about export matters, even in areas that fall outside the usual limits of international banking. If they are unable to provide direct guidance or assistance, they may be able to refer inquirers to other specialists who can. Banks frequently provide consultation and guidance free of charge to their clients, since they derive income primarily from loans to the exporter and from fees for special services. Many banks also have publications available to help exporters. These materials often cover particular countries and their business practices and can be a valuable tool for initial familiarization with foreign industry. Finally, large banks frequently conduct seminars and workshops on letters of credit, documentary collections, and other banking subjects of concern to exporters.

Among the many services a commercial bank may perform for its clients are the following:

- Exchange of currencies.

- Assistance in financing exports.

- Collection of foreign invoices, drafts, letters of credit, and other foreign receivables.

- Transfer of funds to other countries.

- Letters of introduction and letters of credit for travelers.

- Credit information on potential representatives or buyers overseas.

- Credit assistance to the exporter's foreign buyers.

Export intermediaries

Export intermediaries are of many different types, ranging from giant international companies, many foreign owned, to highly specialized, small operations. They provide a multitude of services, such as performing market research, appointing overseas distributors or commission representatives, exhibiting a client's products at international trade shows, advertising, shipping, and arranging documentation. In short, the intermediary can often take full responsibility for the export end of the business, relieving the manufacturer of all the details except filling orders.

Intermediaries may work simultaneously for a number of exporters on the basis of commissions, salary, or retainer plus commission. Some take title to the goods they handle, buying and selling in their own right. Products of a trading company's clients are often related, although the items usually are noncompetitive. One advantage of using an intermediary is that it can immediately make available marketing resources that a smaller firm would need years to develop on its own. Many export intermediaries also finance sales and extend credit, facilitating prompt payment to the exporter. For more information on using export intermediaries see chapter 4.

World trade centers and international trade clubs

Local or regional world trade centers and international trade clubs are composed of area business people who represent firms engaged in international trade and shipping, banks, forwarders, customs brokers, government agencies, and other service organizations involved in world trade. These organizations conduct educational programs on international business and organize promotional events to stimulate interest in world trade. Some 80 world trade centers or affiliated associations are located in major trading cities throughout the world.

By participating in a local association, a company can receive valuable and timely advice on world markets and opportunities from business people who are already knowledgeable on virtually any facet of international business. Another important advantage of membership in a local world trade club is the availability of benefits – such as services, discounts, and contacts – in affiliated clubs from foreign countries.

Chambers of commerce and trade associations

Many local chambers of commerce and major trade associations in the United States provide sophisticated and extensive services for members interested in exporting. Among these services are the following:

- Conducting export seminars, workshops, and round-tables.

- Providing certificates of origin.

- Developing trade promotion programs, including overseas missions, mailings, and event planning.

- Organizing U.S. pavilions in foreign trade shows.

- Providing contacts with foreign companies and distributors.

- Relaying export sales leads and other opportunities to members.

- Organizing transportation routings and shipment consolidations.

- Hosting visiting trade missions from other countries.

- Conducting international activities at domestic trade shows.

In addition, some industry associations can supply detailed information on market demand for products in selected countries or refer members to export management companies. Most trade associations play an active role in lobbying for U.S. trade policies beneficial to their industries. Industry trade associations typically collect and maintain files on international trade news and trends affecting manufacturers. Often they publish articles and newsletters that include government research.

American chambers of commerce abroad

A valuable and reliable source of market information in any foreign country is the local chapter of the American chamber of commerce. These organizations are knowledgeable about local trade opportunities, actual and potential competition, periods of maximum trade activity, and similar considerations.

American chambers of commerce abroad usually handle inquiries from any U.S. business. Detailed service, however, is ordinarily provided free of charge only to members of affiliated organizations. Some chambers have a set schedule of charges for services rendered to nonmembers. For contact information on American chambers in major foreign markets, see appendix IV.

International trade consultants and other advisers

International trade consultants can advise and assist a manufacturer on all aspects of foreign marketing. Trade consultants do not normally deal specifically with one product, although they may advise on product adaptation to a foreign market. They research domestic and foreign regulations and also assess commercial and political risk. They conduct foreign market research and establish contacts with foreign government agencies and other necessary resources, such as advertising companies, product service facilities, and local attorneys.

These consultants can locate and qualify foreign joint venture partners as well as conduct feasibility studies for the sale of manufacturing rights, the location and construction of manufacturing facilities, and the establishment of foreign branches. After sales agreements are completed, trade consultants can also ensure that follow-through is smooth and that any problems that arise are dealt with effectively.

Trade consultants usually specialize by subject matter and by global area or country. For example, firms may specialize in high-technology exports to the Far East. Their consultants can advise on which agents or distributors are likely to be successful, what kinds of promotion are needed, who the competitors are, and how to deal with them. They are also knowledgeable about foreign government regulations, contract laws, and taxation. Some firms may be more specialized than others; for example, some may be thoroughly knowledgeable on legal aspects and taxation and less knowledgeable on marketing strategies.

Many large accounting firms, law firms, and specialized marketing firms provide international trade consulting services. When selecting a consulting firm, the exporter should pay particular attention to the experience and knowledge of the consultant who is in charge of its project. To find an appropriate firm, advice should be sought from other exporters and some of the other resources listed in this chapter, such as the Department of Commerce district office or local chamber of commerce.

Consultants are of greatest value to a firm that knows exactly what it wants. For this reason, and because private consultants are expensive, it pays to take full advantage of publicly funded sources of advice before hiring a consultant.

International Metric Equivalents

Unit	Metric Equivalent
acre	0.404 685 64 hectares
acre	4,046,856 4 meters^2
acre	0.004 046 856 4 kilometers^2
are	100 meters^2
barrel (petroleum, US)	158.987 29 liters
(proof spirits, US)	151.416 47 liters
(beer, US)	117.347 77 liters
bushel	35.239 07 liters
cable	219.456 meters
chain (surveyor's)	20.116 8 meters
cord (wood)	3.624 556 meters^3
cup	0.236 588 2 liters
degrees, celsius	(water boils at 100° degrees C, freezes at 0° C)
degrees, fahrenheit	subtract 32 and divide by 1.8 to obtain °C
dram, avoirdupois	1.771 845 2 grams
dram, troy	3.887 934 6 grams
dram, liquid (US)	3.696 69 milliliters
fathom	1.828 8 meters
foot	30.48 centimeters
foot	0.304 8 meters
foot	0.000 304 8 kilometers
foot^2	929.030 4 centimeters^2
foot	2 0.092 903 04 meters^2
foot^3	28.316 846 592 liters
foot^3	0.028 316 847 meters^3
furlong	201.168 meters
gallon, liquid (US)	3.785 411 784 liters
gill (US)	118.294 118 milliliters
grain	64.798 91 milligrams
gram	1,000 milligrams
hand (height of horse)	10.16 centimeters

hectare	10,000 meters^2
hundredweight, long	50.802 345 kilograms
hundredweight, short	45.359 237 kilograms
inch	2.54 centimeters
inch^2	6.451 6 centimeters^2
inch^3	16.387 064 centimeters^3
inch^3	16.387 064 milliliters
inch^3	16.387 064 milliliters
kilogram	0.001 tons, metric
kilometer	1,000 meters
kilometer^2	100 hectares
kilometer^2	1,000,000 meters^2
knot (1 nautical mi/hr)	1.852 kilometers/hour
league, nautical	5.559 552 kilometers
league, statute	4.828.032 kilometers
link (surveyor's)	20.116 8 centimeters
liter	0.001 meters^3
liter	0.1 dekaliter
liter	1,000 milliliters
meter	100 centimeters
meter^2	10,000 centimeters^2
meter^3	1,000 liters
micron	0.000 001 meter
mil	0.025 4 millimeters
mile, nautical	1.852 kilometers
mile^2, nautical	3.429 904 kilometers^2
mile, statute	1.609 344 kilometers
mile^2, statute	258.998 811 hectares
mile^2, statute	2.589 988 11 kilometers^2
minim (US)	0.061 611 52 milliliters
ounce, avoirdupois	28.349 523 125 grams
ounce, liquid (US)	29.573 53 milliliters
ounce, troy	31.103 476 8 grams
pace	76.2 centimeters
peck	8.809 767 5 liters
pennyweight	1.555 173 84 grams
pint, dry (US)	0.550 610 47 liters